T0313902

PIONEERS OF CAPITALISM

The Princeton Economic History of The Western World

Joel Mokyr, Series Editor

Pioneers of Capitalism

The Netherlands 1000–1800

Maarten Prak
Jan Luiten van Zanden

Translated by Ian Cressie

PRINCETON UNIVERSITY PRESS

PRINCETON AND OXFORD

Published by Princeton University Press
41 William Street, Princeton, New Jersey 08540
99 Banbury Road, Oxford OX2 6JX

press.princeton.edu

All Rights Reserved
ISBN 978-0-691-22987-4
ISBN (e-book) 978-0-691-24246-0

British Library Cataloging-in-Publication Data is available

Editorial: Joe Jackson and Josh Drake
Production Editorial: Jenny Wolkowicki
Jacket design: Katie Osborne
Production: Lauren Reese
Publicity: Kate Hensley and Charlotte Coyne
Copyeditor: Maia Vaswani

Jacket image: Rembrandt, *Syndics of the Drapers' Guild*, Oil on canvas, 1662

This book has been composed in Adobe Text and Gotham

10 9 8 7 6 5 4 3 2 1

CONTENTS

ACKNOWLEDGMENTS

In 1991, we applied together for the joint position of chair of social and economic history at Utrecht University. During the interviews, first separately, then together, we were asked what our combined research agenda might look like. We told the committee that we would want to work on Dutch capitalism. At the time, this was a slightly old-fashioned topic to choose, but nonetheless, we got the job and for the next thirty years remained at Utrecht University. During that period we have each published work in which the word "capitalism" features in the title, but without ever treating the topic comprehensively. Now, on the eve of retirement, still together, we want make good on our promise.

This book started life as a commissioned contribution to a series in Dutch on the history of the Netherlands from the Stone Age to the present. Our brief was to discuss the social and economic developments since the Middle Ages that other authors, perhaps more politically or culturally inclined, were likely to pass over. We connected the intellectual structure of the book to a theme that was, and is today, topical in Dutch public discourse, but has little resonance abroad. The book, published in 2013, was titled—literally translated—*The Netherlands and the "Poldermodel."* In that book we argued that there were three features of Dutch society (collectively referred to in Dutch as the *poldermodel*) that had made the Netherlands into one of the most prosperous countries in the world: relatively low levels of inequality, a strong civil society, and a political culture based on consensus. We traced the origins of these features all the way back to the Middle Ages and argued that they were partly responsible for the increase in Dutch prosperity that began at that early time.

When we started to discuss with Joel Mokyr the possibility of including a translated version of that book in his Economic History of the Western World series, he insisted on two changes. First, he said, we needed to include the Dutch colonial empire. This was the subject of another volume in the Dutch series, and we had therefore more or less ignored the topic. Now,

Joel told us, we could no longer afford to do so. The other revision that he required was to make the text more accessible and relevant to a non-Dutch audience: the *poldermodel* would have to go. It may not have been Joel's intention to steer us in the direction of capitalism, but given the revival of interest in that topic and the promise we'd made on our appointment, we decided to take that course nonetheless. In the process, we have not only revised the original text but overhauled it and added substantial portions, while at the same time dropping the nineteenth- and twentieth-century chapters that had been part of the original book. The result is the work you now have in your hands—or in front of you on the screen.

We have been very fortunate that we could draw upon an expanding body of secondary literature. Over the past thirty years we have ourselves contributed a good deal to this literature, as have many colleagues in the Economic and Social History group of Utrecht University. A great deal of effort by the Utrecht group has focused on the (quantitative) investigation of various aspects of economic growth and on clarifying the role that institutions played in facilitating and inhibiting that growth, as well as on the social consequences of economic development. In addition to the work of our colleagues at Utrecht University, this book also owes much to the Global Economic History Network (GEHN) that, under the leadership of Patrick O'Brien, was created by the Economic History Department of the London School of Economics. Various GEHN workshops and a number of follow-up meetings in Utrecht provided evidence and inspiration for the line of reasoning in this book.

Thanks to the work of this varied but close-knit group of socioeconomic historians, over the past few decades the debate on Dutch capitalism has changed in two ways. First, a solid quantitative foundation has been laid for the debate, one that was largely lacking a generation ago. This quantitative basis has strengthened the relationship with economic theory, which has also made the debate more analytical. Second, socioeconomic historians, following the perspective of new institutional economics, have become much more aware of the institutional context of economic development. The effects of both changes can be found on almost every page of this book.

While working on the Dutch text, we benefited from commentary by Annelies Bannink, Bas van Bavel, Oscar Gelderblom, Ido de Haan, and Paul Schnabel. Bas van Bavel and Oscar Gelderblom have also carefully scrutinized the manuscript of this English edition, as did Jessica Dijkman, Peter Solar, and an anonymous reviewer for Princeton University Press. They identified mistakes and challenged us to improve and clarify our arguments.

Joel Mokyr did the same with no fewer than three different versions of the manuscript; his editorial commitment throughout the process has been truly amazing. Joel's comments and those from our other readers have helped to significantly improve the book, and we are very grateful for the time and energy they all committed to this book. Sometimes we were, however, unable to rise to the challenge, and we must therefore humbly accept responsibility for whatever errors remain. Last but not least, Ian Cressie translated our Dutch text into English and managed to stay calm despite numerous revisions that we decided to make afterward, two remarkable achievements.

Maarten Prak and Jan Luiten van Zanden
Utrecht, September 2021

PIONEERS OF CAPITALISM

1

Introduction

THE MARKET AS A PARTY?

When the Dutch Celebrate their king's birthday—King's Day, on April 27, a national holiday—they don't dance in the streets or drink themselves into a stupor (although that can also occur). No, they play at being merchants. The Dutch call this a *vrijmarkt*, in English literally a "free market," and it works like this: Each family gathers together things that are not used anymore—perhaps shoes that the children have grown out of or books they have finished reading, and lots more. This "merchandise" is displayed somewhere in the town or village center, where it is offered for sale. Cars are banned from the inner precincts of the towns and villages for the duration of the party, and everyone—children and adults—sits on the curb, or on chairs brought along for the purpose, and promotes and sells his or her wares. Those who don't feel like selling their old stuff are potential buyers. Young and old alike celebrate by playing the role of merchant, promoting their goods and haggling over the price, all to earn some extra pocket money, which will often be used to buy things in the same flea market—things that may well be sold again next year because they are too small, have in the meantime been read, or are just a bit out of fashion.

The more creative children play the recorder or violin to earn some money, or they sell homemade cookies. People who do not want to spend hours stuck behind a stall promenade in large herds along the streets in search of bargains. Much-told stories circulate about the purchase of an etching by Rembrandt or an authentic Chinese porcelain vase for next to nothing, but these are probably urban legends. The *vrijmarkt* is, however, under threat from real capitalists: itinerant retailers out to make a profit from the crowds that flock to the market by offering them beer, sweets, or other wares. The municipal authorities regulate all this by supervising these professional traders, and also by setting aside special, attractive parts of the town or village center for children.

That a free market is organized for the country's most important national celebration says something about how deeply the spirit of commerce— buying and selling—is rooted in Dutch culture. The Dutch version of "para- dise" is a free market where everyone can do as they please. It is important to make a bit of profit on the free market, but just as important is the fun of meeting other people and haggling for a bargain. But in order to protect the vulnerable—especially the children—the free market is nevertheless regulated by (in this case) the municipal authorities, who also supervise compliance with regulations and, just as important, deal with any negative "externalities" that arise, notably by efficiently disposing of the mountains of waste left behind after everyone has gone home.

This book is about a country whose economy has been dominated by markets for centuries, a country that can be seen as one of the pioneers of the global market economy as we know it today. The book looks at the question of when this market economy originated and seeks to determine why the Netherlands was one of the forerunners in the emergence of capitalism.[1] In doing so, it links into the ongoing debate about capitalism, about the emer- gence of this economic system and its effects on individual and collective behavior, on economic growth, social inequality, and "broad prosperity." The new history of capitalism has in the last ten years put this topic back on the agenda—after a quasi-absence of this debate during the 1990s and early 2000s.[2] Marxists would even argue that the essence of capitalism is inequality, because it is based on unequal access to the means of production. In their eyes, only a small part of the population is "capitalist" and owns those means of production, while the majority, the workers, have to "sell" themselves on the labor market in order to stay alive. From this fundamen- tal inequality of the capitalist market economy—according to the classical Marxist criticism of this system—originate all other forms of inequality.

So far we have been using the terms "market economy" and "capitalism" interchangeably, but this can easily lead to confusion.[3] A market economy is one in which the most important economic decisions—what to buy, what to produce, where to work—are made on the basis of price. Of course, other sorts of decisions and allocations of resources play a role in every economy— for example, those within the household or by the state—and the share of "pure" market transactions in an economy can vary across time and place. In the nineteenth century and the first half of the twentieth century, married women increasingly withdrew from the labor market under the influence of the "breadwinner model," but the degree to which households were dependent on the labor market hardly decreased as a result. In the twentieth century, social benefit payments associated with the welfare state coexist with income earned from employment. Where the boundary lies between market and nonmarket (e.g., state, household) may vary, but the market has retained its decisive role in economic decision-making.

In order to be able to speak of capitalism, another condition must also be met—namely, unequal access to the means of production. In a capitalist economy, a large part of the working population is dependent on wages, earned on the labor market. A noncapitalist market economy could consist of small-scale providers of goods and services, almost all of whom have some means of production at their disposal. Java in the nineteenth century is an example of what in the literature is called a "peasant economy," because almost all producers in that economy were small farmers.[4]

The founder of the debate on capitalism as a distinctive economic system was Karl Marx, who published the first volume of *Das Kapital* in 1867. Although Marx was primarily interested in industrial capitalism, he saw the roots of this system in what he called "primitive accumulation," the process by which possession of the means of production passed into the hands of a small group. This took place in various parts of Europe, where, according to Marx, small-scale farmers were dispossessed. In Britain, for example, as a result of the "enclosures," peasant farmers lost access to communal agricultural land. At more or less the same time, capitalists began to appropriate the riches of other continents. In Marx's own words:

> The discovery of gold and silver in America, the extirpation, enslavement and entombment in mines of the aboriginal population, the beginning of the conquest and looting of the East Indies, the turning of Africa into a warren for the commercial hunting of black-skins, signaled the rosy dawn of the era of capitalist production. These idyllic proceedings are the chief moments of primitive accumulation. . . . [T]hey all employ the power of the state, the concentrated and organized force of society, to

hasten, hot-house fashion, the process of transformation of the feudal mode of production into the capitalist mode, and to shorten the transition. Force is the midwife of every old society pregnant with a new one. It is itself an economic power.[5]

Marx and, more recently, the new history of capitalism emphasize that capitalism arises from the violent expropriation of the means of production, in which the state and colonialism have played a significant role. The new institutional economics, and in particular the work of Douglass North, one of its founders, sees this in a very different light. The crucial question for North and his followers is under what conditions producers and consumers would willingly become more market-oriented. Such a shift requires institutions that stimulate a strategy of cooperation via the market. For this cooperation, institutions establish the "rules of the game," which determine how people interact with one another. Producing for the market requires trust in its outcomes because all kinds of decisions make the producer dependent on that market.[6] For example, in the fifteenth century, farmers in the province of Holland began to specialize in livestock products—butter, cheese, meat, and hides—in which they had a comparative advantage. In doing so, those farmers made themselves dependent on the market not only for the sale of their butter and cheese but also for the purchase of food products like grain to feed themselves, since they no longer grew their own. According to North, this strategy would be successful only if property rights were protected, to ensure that people could reap the benefits of their market-oriented activities.

In North's view, the elites, and the state they controlled, were the most acute threat to market exchange. He was keenly aware of the role of violence, especially that of the state, which has the power to skim off any gains from specialization through taxation or simple expropriation. Constraining the executive is thus one of the major themes of new institutional economics—for example, through the development of democratic institutions such as parliaments. The most important breakthrough, according to North and Weingast, was therefore the Glorious Revolution of 1688–89, which restricted the power of the British monarch; the French Revolution in 1789 did the same in mainland Europe.[7] Acemoglu and Robinson, in an equally seminal statement, have argued that "inclusive institutions" are necessary for economic development, and that "extractive institutions" hinder economic growth.[8] The general idea of new institutional economics is that sociopolitical structures, the distribution of power in a society, determine whether the proper preconditions for economic development through the market are present.

Through his American lens, North saw the state, alongside its role as a guarantor of the rules, as a potential predator; he paid much less attention to the possibility that it could also protect weaker participants in the market (just as Dutch municipalities do by setting aside a special place for children in the free markets held on King's Day). In the premodern period, most states were barely able to play this role. Their authority was undermined, among other things, by independent lords, who could please themselves in the areas they controlled. On the other hand, there are other institutions that did play an important role in the early history of capitalism, as Max Weber realized a hundred years ago. Weber, most famously, claimed that Protestantism laid an ideological and psychological basis for capitalism.[9] But he also pointed out another peculiarity of medieval Europe: autonomous cities and their citizens. This draws attention to the possibility of a role played by civil society in the emergence and development of the capitalist economy. The bourgeoisie were not only people tempted by the enticements of profitable transactions but also citizens of cities, through which they tried to create their own political and economic space.

Political scientist Robert D. Putnam is the standard-bearer of a neo-Weberian group that attaches great importance to "civil society," with "social capital" as its active ingredient.[10] In essence this means that citizens organize themselves as collectives, within which they create mutual relationships (social capital) that enable them to act in the public domain. Some of these civil organizations are independent of the government—for example, sports clubs, choirs, and charities. Other organizations, however, have major dealings with governments, such as trade unions, consumer organizations, and political parties. In this book we consider their predecessors: guilds, neighborhood communities, civic militias in the cities, and polder administrations in the countryside. On paper, such organizations may appear to be opponents of the government, but in practice they can just as often help the state to find out what citizens really want, or to create support for difficult decisions.

Putnam concludes that societies with a strong civil society, and therefore a lot of social capital, perform better—like Douglass North, he sees civil society and social capital as bringing balance to society, providing organized countervailing forces that prevent the corruption that grows out of unbridled power. In theories like this, citizens are no longer regarded as "wage slaves," passive instruments in the hands of the elite or of capitalists, but as people with their own economic and political agendas. The underlying rationale in Putnam's work and that of his associates is that societies and their economies function better when there is active popular support for governmental policies and economic activities, because citizens can see the benefits of the government's efforts and of their own labors.[11] From our perspective, this means that we need to investigate the nature of the relationship between citizenship and social capital and the rise and further development of capitalism. Incidentally, there are also critics who think that this works the other way around: prosperous societies can afford to maintain the expensive consultations that accompany a high level of citizen participation.[12]

In classical Marxist theory, capitalism emerged from feudalism. Feudalism is in many respects the antithesis of capitalism: markets are marginal; the elites live from agricultural surpluses—the labor of serf farmers skimmed off by force. Ultimately, the system is static since it does not generate economic growth. The transition debate among Marxists mainly concerns whether feudalism perished owing to internal contradictions—an endogenous crisis in the system was needed to make room for the forces of capitalism, which then further undermined the system—or whether it was exogenous developments, in particular the rise of cities and international trade, that were responsible for the disappearance of this sociopolitical system.[13] The Netherlands was located on the margins of the region in which classical feudalism was concentrated, the area between the Seine and Rhine rivers. The country displayed a significant variation in terms of population density, urbanization, and rural soil conditions, as well as governance structures. While the southern regions of the Netherlands and the lands bordering these major rivers fell within this core of feudalism, the northern regions did not, because, as we will see later, "Frisian freedom" came to prevail. This makes the Netherlands an interesting case for studying the transition from feudalism to capitalism: how did it take place in the "feudal" and "nonfeudal" parts of the country?

Feudalism is traditionally seen as a rigid hierarchical system that suppresses market flows and is essentially based on coercion; Wickham, for example, in a recent review describes the core of feudalism as "surplus extraction: peasants having to give their products to lords, with the implicit threat of force."[14] Feudalism usually also refers to a sociopolitical structure (following Bloch) based on oaths of allegiance between lord and vassal as the primary structure of (the upper layers of) the state.[15] This view has been strongly criticized by Reynolds, but appears to fit well the development of feudalism in the Netherlands, as we hope to show.[16] However, regions with a strong feudal tradition would, as Jan de Vries has emphasized several times, have been less suitable for the development of capitalism.[17] The rise of capitalism in the Netherlands would, in this view, be the result of the absence of feudalism in the areas that were later to become the core of the Dutch Golden Age. On the other hand, however, the rise of feudalism in western Europe did actually stimulate economic development: the efficient extraction of production surpluses that feudalism made possible created a relatively wealthy elite (nobility and Church), with money to buy luxury products, which gave a significant boost to international trade.[18] And was feudalism really so hierarchical, anyway? The reciprocity between lord and vassal resulted in a division of power, making it possible for institutions to emerge, such as parliaments, in which this reciprocity—balance of power— was expressed. And just as the feudal monarch negotiated with his vassal, he in turn negotiated with the emerging cities, which could claim a more or less autonomous position in this system. In short, perhaps feudalism provided the breeding ground for capitalism.[19]

The gradual replacement of the feudal economy by a capitalist economy meant a fundamental revolution in the organization of society, economically, but also socially, politically, and culturally.[20] There is broad consensus that a market economy can provide the sort of economic growth that Adam Smith analyzed in *The Wealth of Nations*: trade and growing market exchange lead to specialization—between regions, between urban and rural areas, between professional craftspeople—like the famous workers in the pin factory, who could become much more productive by each taking one of the tasks involved in making a pin rather than if they personally had to complete the entire production process for each pin.[21] This "Smithian growth" has many facets, and includes the efficiency effects of better institutions. Another famous example, by David Ricardo, concerns the Portuguese trading wine for British textiles; large productivity gains could be achieved in both countries because the relative productivity of making such goods differed strongly between England and Portugal. It is embedded in the logic of the market economy that such productivity gains be systematically identified and exploited. But is that enough to get the process of "modern economic growth" going? Smith himself was not optimistic: he believed that after a phase of growth a "stationary state" would emerge, as productivity gains became exhausted. What is more, he described Holland as the most developed economy in the eighteenth century, but at the same time an example of an economy that was approaching this stationary state.[22]

Marxists like Brenner argue that persistent growth requires capitalism.[23] If the majority of the population are small-scale producers—as in a peasant economy—productivity gains from market production will remain limited. It is assumed that peasants work largely to provide for their own subsistence, as a result of which the core activity—small-scale farming for food—escapes the discipline of the market. Real economic growth, therefore, requires the "primitive accumulation of capital," which means that agricultural activities take place on large, capitalistic farms that make use of wage labor. Then, when the capitalist entrepreneur takes charge, a process of capital accumulation can begin that, in this view, is the driving force behind modern economic growth. English agriculture as created by the enclosures of the sixteenth century was the model for this line of thinking.[24]

This touches on the discussion about the nature of economic growth in the period prior to the Industrial Revolution of the late eighteenth and nineteenth centuries and the identification of the causes of this growth.[25] Is this Smithian growth, the result of specialization and the improved institutions that promote increased market production?[26] Or is it Marxian growth, the result of economies of scale made possible by proletarianization? Were large capitalist farms in England, for instance, far more productive than small family farms elsewhere? What is clear about the Dutch case, however, is that Malthusian forces—population growth causing a decline in availability of agricultural land and resources in general—play a very limited role in this Smithian/Marxian economy, where in the long run population growth correlates positively with economic growth (as we will see in chapter 2).

Was there a major economic cycle in the Netherlands between 1300 and 1800, with its peak during the seventeenth century? In its Golden Age of the late sixteenth and seventeenth centuries, the Dutch Republic played a leading role on the world stage: not only could the Dutch be found in every corner of the globe, they were also able to accumulate enormous wealth, making the Republic the most prosperous country in the world during the seventeenth century. But that period of economic success was followed by a period in which the Dutch Republic had to relinquish its central role, especially to the British. Was this sequel to the Golden Age inevitable, and did it lead to a downturn in the economy? Or did the trend of productivity and income growth continue after the boom? How should we interpret these patterns spatially, given that the economic center of gravity within northwestern Europe shifted from Flanders (Middle Ages) to Brabant (sixteenth century), and later to Holland (seventeenth century), and later still to England (eighteenth century)?

At the heart of the debate on capitalism is the issue of social inequality, as was highlighted by Catharina Lis and Hugo Soly in their 1979 book on poverty in preindustrial Europe.[27] The issue has recently returned to the political agenda following the publication of Thomas Piketty's book *Capital in the Twenty-First Century*.[28] Capitalism is associated with exploitation and unequal exchange, with the result that the poor become poorer and the rich richer. The new history of capitalism has in particular stressed the link with slavery, which is seen as a capitalist institution that played a major role in the rise of the capitalist world economy.[29] Did slavery play such a role in the rise of capitalism in the Netherlands? Was extreme inequality the result of this pioneering economic development by the Dutch? And in what forms did these inequalities manifest themselves? In chapter 8 we look at several dimensions of inequality to find out whether, and to what extent, it did increase. Inequality also has an important international dimension: economic expansion—Dutch capitalism—stretched far beyond the borders of the Republic, to South Africa, Ceylon (Sri Lanka), the East Indies, Surinam, and other Caribbean colonies. In a previous study on merchant capitalism, Van Zanden argued that this stage of capitalism was an open system that used the flow of cheap labor—migrants, protoindustrial workers, and slaves—to enhance its profitability and success.[30] Slavery on the one hand was an integral part of the system but, on the other hand, as we will see, never became an indigenous institution in the Netherlands. Slavery had a disastrous impact on the well-being of those enslaved, and on the long-term development potential of both the regions where they were captured and those where they were taken, but it hardly affected the institutions of the Netherlands itself.

The story of capitalism, according to its critics, does not end with the increase in socioeconomic inequality. Greater inequality can affect the quality of the political system, lead to corruption, result in exclusion of groups within the population, and, more generally, lead to economic and sociopolitical behavior aimed at short-term gain, at the expense of citizenship and civil society. "Greed is good" summarizes the type of behavior that, critics claim, is encouraged by capitalism. Does the triumph of capitalism lead to erosion of the values and norms that, according to new institutional economics, made that system possible?[31]

The idea that this outcome is not entirely inevitable is derived from Sam Bowles's book *The Moral Economy*, which deals with the temptations to which the "homo economicus" is exposed. An interesting example is the behavior of diplomats at the United Nations in New York, who enjoy diplomatic immunity and can therefore park their cars wherever they want.[32] They do get a fine (a parking ticket) for this but do not have to pay it. Statistics on these violations have been kept for a number of years. Diplomats from some countries make heavy use of their immunity: Egypt topped the league with 140 tickets per year per diplomat; Bulgaria was a close second with 117. Yet not one Dutch or British diplomat was ever issued a ticket, nor were their Swedish, Norwegian, and Canadian counterparts. Bowles speculated that this was because of the "admirable civic cultures of many of the long-standing capitalist economies," and explicitly linked this with the long capitalist history of these countries.[33] Can capitalism, under some conditions, still coexist with good citizenship, or is it only with good citizenship that capitalism can flourish? But what, then, prevents good citizenship from being undermined by greed and the pursuit of profit on the Amsterdam Exchange or Wall Street?

The parking behavior of UN diplomats indicates that several sorts of capitalism exist. This is the crux of the discussion about "varieties of capitalism." As new institutional economics emphasizes, markets are always embedded in a system of institutions, aimed at, among other things, increasing confidence and limiting negative excesses. However, the extent to which those aims are achieved differs from society to society, from century to century, and perhaps even from market to market. The state almost always regulates the currencies and the weights and measures used in markets, as well as the taxes to be paid on market transactions. Sometimes, however, the state—or a party authorized by the state, a city or another competent body, such as a guild or trading company—determines who can conduct which transactions; not everyone is allowed to call themselves a doctor or notary, for example. The balance between the market and other forms of coordination is different in every capitalist society, which can have major consequences for the degree of inequality that exists, since many interventions in the market are motivated by the desire to counter extreme inequality. This alerts us to the dangers of general statements about capitalism, and at the same time underlines the importance of a historical approach that can account for specifics of time and place.[34]

To sum up, in this book on the role of the Netherlands as a pioneer of capitalism we are interested in finding answers to a number of questions. A first set of questions deals with the "how" and "why" of the emergence of a capitalist market economy. Why was the Netherlands—a fairly marginal region of western Europe until 1300—one of the pioneers of the market economy and capitalism? What role did feudalism play as a social structure preceding this emergence? Was there a violent transition—one in which the Dutch Revolt of 1566–1648 may have played a key role—or was the rise of capitalism mainly the result of voluntary choices made by market participants? What role did civil society play? Did it precede the breakthrough of the capitalist market economy or was it actually a consequence of that development? What role did slavery play in the emergence of Dutch capitalism?

A second set of questions deals with the impact of the emergence of capitalism on the nature of society and the economy—at home and abroad. Was this pioneer of capitalism subsequently derailed by the negative consequences of rapidly increasing inequality? Was the impact of capitalism at home, within the Netherlands' borders, different from that overseas, in Indonesia, South Africa, or Surinam? Did Dutch capitalism dig its own grave? Was the relative decline of the eighteenth century a consequence of the dynamics of capitalist expansion, or should we see the problems of that century in a completely different light?

Within the overall context of capitalism, we do not regard its history in the Netherlands from a national perspective but, rather, as stage in the realization of a global process. As a short-lived leader of the budding world economy, the Netherlands played an important role in the rise and shaping of early capitalism.

We have restricted our focus in this book to the medieval and early modern periods. The history of the Dutch economy and society throughout the "long" nineteenth century (1780–1913) has already been described by Jan Luiten van Zanden and Arthur van Riel in their book *The Strictures of Inheritance* (2000), while the twentieth century is described in Jan Luiten van Zanden's *Economic History of the Netherlands, 1914–1995* (1997).[35] Although those two books are organized around the concept of economic growth, they can nevertheless easily be read as sequels to this book. For the present book, however, we have used the organizing principle of chronology. After a brief, quantitative overview of major events and themes in economic growth and well-being from 1000 to 1800 (chapter 2), chapters 3 and 4 sketch the emergence of the typical medieval institutions of western Europe and, more importantly, how the market economy and capitalism arose from this. Subsequently, our focus shifts to the economic acceleration of the seventeenth century, in which Dutch capitalism accelerated and developed into a pre-eminent model. But this book is also about the "political economy" of a region that would not itself become a state—and then only through political revolution—until around 1600. The Dutch Revolt, we argue in chapter 5, contributed greatly to the economic dynamism of the period that followed by giving the towns of the Netherlands their own state. The period roughly coinciding with the seventeenth century that is known as the Dutch Golden Age is analyzed in chapters 6 and 7. The legacy of Dutch medieval institutions remained visible and active even after the Revolt; to a certain extent these institutions were even consolidated and reinforced during the course of the revolution. In the last chapter we examine the consequences of Dutch capitalist expansion for different groups within the Dutch Republic and for peoples outside Europe who were absorbed into the Dutch capitalist economy.

Since the fall of the Berlin Wall in 1989 and the economic transformation of China into a market economy, one could reasonably say that capitalism is the "only show in town."[36] There is a great deal of agreement about the benefits of this economic model: it has enabled enormous growth in the prosperity of humanity as a whole. Its major drawbacks are also easy to identify in 2022: enormous inequality, between both social classes and regions, along with depletion of natural resources. The latter is mainly a consequence of the Industrial Revolution, and for this reason we have not discussed it in this book. However, with the economic history of the Netherlands in mind we are able to comment on the former. The lack of a serious alternative to capitalism underscores the urgency for finding answers to the question of how the capitalist economic system can be improved. Knowledge of the history of capitalism offers useful material for meeting this challenge.

Two practical issues need to be clarified before we can finally launch into our story. The first is timing. This book is dealing with the country currently indicated on the world map as "the Netherlands"—officially, the "Kingdom of the Netherlands." However, a country with some resemblance to the present Netherlands emerged only in the decades around 1600, during the revolution called the Dutch Revolt. This Revolt is the subject of chapter 5, but it means that chapters 3 and 4 in particular are discussing a country that did not, as such, exist. However, its constituent parts, called "provinces" after the establishment of the country, did exist, and we will be using those as the units of analysis, not only in chapters 3 and 4 but also very often in the other chapters of the book. The second issue is geography. Confusingly, the country we are discussing in this book has been known under various names during the period covered here. Presently it is the Netherlands, but that country is also often called Holland. Between roughly 1600 and 1795 the country was known as the Republic of the Seven United Netherlands, or Dutch Republic for short. Holland was its most important province, but there were six other provinces that also participated in the Dutch Republic. Before 1600, the Dutch provinces were part of an area known as the Low Countries, which also comprised two other independent countries within the modern European Union: Belgium and Luxemburg. After the split of the Low Countries around 1600, what we nowadays know as Belgium continued as the Spanish, and later Austrian, Low Countries, after the Spanish and Austrian Habsburg dynasties that in turn ruled these parts. These were also known as the Southern Netherlands.

2

Eight Hundred Years of Economic Growth, 1000–1800

In the nineteenth century, Marx investigated the roots of the revolutionary transformation that western Europe's economy and society were undergoing at the time, a transformation known to us as the Industrial Revolution. He wondered whether this was the moment when the dynamics generated by the market economy and capitalism took hold. Or did the impetus for economic growth occur much earlier? Here we will look back well before Marx's time to see if we can detect earlier economic growth and improvements in human welfare in the Netherlands and to put these developments into a European perspective. We will focus on people and gross domestic product (GDP) per capita first—the measures most often used to chart economic development. Next, we will follow the "beyond GDP" debate and chart the long-term trends in dimensions of well-being.

People and GDP

This chapter presents an overview of the long-term development of the region now known as the Netherlands from the year 1000 to 1800—the period covered by this book. We start with the most basic numbers: What was the size of the population of the Netherlands in this period? Figure 2.1 shows estimates of population numbers for the Netherlands since 950, based on a recent update of the demographic history of the Netherlands in this period by Paping, who has synthesized research carried out since the last

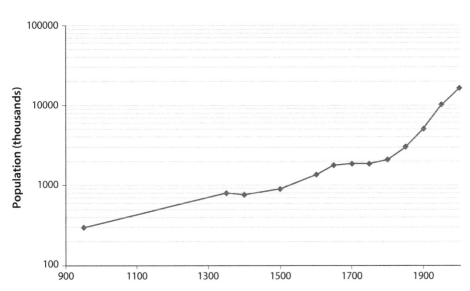

FIGURE 2.1. Estimates of the population of the Netherlands, 950–2000 (in thousands, semi-log scale).
Sources: Paping 2014; Bavel and Van Zanden 2004; after 1800: Maddison database, see Bolt and Van Zanden 2020.

overview, that of the Wageningen research group in the 1970s.[1] The rising long-term trend is the most striking feature, but we can also see three major cycles. The first boom starts at about the year 950, around the time when our story begins. The Netherlands had a population of an estimated 300,000 people—because of the margins of uncertainty, let us say the total was somewhere between 250,000 and 350,000. By the end of the great medieval boom—around 1350—this had nearly tripled to an estimated 800,000. And while the Black Death, which began in 1348, had a radical impact on the population of Europe, its overall effect on the population of the Netherlands remained limited: by the year 1400 this population still numbered 765,000, while by 1500 it had increased to 900,000, well beyond the 1348 level.[2]

The next cycle starts in the fifteenth century. Population numbers increase from just under 1 million in 1511 to just over 2.1 million in 1800. The population increased throughout almost the entire period; only around 1740 is some hesitation in the rate of growth visible. Cities grew faster than the countryside: the degree of urbanization rose from 36% in 1511 to 40% in 1800, quite a modest increase considering the Netherlands was already by 1500 probably the most urbanized region in the world. At that time, the County of Holland had an urbanization rate of 45%, which rose to 60%

by 1800.[3] However, the drawing power of Holland's rapidly growing urban system caused a decline of urbanization in the rest of the country, from 32% to 27%. This reflects a process of internal divergence, with Holland undergoing strong economic development while other parts of the country lagged behind.

One of the most exciting developments in the study of economic history in recent years has been the work on the quantification of economic growth in the period before 1800. In the footsteps of Simon Kuznets and Angus Maddison, who started this research and extended it to the preindustrial period, scholars have now published time series of the long-term evolution of GDP per capita of "their" countries, including China, India, Japan, Peru, Mexico, and the Ottoman Empire, as well as European nations such as England, Holland, Italy, Spain, Portugal, France, Germany, and Poland. Integrated into a single system of international benchmark estimates (as developed by Maddison), these estimates give a broad picture of the long-term trends in the world economy in the centuries before the Industrial Revolution.[4] Figure 2.2 presents a selection from this rich data set, the series estimates of the GDP per capita of England, Holland, northern Italy, and China (for the last, only point estimates at irregular intervals). A minimum, near-subsistence level of income per capita in each of the four countries across this period would be about 600 dollars (of 2011). The lowest estimates—for England in the years around 1300 and China after 1750—are at the level of about 1,000 (2011) dollars. The line representing England shows a jump immediately after the Black Death of 1348, which almost halved the population but led to a much higher GDP per capita for those who survived, followed by a plateau between 1400 and 1650, and then consistent growth starting in the middle decades of the seventeenth century. By contrast, northern Italy, in the Middle Ages much more prosperous than England, shows long-term decline resulting in a much lower GDP per capita at the start of the nineteenth century. A similar long-term stagnation can be found in China before 1650, followed by decline during the Qing period after 1644.

This is the broad picture against which the Dutch case must be understood. Unfortunately, we do not have reliable estimates for the Netherlands as a whole, but a continuous series for the province of Holland starting in 1348, just before the bubonic plague pandemic struck for the first time. At that time, Holland's GDP per capita was at about the same level as that of England, and much below that of northern Italy, albeit the size of the gap between the countries of the North Sea area and northern Italy is still a matter of some debate.[5] There are no reliable estimates for Chinese GDP in

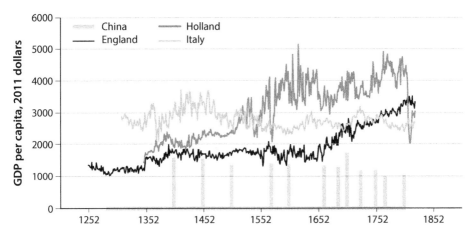

FIGURE 2.2. Estimates of the GDP per capita of England, northern Italy, China, and Holland, 1252–1800 (in 2011 international dollars).
Source: Bolt and Van Zanden 2020.

the fourteenth century, but probably the empire was at about the same or a somewhat higher level; in the most developed part of China, the Yangtze Delta, GDP per capita must have been substantially higher. In short, around 1350 Holland (and the Netherlands as a whole) was at a level of income per capita that we could consider "normal" for a preindustrial society, but this changed dramatically in the three following centuries, as figure 2.2 shows clearly. A consistent process of economic growth set in, which made Holland into the most prosperous country in the world, with a GDP per capita fluctuating wildly at levels between 3,000 and 4,500 dollars (of 2011).[6] A problem with these estimates is that annual fluctuations are huge, owing to changes in international trade and shipping, which were heavily affected by exogenous shocks (war, harvest failures) that also had a large impact on the rest of the economy. These fluctuations in a way overshadow the long-term trends, and make it difficult to determine when growth began and when it ended. A first glance may suggest that there was one long period of growth, between 1350 and about 1630, followed by 170 years of stagnation at a high level, but econometric testing for trends and breaking points tells a story of an unchanging process of economic growth over the entire period from 1350 to 1800.[7] Around this constant trend of about 0.18% growth per year, swings occurred, leading to temporarily higher levels of GDP per capita in the 1620s and 1630s, and low-level "outliers" between 1650 and 1680.[8]

This constant rate of growth after 1350 is a significant result for a number of reasons. One is that economic growth preceded the Golden Age of the

seventeenth century—the classic period of Dutch economic expansion—
by 250 years. The economy of Holland was already modernizing and pro-
gressing dramatically in the two centuries between 1350 and 1580, before
the Dutch Revolt (of 1572) and the mass migration from the south to the
north further contributed to the dynamic expansion. The crucial "takeoff"
(if this term is allowed here) that set in motion an irreversible process of
economic development occurred between 1350 and 1500 (and perhaps
already by 1400), when the urban economy of Holland started to change
(see chapter 4). We will demonstrate in this book that at the same time a
capitalist market economy emerged, characterized by efficient markets for
commodities, labor, capital, and land (following, amongst others, Van Bavel,
who has developed a similar argument).[9] In order to explain the specific
path of growth in Holland, we have to determine the causes of the start of
economic growth in the late medieval period—and therefore the emergence
of capitalism in that period.

A second important point to be made is that according to these estimates
and the econometric analysis based on them, per capita economic growth
continued after 1670. To the Dutch of the late seventeenth and eighteenth
centuries, this growth was perhaps less dramatic than that during the preceding century, giving rise to complaints about (relative) decline and stagnation (see the discussion in chapter 8). The well-informed Adam Smith
theorized at the time that, in the long term, highly developed economies
had the tendency to enter a "stationary state," and he clearly had Holland in
mind when he discussed this possibility.[10] But the estimated development of
GDP per capita suggests that the eighteenth century was not characterized
by substantial economic failure, and that the underlying process of (slow)
productivity growth continued, despite the Dutch Republic having to contend with worsening international conditions and increased competition.

In the fourteenth century, Holland embarked on a process of economic
growth that by the start of the seventeenth century had made the Dutch
Republic into the richest and most productive economy in the world.
This is one of the central topics of this book, and explaining this "birth of
capitalism"—and hence the spectacular growth path of this region—is one
of our aims.

We emphasize the consistent positive trend of growth between 1350 and
1800. Moreover, GDP growth and population growth were positively cor-
related—in particular, the economic growth spurt of 1500–1650 coincided
with rapid population growth.[11] However, we do accept that growth after the
Industrial Revolution was of a fundamentally different nature. After about

1820 an acceleration of growth is clearly visible in the available GDP per capita time series.[12] Growth after 1820 was based on the exploitation of a knowledge base that was rapidly expanding, resulting in the kind of cumulative technological change that still dominates the world economy today.[13] Such an engine of growth was lacking before 1820. Technology did change, but at a much slower rate, and was not driven by the systematic, cumulative growth of useful knowledge that was the result of the Enlightenment (although useful knowledge did of course grow). Pre-1820 growth is usually characterized as "Smithian": the result of growing market production, specialization, and the technological change commercialization induced. In that sense pre-1820 growth is even more intimately linked to the emergence and development of a market economy. It was the market and the specialization it induced—as analyzed very clearly for the first time by Adam Smith—that was the direct driver of growth, and not a (more or less) independent process of technological change that caused productivity to rise.

How exceptional was the pattern of economic growth that we find in Holland between 1348 and 1800? There is an influential tradition regarding economic development in the preindustrial period that focuses mainly on the ups and downs of these economies. Jack Goldstone is an outspoken proponent of the cyclical nature of growth before 1800.[14] A particular region—for example, the Middle East after 800, northern Italy in the High Middle Ages, or the Netherlands in the seventeenth century—would for certain reasons experience a period of strong growth, but after a number of generations it would come to an end, and a decline would set in, although this did not wipe away all gains: on balance, a more developed economy with a higher level of income remained at the end of the cycle. Van Bavel, another proponent of this view, considers economic growth in all periods—both before and after 1800—as a cyclical phenomenon. In his view, a growth spurt is triggered by rising pressure from capitalist market forces, but the increasing inequality that results in the long run undermines the economic momentum, which then, consistent with Goldstone, degenerates into stagnation and even decline.[15] The two economic historians differ, however, in what they believe determines this cycle: according to Goldstone it is mainly exogenous influences, while Van Bavel considers these influences to be predominantly endogenous.

The interpretation of Jan de Vries and Ad van der Woude, presented in their path-breaking book *The First Modern Economy*, can be considered as another version of the view that stresses the cyclical nature of growth. Their main point is that the Netherlands during the period 1500–1800 was a "modern" market economy, not dominated by Malthusian forces but characterized by "modern" institutions, which supported a process of sustained growth lasting from 1500 to 1670. Growth was based on "modernizing, dynamic processes" such as "urbanization, education, mobility, monetization, and political and legal development." "These features of Dutch society in the seventeenth and eighteenth century placed the rational actor, the homo oeconomicus, in a dynamic setting conducive to innovation." "The economic experience analyzed in this book," they continue, "constituted modern economic growth." Moreover, growth did not stop in the 1670s because of population growth and declining returns in agriculture, or because of "supply constraints of inelastic energy sources, but because of economic circumstances that limited demand."[16] The paradox that this "first modern economy" experienced cyclical growth can perhaps be explained by the fact that the global economy as a whole was also experiencing a long cycle of growth—the secular trends that we alluded to earlier in this chapter.

How can we reconcile these studies, stressing the cyclical character of growth before 1800, with the evidence about the development of GDP per capita between 1350 and 1800 presented earlier? Firstly, Holland was the exception, and possibly the only example of a capitalist market economy generating consistent growth. Secondly, De Vries and Van der Woude were not radical enough in their assessment of the performance of the "first modern economy," because they lacked the statistical data to gauge the true extent of the process of economic growth (and, as argued elsewhere, overlooked the medieval roots of the growth process).[17] An additional explanation is offered by De Pleijt and Van Zanden, who have argued that what looks like a cycle (or cycles) is in fact a shift in location of the core of a much larger economy. In their alternative interpretation, the North Sea region as a whole is the relevant unit of analysis for the study of preindustrial growth. Within this region, the center of economic growth was located during the Middle Ages in Flanders (Bruges, Ghent), then shifted in the sixteenth century to Brabant (Antwerp), before moving north after 1585 to Holland (Amsterdam), and finally, around 1700, to England (London). The region as a whole, however, experienced continuous growth for the best part of a millennium, owing to the emergence of a capitalist market economy there in the late medieval period. The shift, for example, of the economic center of the North Sea region from Antwerp to Amsterdam at the end of the sixteenth century brought about a deep crisis in Brabant and Flanders, while Holland, on the other hand, enjoyed a huge boost. So when Flanders is seen in isolation, Flemish growth may appear cyclical, but within the context of the North Sea region as a whole, the decline of one region is compensated by the expansion of other regions. Similarly, the English growth spurt starts only in the middle decades of the seventeenth century, because the highly productive international activities of the North Sea area before 1650 were mainly concentrated in the Low Countries. After 1650, with the dramatic expansion of London and the growth of the Atlantic economy, England became the core of the North Sea region.[18] The Dutch "Golden Age" was thus part of this much wider process of growth in the North Sea area, and what appears to be a growth cycle is just the century of Holland being the "core" of this region on the long road from 1350 to 1800.

Other Measures, Other Dimensions of Well-Being

It is well known that GDP estimates have serious limitations as a measure of economic development. In the "beyond GDP" debate, it has been argued that income is only one dimension of well-being. Other dimensions—life expectancy and health, education, exposure to crime and violence, political rights, a clean environment—matter as well.[19] Moreover, the available GDP series start in fourteenth century, so we need other data to find out what was happening before that moment. Ultimately, economic development—as expressed in the vision of Nobel laureate Amartya Sen—is about increasing freedom, creating space for people to make meaningful decisions about their own lives. From this perspective, economic development is a much more complex process, and its evaluation requires a much broader view of the economy and society, including, for example, gender relations and the occurrence of coercion in the form of serfdom or slavery.[20]

A study of the other dimensions of well-being requires other measures and other data. New work on the economic history of artifacts has contributed to this. Economic activity in the past has left a material heritage— books, manuscripts, paintings, churches, castles, urban agglomerations— which is still (more or less) intact and testifies to the wealth (or poverty) of societies in the past. In principle, these artifacts, found in museums, libraries, or simply in the public space, can be quantified, and big data sets are available (including, for churches, Google Maps) that contain a wealth of information. Estimates have to be made to transform this data into the real output of number of books written or churches built during historical times, but much work on this has been done—by historians of medieval manuscripts, for example, who have estimated how much of that particular type of historical source has been lost over the years.[21] Ad van der Woude has used this kind of information for his reconstruction of the production of paintings in the Dutch Republic in the seventeenth century.[22] One of the advantages of the study of artifacts is that this research is not restricted to periods for which there are surviving written sources. In chapter 3 we present estimates of the evolution of the building of great churches in a large part of Europe—medieval cathedrals that are (with a few exceptions) still visible in the centers of European cities and for which the building history has often been documented or reconstructed in detail. Church building was linked to fund-raising by the Church and to agricultural output (via tithes, for example), the skilled labor of artisans, and the growth and prosperity of cities, and can therefore be considered an index of economic activity.[23] And we can study church building in the centuries before 1300, when other sources are much more scarce. Compared with the rest of western Europe, until the fourteenth century there was little church construction activity in the Netherlands, whereas Flanders was part of the core region of relatively intense building activity stretching from the Rhineland to northern France (the region of classic feudalism as described by Bloch).[24] But after 1350 building activity in the Netherlands exploded, and the region became the most dynamic and active center of the building industry. Church building in many ways seems to mirror the process of growth of GDP per capita presented in figure 2.2.

The Netherlands lagged far behind the rest of western Europe in church building during most of the Middle Ages, but suddenly began to catch up and even overtook its peers in the fourteenth and fifteenth centuries. A similar development can be found in a very important dimension of well-being, human capital. The reconstruction of the production of manuscripts and books, based on the research by Buringh and Van Zanden, can be used as a proxy for the growing importance of literacy at this time (tables 2.1 and 2.2). Over the entire period, growth in book production is spectacular: between the sixth and eighteenth centuries, in per capita terms, European book production increased by a factor of more than ten thousand. The position of the Netherlands also changed dramatically. In the Middle Ages, the country—still on the fringes of Europe—was not an important center for book production: in per capita terms its output amounted to no more than 20%–30% of the average western European level. Yet in the fifteenth century this suddenly changed, with the Netherlands producing more than double the European average of manuscripts, and lagging behind only Belgium. With the invention of book printing, its relative position remained intact: between 1454 and 1500 the Netherlands appears to have printed more than

TABLE 2.1. Per Capita Consumption of Manuscript Books per Annum (per Million Inhabitants), Sixth to Fifteenth Centuries, Key Countries

	Century									
	6th	7th	8th	9th	10th	11th	12th	13th	14th	15th
Britain	0.9	11.4	54.7	61.0	54.4	88.5	270.1	466.6	370.3	485.4
France	3.5	5.1	32.5	142.7	22.0	62.6	217.4	384.1	418.2	919.8
Belgium	0.0	4.2	37.0	101.0	38.9	170.6	540.2	1087.2	1061.5	5721.2
Netherlands	0.0	1.3	3.0	4.1	1.9	8.9	34.6	29.5	188.3	2149.7
Germany	0.0	0.0	23.4	181.1	134.4	130.4	333.8	360.5	376.7	660.4
Italy	25.5	12.4	17.2	47.2	31.7	71.8	146.5	294.2	1034.5	1674.9
Iberia	3.7	6.4	9.7	51.7	110.8	83.4	193.9	312.9	453.0	550.0
Western Europe	6.5	5.3	20.9	88.1	52.6	70.2	206.1	330.0	507.8	929.2

Source: Buringh and Van Zanden 2009.

TABLE 2.2. Per Capita Consumption of Printed Books per Annum, 1454/1500–1751/1800 (per 1000 inhabitants), Key Countries

	1454–1500	1501–1550	1551–1600	1601–1650	1651–1700	1701–1750	1751–1800
Great Britain	2.0	14.6	27.3	80.0	191.8	168.3	192.0
France	3.2	29.9	33.7	52.2	70.1	58.7	117.9
Belgium	4.7	17.7	48.2	33.2	73.6	30.7	44.5
Netherlands	7.9	14.2	33.5	139.0	259.4	391.3	488.3
Germany	4.1	21.2	43.4	54.0	78.7	99.7	122.4
Italy	6.8	21.3	51.0	42.1	56.3	48.4	86.5
Spain	0.9	4.2	4.3	8.8	14.3	18.5	28.3
Sweden	0.2	0.8	1.1	39.7	58.5	83.8	208.9
Western Europe	3.1	17.5	29.1	40.6	66.7	66.7	122.4

Source: Buringh and Van Zanden 2009.

double the European average number of books, with the Hanseatic town of Deventer as the most important center of this new industry. In the sixteenth century, book printing in the Low Countries was initially concentrated in Antwerp, but after 1585 production in the northern Netherlands skyrocketed, reaching an average per capita output that was consistently three to more than four times that of Europe as a whole.[25] During the seventeenth century, Holland became the "bookshop of the world."[26] Exports of books were important, but the domestic demand for print was equally large.

It has been argued that the marriage system found in western Europe, where marriage was based on consensus and women had a relatively strong position as a result, contributed to this favorable environment for human capital formation. The Reformation, with its emphasis on independent reading of the Bible, further contributed to rising levels of literacy. As late as the beginning of the nineteenth century, the Catholic provinces of the Netherlands were much less literate than the Protestant ones. Indeed, although poor and sparsely populated, the Protestant province of Drenthe was a frontrunner in literacy, owing to strong promotion of primary education by the regional government. Around 1815 in the Netherlands, the proportion of brides capable of signing their marriage certificate—a test of minimal literacy–was almost 60%; approximately 75% of grooms could do the same. The northern parts of the Netherlands scored best in all respects (70%–75% brides, 85% grooms), and the Catholic south the worst (Limburg: 42% brides, 68% grooms). These percentages were high by international standards: only countries such as Sweden and Prussia, with their tradition of state-organized education—as inspired by Luther—surpassed Dutch figures.[27]

The third dimension of well-being that, together with real income and literacy, makes up the Human Development Index is life expectancy.[28] There is no good overview of the development of life expectancy over these centuries, but we cannot be very optimistic about it. Cities were very unhealthy places, and growth of the urban population will certainly have had a negative effect on life expectancy (this is known as the "urban graveyard effect").[29]

The Black Death in 1348, and periodic outbreaks of the plague that followed until 1665, certainly had an adverse effect on life expectancy.[30] There are also indications that malaria—in part the result of increasing brackishness in some areas of inland water, such as the IJ—continued to spread and had perhaps an even greater adverse impact on life expectancy. The discontinuity in the population growth trend around 1740 may have been related to virulent malaria epidemics in the period, which continued into the nineteenth century. Nevertheless, there were also some positive developments: Neil Cummins has shown that the life expectancy of nobles in northwestern Europe began to increase in the fifteenth century and did so again after 1650, thus displaying an upward trend well before the Industrial Revolution.[31] De la Croix and Licandro identified a similar break around 1650 among a set of three hundred thousand "famous" northwest Europeans, for which they had reconstructed the demographics.[32] So, among the elite—the nobility, the "famous people"—the beginning of the seventeenth century marks a turn toward an increase in life expectancy. In Holland, urban elites started to acquire or build country houses in the seventeenth century, allowing them to escape both the bad odors and the pollution that afflicted the towns during the summer months.[33]

An indicator closely related to life expectancy is body height, data for which are usually derived from archaeological research on human remains (in a way, also artifacts) for periods before armies started to measure their recruits. Height depends on the general state of health and nutrition, especially during childhood. Thanks to extensive research into the "biological standard of living," much is known about long-term trends. The archaeologist Maat published an overview of the research findings in the Netherlands that had produced data on the body sizes of the interred. Those data show a long-term decline from the Roman period to the mid-nineteenth century, which he links to population growth and urbanization. It seems that this decline accelerated in the late medieval period, but the sample sizes were small and the social composition of the samples changed over time (it is no surprise that well-fed medieval monks are taller than the working-class inhabitants of an industrial town such as Leiden).[34] A much more comprehensive study, covering Europe as a whole, and making it possible to control for place and social group, shows that the long-term decline in stature from the early Middle Ages was a pan-European process. Body height seems to have peaked around the year 500, gradually decreasing with the return of "civilization" until sometime between 1800 and 1850. In northwestern Europe, the decline, especially among women, was more modest than elsewhere, although there, too, a decrease in body height did take place in the early modern period. The data suggest that, overall, little or no gain in body height was made before 1800—which seems consistent with the rather pessimistic picture of life expectancy—although regional differences may have favored northwestern Europe somewhat.[35]

A trend that is strongly supportive of an increase in the standard of living concerns security and crime. Several authors have reconstructed trends in the statistics of numbers of victims of murder and manslaughter, which provide a clear picture for the Low Countries. In the late Middle Ages, the Netherlands (and Europe as a whole) was by the standards of today an extremely violent place: the homicide rate was at a level comparable to that of South Africa today, and, at around 45 homicides per 100,000 inhabitants, was double that of modern Brazil, two countries notorious for their levels of violence. By the sixteenth century the rate in the Low Countries had fallen to 25 per 100,000 inhabitants, and in the seventeenth century to less than 10, reaching 4 per 100,000 by the second half of the eighteenth century—a decrease of more than 90%.[36] Moreover, the social distribution of violence may have changed; in the Middle Ages it was members of the nobility who were mainly responsible for homicides. But this kind of violence perpetrated by the rich and powerful gradually diminished, and interpersonal violence was increasingly committed predominantly by those at the bottom of the social pyramid.[37] In other words, the elite was pacified and no longer used personal violence to impose its power, but relied more and more on the state and related institutions. During the early modern period, the rest of the Dutch were also "pacified," and violence was largely banished as a means for settling interpersonal conflicts. The driving force behind this process was, as has been argued by Steve Pinker, the increasing appropriation by the state of a monopoly on the use of violence, replacing it with formalized, state-regulated processes of conflict resolution, and, ultimately, more generally "civilized" behavior by Europeans during the period.[38]

We have already reviewed quite a few dimensions of well-being, inspired by the analytical framework developed by the Organisation for Economic Co-operation and Development's Better Life Initiative. The dimension of gender inequality also has a place in this review.[39] Much research has shown that the position of women in the Netherlands in the late Middle Ages and early modern times was fairly strong, and that women had a relatively large influence on important decisions in their lives. From the late Middle Ages onward, marriage was based on consensus (consent by husband and wife), literacy among women was relatively high, and many women had access to labor and capital markets—all matters to be dealt with in chapters to come.[40]

Another important, positive aspect of social relations in the Netherlands was the almost complete absence, after 1300, of forms of coercion such as serfdom and slavery, at least in the territory of the Dutch Republic itself (we return to this in chapters 6 and 8). We will also see that a strong civil society arose in the Middle Ages, and that political institutions allowed much space for "bottom-up" opinions and initiatives.

In sum, several indicators of well-being show a strong increase in living standards. Rising average income and educational level and the decreasing homicide rate are strong indicators of improvement. The level of political participation was relatively high (for a premodern economy), and gender inequality was relatively low. These positive signs need to be set against stagnant or perhaps (particularly in the larger cities) declining life expectancy and health status as measured by stature. Note that all these data are limited to the inhabitants of the Netherlands, and that, for example, the impact of slavery as a result of Dutch activities in Asia, America, and Africa has not been included here (see the discussion in chapter 8).

All told, we see before us a remarkable picture: the capitalist market economy, which had already become dominant in large parts of the Netherlands in the late Middle Ages, led to broad growth in prosperity. How could an economic system based on the exploitation of labor by the holders of capital produce such an outcome? That question is the focus of the chapters to come.

3

Between Feudalism and Freedom, 1000–1350

A thousand years ago, around the year 1015, the monk Alpert of Metz visited the region we now call the Netherlands. Among other things, he described how the merchants of Tiel—at that time the most important trading center in the region—were members of an association that organized banquets and enjoyed certain rights, claiming to have had a privilege granted to them by the emperor of the Holy Roman Empire. They also maintained their own system of justice, which deviated from canonical law. These merchants complained about an illegal toll that Count Dirk III of Holland, who controlled access to the sea through the present-day North Sea port of Vlaardingen, levied on their trading goods. To support "his" merchants, the emperor, Otto III, organized a punitive expedition against Dirk III, who, because Holland was part of the Holy Roman Empire, was formally his subject (although the medieval term vassal would be a better description of the relationship). This expedition failed miserably: the emperor's troops were defeated, confirming Dirk's virtually independent status.[1]

This story serves to illustrate some of the essential characteristics of medieval relations. For a start, here we are dealing with typically feudal sociopolitical structures. Although the Netherlands was part of the larger Holy Roman Empire, the emperor's vassals, such as Dirk III, often behaved as more-or-less independent rulers of their own portion of the empire. Indeed, the emperor proved unable to keep his vassals in line. This is the period of transition from the great, fairly loosely organized Holy Roman

Empire that had reached full maturity in the eighth century under Charlemagne (747–814 CE) to much smaller political units, of which the Holland of Dirk III is an example. These new units would come to occupy an increasingly strong position and eventually become the building blocks of the "modern" states of the period after 1500.

Equally interesting in this story is the leading role played by the merchants of Tiel. They enjoyed a certain degree of independence, which was bestowed on them by the emperor (unfortunately we do not know which emperor granted this privilege, nor when) and thereby created a special relationship with him, putting them in a position to ask him to take action for their benefit. These merchants owed their success to the fact that they were organized. This first-documented merchant guild in Dutch history—and that is how historians see it—was a precursor to various kinds of "collective action" that are characteristic of the Middle Ages. Merchants' guilds were the pioneers, but from the twelfth century onward they were followed by guilds of all kinds of craftsmen and craftswomen, which would shape the nature of large parts of the economy in the centuries leading up to 1800. Merchant organizations predated the "communes"—organizations of the inhabitants, or citizens, of a city, which obtained urban privileges from the monarch and on a small scale attempted to establish their own constitutional body in the feudal world of the tenth and eleventh centuries, where law and order were often lacking.[2]

Cities and citizens with their own privileges were to play a central role in the sociopolitical history of the centuries to come. The merchants of Tiel used drinking societies to strengthen their mutual bonds, fostering trust and thus simplifying mutual trade. According to one interpretation of the writings of Alpert of Metz, they even pooled a portion of their capital and knowledge, thereby limiting the risks inherent to trading over long distances. Cities and guilds would become the core of the civil society that emerged in western Europe in the centuries that followed 1015, and in this way they became a breeding ground for a variety of different forms of participation and representation.

The third party, next to the feudal state and the emerging communes, is the chronicler, the monk Alpert of Metz, who represented the Church, which at that time of a "failing" empire was calling for peace, for "law and order." He was annoyed by the customs of the merchants, with their own legal rules and pagan drinking societies, which indeed remind one of Germanic rituals from an even more distant past. Alpert represented the "peace movement" that had started in France, where the state had almost completely imploded, and which by the year 1000 had spread to large parts of Europe.[3] This same Church—the institution—had major secular interests: it controlled sizeable possessions (especially land, but also tithes) and much of the "human capital" of medieval society. Monks were often literate and, thus, like Alpert, were able to record their findings and experiences in writing. Outside the church and monasteries literacy was low, and royalty had to call upon the clergy to produce their chronicles and charters. In 1015, the Catholic Church stood on the threshold of the Investiture Controversy, a dramatic struggle between the Church and imperial secular power, which peaked some sixty years later with Emperor Henry IV's walk to Canossa.

In a nutshell, this story of 1015 foreshadowed trends that were to continue for hundreds of years thereafter and that would make Europe a continent with its own identity and institutions. And that is what this chapter is about: feudalism, cities and guilds, and the role of churches and monasteries in these changes. It joins the discussion about the negative image attached to the Middle Ages. When various sorts of misconduct come to light, we often describe them as being "medieval." Even the name of the period is not very positive: it implies that these were centuries sandwiched in between periods when something of real importance happened—between the golden age of Roman antiquity and the Renaissance of the fifteenth and sixteenth centuries. Our story is very different, however: in the centuries that came after Alpert of Metz wrote his chronicle, the foundations were laid for capitalist society as we know it today.

Feudalism or "Freedom" in the Countryside

Around 1000, the Netherlands was an empty country,[4] then at the margins of the European economy and European society. Several decades before Alpert of Metz's travels, around 965, Ibrahim ben Jacob, a Jewish merchant and diplomat from Tortosa in Spain, visited western Europe as a member of a diplomatic mission on behalf of the Caliph in Cordoba to the court of Otto I (in Mainz). Ibrahim ben Jacob's travel diary included a description of the city of Utrecht and its surroundings:

> It is a large city in the land of the Franks with extensive estates. The soil is saline and seeds and plants hardly grow there. People derive their livelihood from cattle, milk and wool. There is no firewood in the area, but the inhabitants have some kind of mud that they use as fuel. What happens is this: in the summer, when the water level is low, they go

into the fields and cut the mud with axes into the shape of bricks. Each household cuts as much as it needs and spreads the pieces out to dry in the sun. This makes them very light, and when they come near a flame they ignite. The flame burns just as it would with wood and gives off a lot of heat, just like the fire in the furnace of a glassworks. When a piece of this mud is burned, ashes remain, but no charcoal.[5]

It is striking that he called Utrecht a "large city." Later travel accounts from the eleventh and twelfth centuries would emphasize the rural character of the area and subsequently pay ample attention to agricultural practices, of which animal husbandry was relatively important. Small amounts of grain were grown and there was peat cutting, which in particular appealed to the imagination of the observers. Peat cutting was practiced on a small scale: each family cut just enough peat for itself, indicating a low level of division of labor. This description already provides a glimpse of a special economic structure that would arise in western parts of the Netherlands, focusing on peat, milk, and livestock.

Around the year 1000, the region that is now the Netherlands was very sparsely populated, with a total of some 250,000–300,000 inhabitants, almost all of whom lived in the countryside. Perhaps 5%—about 15,000 people—lived in towns and cities. No city at that time is believed to have had more than 5,000 inhabitants. A handful of areas were more intensively inhabited, such as those surrounding the major rivers (the Rhine, Maas, and Waal) and southern parts of Limburg, and in the north, on the clay soils of Friesland and Groningen, where fairly high densities of inhabitants could be found living on *terpen* and *wierden*, man-made mounds to avoid flooding in what was otherwise flat terrain. In the middle lay the city of Utrecht, in 1015 the undisputed center of the region we now call the Netherlands, which at that time largely coincided with the Diocese of Utrecht. The city was, just like the trading city of Tiel, located on the border between the Frisian and Frankish spheres of influence. Although the entire region had become part of the Carolingian Empire during the eighth century, the influence of the state and its associated nobility in the south was much greater than it was in the north. The location of the Netherlands on the fringes of the Carolingian and, later, Holy Roman Empires ultimately placed limitations on the power the emperor could exert there. In the period of "Frisian freedom" after 1000, the north would again in large measure detach itself from the embrace of emperor and feudalism. South of the river IJssel and the IJ sea arm, the decline of central authority eventually led to the formation of much smaller, but more integrated, political units. Flanders, Brabant, Utrecht, Holland, and Gelderland grew into relatively strong states. But because they arose from the disintegration of the Carolingian Empire, their "independence" was not complete: Holland and Utrecht remained part of the German Empire, and the king of France claimed supreme authority over Flanders.

As elsewhere in Europe during the period, this gradual process of state building was accompanied by an increase of state power at the lowest level. In the turbulent tenth century, a time when central government was already severely undermined, local lords began to fortify their family properties, or the villages over which they held control. Their ring-shaped fortresses (or *mottes*), built first of wood, later of stone, grew into local centers of power, where taxes were levied and judgements passed, and where local people could find protection in times of danger, such as an attack by the Vikings.[6] The local lords who thus expanded their power were connected through family networks and oaths of mutual allegiance to a central authority—a count (in Holland) or duke (in Brabant)—and through them to the Holy Roman Empire. When the count went to war, he could appeal to these lords and their entourage. This is how classic medieval knighthood was born: power shifted to men on horseback, wearing heavy armor, who were all linked together through bonds of mutual allegiance.[7]

The heart of classical, feudal Europe lay in the lands between the Seine and the Rhine, from northern France to the Meuse delta. In the north of the Netherlands, the process of state formation and concentration of power at a local level did not take place to the same extent. In the Frisian territory, between the IJ and the Lauwerszee, and in the region of Drenthe, another type of society developed in which the state—or, to be more precise, the structures of Carolingian power—lost its effectiveness. This implosion of the state did not, however, lead to a complete power vacuum. Small-scale farmer republics based on basic "democratic" principles developed: judges, for example, were originally chosen by the *meente*, an informal meeting of farmers. But in these republics, too, the "iron law of oligarchy" was in force, and eventually distinct social differences evolved between individuals and, especially, families, based in part on differences in land tenure.[8]

Families and clans, often led by "strong men," dominated political and military affairs in the villages and surrounding countryside, and were able to mobilize support from groups of residents in return for providing protection. Gradually *mottes* sprang up across the Frisian countryside, from where the "headmen," as the local elites were called, tried to govern the surrounding areas, but this process began only in the thirteenth and fourteenth centuries.

Local lords and peasant communities collaborated in the formation and governance of districts, which gave a certain degree of stability. This developed without involving a central power. In general, social inequalities remained smaller in the north than in the feudal center.[9]

The extent to which people were involved in warfare illustrates the differences between the two regions—the "free" north and the "feudal" south. In feudal Europe, war became the monopoly of a small group of specialists: knights and their entourages. The rest of the population did not usually possess weapons and relied on the institution of knighthood, with its castles, for protection. This development—the disappearance of peasant armies—had been underway in much of western Europe from as early as the eighth and ninth centuries, strengthening the power base of the knights and nobility. In the northern Netherlands, however, in Frisia (and Drenthe), broad sections of the farming population continued to be actively involved in the defense of their land, perhaps because knights on horseback were less effective there, given the number of rivers and other waterways. Their skill as fighters and their weapon of choice—long lances were their specialty—meant that groups of Frisians would play an important role in the Crusades. There they were known as the "tall Frisians"; their large body size seems to indicate a favorable nutritional base, possibly because they possessed large numbers of livestock and therefore consumed more meat and milk than people elsewhere in Europe.[10]

The Frisians were commonly reported as being difficult to control (as members of the crusading armies): they had their own ambitions and ideas, and did not easily take orders from feudal lords. For the most part, in the core areas of Friesland there was practically no serfdom. That people were aware of this exceptional position is evident, for example, from the words of Emo, Abbot of Wittewierum (*ca.* 1170–1237), who wrote in his chronicle:

> Friesland may be able to boast its many monasteries of the religious, who continuously pray for the country with pious intentions, but because it stands out due to its large population and is rich in freedom, which applies equally to the poor and the wealthy (an invaluable asset), and is prosperous and blessed due to a multitude of livestock, and its ample pastures and the fertility of its field crops, it may perhaps be guilty in the eyes of the Almighty of ingratitude for all these benefits, so great and so many.[11]

And a few years later he wrote: "because by God's grace we live in Friesland in such great freedom that neither the bishop nor his henchmen could not forcibly rob us of even a chicken."[12] In the terminology of the modern economy, freedom meant, therefore, the protection of property rights, even down to a chicken. And despite a lack of central authority, Friesland around the year 1200 was rich: rich in livestock, rich in field crops, rich in population, and also rich in monasteries.

The neighboring district of Drenthe provides another example of shifting relationships on the frontier between feudalism and "freedom." In the ninth century, when it became incorporated into Charlemagne's empire, Drenthe entered feudal waters, although the number of serfs was probably small and that of free farmers relatively large. As will be seen later, this transition did bring new impulses to population growth, land reclamation, and the emergence of communal farming on the common fields, which remained characteristic of the region until well into the nineteenth century. Initially, the grip of Drenthe's feudal rulers tightened: it became a county within the German Empire, and the typical court structures of the count gradually spread throughout the area. The city of Groningen, located at the northern tip of the Drenthe sand plateau, developed from such a court structure into an urban settlement. After Emperor Henry III in 1040 gave the jurisdiction of the County of Drenthe to the bishop of Utrecht, it was added to the vast possessions of this ecclesiastical and secular ruler.[13]

Yet in a series of bloody conflicts, climaxing with the Battle of the Ane of 1227, Drenthe managed to shake off the rule of the bishop. Drenthe's resistance was led by the same official whose responsibility it was to represent the authority of the bishop—namely, the Viscount of Coevorden. But the core of the resistance comprised the free farmers of Drenthe, who, like the Frisians, had maintained a tradition of bearing arms—and, also just like the Frisians, excelled in using the long lance. By 1233, the bishop of Utrecht had actually resigned himself to the semi-independence of the region.[14] The local assembly, or *etsenstoel*, subsequently developed into an administrative body and, in particular, a court of law.[15] In other words, what had once been the prefecture of a bishop became the community of the "Sworn of Drenthe" (*iurati et universitas terre Threnthie*), a terminology reminiscent of urban communes, which were also communities bound together by an oath of citizenship.[16]

The fact that large parts of the Netherlands remained removed from European feudalism had complex consequences for its economy. The feudal system was an effective way of skimming off the surpluses of farmers, especially through various kinds of compulsory male service and the so-called banal rights of the lord. This led to a concentration of income among a small group of nobles and clergy, since the Church also participated in the system.

Feudalism was accompanied by the creation of great domains (although these remained rare in the Netherlands), worked directly by farmers for the benefit of the landed nobles or Church.[17] Noble families also sought to strengthen their ties with the Church—which was to provide for their salvation—through the donation of large tracts of land to monasteries and other ecclesiastical institutions. Nobility and clergy spent their newfound wealth on luxury goods—from expensive hand-copied manuscripts to exotic robes to delicacies such as spices and sugar. Indeed, feudalism stimulated trade, since those expensive items had to be imported from afar.[18] Noble gentlemen even discovered that they could also take advantage of the flourishing trade, by bestowing on their subjects the right to establish markets (and levying a modest tax on what was sold), and by granting privileges to groups of traders. These markets could eventually develop into cities, with privileges known as city rights.[19]

In the north of the country, however, such changes evolved at a much slower pace. There, the elite with a strong demand for luxury goods from outside the region was much smaller in numbers, although a lively trade had emerged nonetheless. Why in the Middle Ages the Frisians excelled in this and dominated the trade of the North Sea region—between England, Scandinavia, northern Germany, and northern France—is not entirely clear. It is likely that the north of the Netherlands did not produce the range of products necessary to support itself reasonably well. On and around the *terpen* of the Frisian heartland—an area regularly flooded by seawater—keeping livestock was much easier than arable farming. For this reason, the abbot of Wittewierum extensively praised "the multitude of cattle" and "the many pastures" before he mentioned field crops. Furthermore, people traditionally excelled in textile production, but, again, this may have been a necessity, a product to sell to enable them to buy in exchange the grain necessary for making bread. It is no coincidence that Tiel was then still a town dominated by Frisian merchants. While elsewhere in the Netherlands the use of coinage was minimal—as in the rest of western Europe around 1000—archaeological finds show that the Frisians routinely used gold and silver coins on a fairly large scale.[20]

Clearly, in the Netherlands there were large differences in sociopolitical structure owing to its situation on the boundary between the "free" north and the "feudal" south. In the north, "Frisian freedom" applied to a large extent. Regions such as Zeeland and the River Area, on the other hand, were characterized by the existence of a powerful noble elite and—especially in the River Area—showed all the hallmarks of classical feudal structures: large agricultural domains and serfdom.[21] The peatlands of Holland and Utrecht straddled the border. At the turn of the millennium, they were almost empty: only along the dunes, and on the banks of major rivers, did concentrations of population exist (e.g., Dordrecht, Vlaardingen, Rijnsburg), but the central area was a vast peat bog that included the current province of South Holland and the western half of what is now the province of Utrecht. This terrain was used for grazing livestock, for fishing (in the peat ponds), and for collecting wood and peat. The concentration of the population on the margins of these marshes was partly due to the fact that arable farming was possible only on the sandy soils of dunes and along riverbanks.

The middle of the tenth century saw the first of many projects to make the central peat bog suitable for arable farming, and thus for the cultivation of the essential bread grains. Presumably this was made possible by climatic changes—the second half of the tenth century was remarkably dry, allowing easier access to and work in peat bogs. In addition, a new series of dunes formed along existing dune banks, at the expense of existing cropping fields, and this also pushed the population towards the peatlands. The bogs in this area were at a relatively high altitude, owing to the growth of the peat moss throughout previous centuries. Natural drainage was therefore possible, but drainage channels had to be dug first, and dikes had to be constructed to keep out surplus water from elsewhere.

There are indications that around the mid-tenth century farmers took the initiative and started draining the peat bogs themselves. At the same time, the first plans for larger-scale reclamation of the bogs took form, with the administrative body of the feudal court serving as a coordinating mechanism.[22] The Count of Holland and the bishop of Utrecht soon recognized the gains that could be made for the benefit of their "subjects"—as well as themselves. They claimed, like other feudal lords, that they owned these "waste lands," thus giving them the right to decide how they were to be cultivated. Subsequently, they began to recruit *locatores* (or "project developers") among the lower nobility to reclaim certain areas. These developers then entered into a contract (called a *cope*) with groups prepared to carry out the reclamation works, with this contract stipulating the exact conditions to be met and, in particular, the tax that would have to be paid to the landowner (the count or bishop) in the future. These reclamation groups were in fact farmers keen to improve their financial and social position. They could presumably—this is not always clear owing to a lack of written sources—obtain release from their serfdom in this way and become free farmers with property rights to their land. These planned developments produced clean lines in the landscape and farms of identical size (approximately 14 hectares).[23]

Regional historians of Holland and Utrecht still disagree about who first developed this reclamation "model." Holland has traditionally had the strongest claim.[24] Whatever the case, it is certain that the model took shape in the eleventh century and it worked so well that already by 1113 it had been copied by the bishop of Bremen, who signed an identical contract with a group of Hollanders for the reclamation of a swamp in his diocese.[25] This model of self-organization with a degree of central authority had two advantages: "free riders" could be forced to abide by the rules, and conflicts beyond the village community level could be resolved through mediation, and if necessary through the pure power—direct intervention—of the count or bishop. Reclamation and drainage in one place inevitably had consequences for other places—downstream, for example, or for users of natural watercourses (fishermen, ships' masters) who saw their interests jeopardized by dikes and the construction of locks and dams. At the same time, the extraction of peat led to an almost unstoppable fall in ground levels, owing to subsidence and erosion of the peat, thus creating an environmental time bomb that eventually led to large-scale flooding and decreasing crop yields, thereby undermining the foundations of agrarian life. There are indications that as early as the twelfth century the first phase of the "major reclamations" in central Holland came to a halt precisely because of this problem. Windmill-driven pumps for draining land, which might have provided an escape, were not available in Europe before the 1400s.[26]

Predictably, the local communities that emerged after reclamation works also played an important role in the water management of their surroundings, setting up local drainage boards governed by local officials (such as the bailiff) often appointed by the count or bishop, and in some cases by specially selected, and perhaps even elected, authorities: *heemraden*, or dike boards. Early examples of this can be seen during the first crisis of the late twelfth century, when attempts were made to dam the Oude Rijn at the Holland–Utrecht border to stop an influx of unwanted water from the Utrecht side. For understandable reasons, this met with resistance from Utrecht. Only supra-state consultation, involving the Duke of Brabant and the German emperor, as well as the Count of Holland and the bishop of Utrecht, led to a compromise solution.[27]

The next and perhaps the decisive step in the reclamation process was taken in 1253. By this time, the count's council had developed into an important instrument for policy making, one that Count William II (who at the time was also the king of the Holy Roman Empire) made extensive use of. After obtaining advice from his council—"the common council of our nobles, servants and vassals in Holland, and of other good men"[28]—in that year, William decided to build a large lock in Spaarndam. This was an important innovation— one of the first locks ever to be built had just been constructed in Bruges—that allowed a reconciliation between the interests of trade and transport, on the one hand, and those of water management, on the other. This was probably an initiative "from the bottom up" of the city of Haarlem and those involved in the water management of the Rhineland.[29] Building the lock was a very costly project aimed, among other things, at easing the movement of shipping traffic between the Zuiderzee and the lands to the south (see chapter 4).

The counts of Holland recognized and encouraged the new form of collaboration that had begun in Rhineland: additional charters (in 1255 and 1286) confirmed and regulated the existence and authority of the dike boards. The first "modern" drainage board—or, rather, super-drainage board, because it administered an area containing many relatively autonomous polders—was the result of a subtle game of institution building by which "bottom up" and "top down" elements were brought together. More or less voluntary contributions by large numbers of individual land users, both owners and tenants, had to be encouraged by allowing them a certain amount of agency. At the same time, their contributions had to be coordinated by a committee with sufficient power to do its job. Balancing these two would become the challenge for not only water management but also most Dutch institutions.

The relative advantages of embedding an organization responsible for water management in the structures of state were also evident in comparable processes occurring in "free" Frisia. Along the entire coast of the Netherlands, large-scale reclamation and dike construction took place between 900 and 1300. North of the IJ, however, rather than relying on official organizations, the mostly autonomous village communities themselves were responsible for these works and their coordination. In some cases, monasteries with ambitious reclamation plans also played a significant role. However, it was not always easy to coordinate these activities, nor to find solutions for the inevitable subsidence of peat soils. Particularly in North Holland, subsidence resulted in the loss of much of the reclaimed peat country, and large peat lakes (Beemster, Purmer, Schermer) developed, which were finally drained only during the seventeenth century.

The dike surrounding West Frisia (a large area in Holland, north of Amsterdam) is another example of the problem of coordination without a feudal state. The conquest of this area by Count Floris V in 1280–82, the imposition of central authority, and the introduction of a general, compulsory dike levy for "all who have land, be it monastery, be it knight, be it the Pope, all are equally liable," helped to improve the dike and the related water management. As this quotation, from the thirteenth-century dike letter, shows, everyone was required to do their bit—including the Church and the nobility, two groups that often demanded exemption from all sorts of obligations. The construction of a number of fortresses along the dike certainly also helped to deal with the "free rider" problem.[30]

The great reclamations benefited from the structures of the feudal state in which they were carried out: the count and the bishop and their vassals, the *locatores* or project developers, acted like genuine entrepreneurs to take advantage of the new opportunities that arose and ensure that adequate organizational structures were in place for these infrastructural "megaoperations." This would not have been possible without the flexibility of feudal relations (in which feudal vassals could act as entrepreneurs), a relatively efficient state (in which the count was advised by his council), and new forms of contract such as the *cope*. At the same time, a new class of free farmers emerged that was distinctly different from the serfs of feudalism. Like free citizens elsewhere, members of this new free-farmer class were obliged to support and accompany their lord in his wars and man his warships (cogs); like the free Frisians, these free farmers were considered capable of going to war.

In a sociopolitical sense, Holland moved in the direction of the "free" north; because of the great reclamations, feudalism became a marginal phenomenon that was relevant only for a small number of nobles and an even smaller ecclesiastical elite. This resulted in a state with a substantially centralized authority; that is, the benefits of feudalism—which was based on relatively free farmers paying taxes and committing their lives and arms—without its drawbacks.

Major reclamation activity took place not only in the low-lying parts of the Netherlands: it was a European phenomenon. As a consequence of the strong population growth between 900 and 1300, agricultural lands were expanded everywhere at the expense of natural land cover, such as forests. This process also led to institutional changes in the eastern and southern Netherlands. In Drenthe, which we know relatively much about, the turning point came with the integration of the region into the Carolingian Empire.[31] Before then, agriculture had taken place in open spaces within the existing primary forest. But from the ninth century onward, larger complexes of fields and pastureland arose around farms, which tended to conglomerate. At the same time, the three-field system of rotation was introduced, whereby the fields produced a winter harvest for one year, a summer crop the following year, and were left fallow the year after that. The scale of farms also increased sharply: the average holding in the tenth century was three to five times larger than that in the seventh century.[32] It is not yet clear whether such radical changes were the result of greater political stability arising from integration into the Carolingian Empire or, in particular, of technical developments such as a new type of plow, ox traction, or the three-field system. Each development was probably interrelated with the others.[33] They certainly laid the foundation for the sharp increase in population that occurred in the period 950–1300, and also clearly demonstrate that in the tenth and eleventh centuries Drenthe was a relatively prosperous region, one from which the bishop of Utrecht could extract a large income. It seems that feudalism as introduced by the Carolingians heralded a phase of economic and population growth. Moreover, as farmers settled more closely together, the village community emerged as a new institution—first as an informal organization of farmers dealing with matters that directly concerned them, but gradually starting to deal with all sorts of formal matters.

The management of "common land"—the unallocated land found outside fields, gardens, and cattle pastures under private ownership—was one of the matters that village communities became involved with. *Woeste grond* (uncultivated terrain such as heath, peat bog, or marshland), as it came to be called in the nineteenth century, was in 900 not really a scarce phenomenon. Villages and farms were often located in a "sea" of space, and in large parts of the eastern Netherlands landowners often failed to establish their claim to ownership of these lands. This changed between 900 and 1300: from around 950 onward new villages and farms were rapidly established, while older ones expanded their borders. As a consequence of population growth, land became a scarce commodity. At the same time, much of the land was not used intensively enough for it to be divided up into private property, and land continued to be mainly used for cattle pasture.

To manage these common lands, and to safeguard and protect them from overexploitation, organizations often called *marken* (sing. *marke*), another typical medieval institution, emerged in the east of the Netherlands in the course of the thirteenth and fourteenth centuries.[34] In Drenthe, *marke* and village often coincided, and it was simply the neighboring farmers who established the rules for their use: how many horses, cattle, sheep, and pigs could be grazed, or how much peat or wood was to be cut.

Common property was secured by delineating the properties of the neighboring farmers—often by placing large boulders. Where ownership of large tracts of the countryside was more prominent, south of the river Ane, in Overijssel, a separate institution, also called a *marke*, was often established, through which it was decided which farms—and thus which owners—had access to precisely which parts of the common lands. *Marke* meetings, usually held once a year, drew up guidelines on land management, determining who benefited and how much from, for example, grazing pigs in woodland, cutting peat (for heating) or heathland sods (for fertilizer), or, sometimes, the division and "privatization" of a part of the pasture land. Only in the long run (fifteenth–sixteenth centuries) did it prove impossible to prevent forest area from shrinking further, giving way to rather poor heathland with a much poorer yield. In parts of the eastern Netherlands (Salland, and the Achterhoek), ownership of large tracts of land was dominated by the original feudal lords. There, the lord, who was also chairman of meetings of the *marke*, firmly put his stamp on its fortunes, even though the actual use of the land was dictated mainly by local custom.[35]

It is probably typical of the spatial variation found in these kinds of institutional solutions that south of the great rivers no independent institutions like *marken* emerged to manage the forests and meadows, but that these "common lands" were in effect claimed by, for example, the Duke of Brabant. From about 1300 these *gemeynten* began to be sold by the landlord to the village communities that had sprung up around them. In this way, the communities acquired an important role in the management of the land.

Urban Charters and Urban Trade

After the collapse of the Roman Empire, not only did its territorial authority in western Europe (with its associated legal system and international trade) disappear, its cities, once the backbone of Roman civilization, also declined. Their influence may not have been completely absent from early medieval society, but their role had become marginal. And although in the Low Countries here and there one could speak of continuity—in Maastricht, Nijmegen, and Utrecht—in most places the process of urbanization that began around the year 1000 was without precedent. This was mainly because cities in western Europe, unlike most other parts of the world, managed to achieve a somewhat autonomous position early on. We have already outlined the roots of this development—the power vacuum of the tenth and eleventh centuries, and the merchant organizations that emerged during this period.

Beginning in the mid-tenth century, Italian cities were the first to develop into "communes": collectives of citizens who swore to defend the rights of their city, rights acquired within the larger state of the Holy Roman Empire and recorded in charters.[36] This movement spread to northwestern Europe (northern France, the Rhineland), and in 1122 reached Utrecht, the most important city in the northern Netherlands. With the acquisition of city rights, a separate jurisdiction arose within the feudal state—the city—with its own rights and customs. This gave citizens, too, a separate legal status.

The fact that the Netherlands was on the margins of feudal western Europe also had consequences for the development of its cities. Almost everywhere else in Europe, episcopal cities formed the core of the urban system, with the income from the (arch)bishop's large ecclesiastical possessions boosting the urban economy. This resulted early on in the construction of large cathedrals (a cathedral is the principal church of a bishop, containing his cathedra, or official throne), first in the Romanesque style, later in the Gothic form. But as one moved north, episcopal cities became scarcer, and north of the great rivers there was only one: Utrecht. In a way, the spatial structure of the Church still reflected that of the Roman Empire from which it had arisen. Utrecht therefore profited enormously from the extensive possessions of ecclesiastical institutions in the Low Countries; other urban centers lacked this asset for expansion. This and, more generally, the lack or weakness of feudal power structures above the major rivers, explains why the cities there—with the exception of Utrecht—were late in developing and remained relatively small until about 1300. On the other hand, the less dense ecclesiastical network of the Low Countries provided, as we will see in the next chapter, more room for alternative religious movements, such as the Sisters and Brothers of Common Life.

The economic development of the region is clearly reflected in the increase in—largely urban—church-building activity in the Middle Ages. The heat maps in figure 3.1 are based on an extensive study of the history of the construction of 1,144 large churches in western Europe in the period 700–1500.[37] The maps show the density of building activity in each period. It is clear from the map of the period 700–1000 that there was hardly any construction in the Netherlands; the European center of church construction activity was mainly in northern and central Italy, although the region around Aachen also shows a relatively high activity level. In the period 1000–1200, northern France (where Gothic architecture originated) and Belgium "light up," as well as, again, northern Italy. Between 1200 and 1348, these two poles of activity are even more evident—again, northern France–Belgium and, now, central Italy, while the northern Netherlands is to some extent

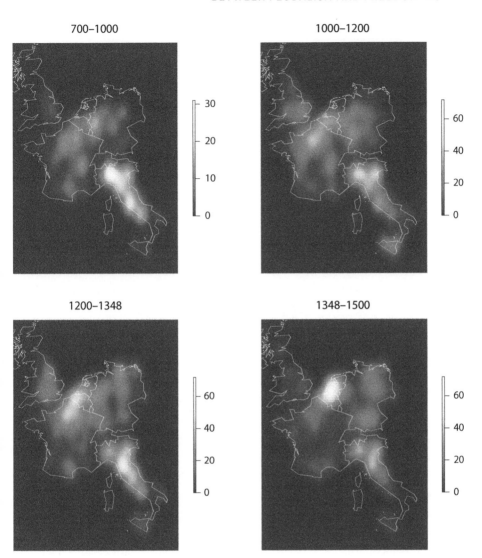

FIGURE 3.1. Heat maps of church-building activity in Western Europe (cubic meters per square kilometer), 700–1500.
Source: Buringh et al. 2020.

affected by these developments. In the latest period, 1348–1500, the topic of the next chapter, curiously enough, Italy—where the Renaissance was at its peak—is less prominent and the Flanders–Low Countries region dominates.

As a bishop's see, Utrecht was representative of the normal western European pattern. The economy of the city was geared to the consumption of luxury goods by an elite that mainly derived its income from the exploitation of land. Other cities were oriented more toward international trade; Zutphen and other towns along the river IJssel are typical examples of this. Cities that emerged as agricultural centers but lacked an exploitative elite were a third type, of which Amsterdam was, at this point in time, an example. Each of these city types also had its own sociopolitical structure.

Utrecht had been created from a *castellum* built on the limes, fortified frontiers, of the Roman Empire. For a long time it was believed that the site had been uninhabited for several hundred years after the departure of the Romans at the end of the third century.[38] Recent excavations have, however, revealed traces of habitation spanning the fourth, fifth, and sixth centuries. Probably only a small number of people lived there—a few hundred at most. Utrecht's revival began in the last decades of the seventh century, when several missionaries from the British Isles visited there. The most important of these was Willibrord, who was ordained archbishop of the Frisians in 695 and chose Utrecht as his see. This made Utrecht an important ecclesiastical center. The revival of the regional economy was initially concentrated in Dorestad, twenty kilometers to the south, but when it was destroyed in the middle of the ninth century by Viking invaders, Utrecht was able to take on some of the international trade.

So, the Church was of crucial importance for Utrecht's revival.[39] There were two reasons for this. Firstly, an ecclesiastical "headquarters" of a large region usually created a great deal of direct employment. Not only was the bishop of Utrecht an important ecclesiastical authority, he also had a strong voice in shaping politics in the region. His court comprised a fairly large group of people who supported him, who were not only large in number but often also wealthy. Together they were able to maintain the Utrecht cathedral and— this is the second reason—over time they would endow the Church with large amounts of their personal wealth. In the eleventh and twelfth centuries, this influx of income increased sharply as the Church began to cultivate large tracts of its own land that had previously been desolate and uninhabited.

The bishop and his court lived behind walls built on the exact same site as the Roman *castellum*, in a river bend known today as the Old Rhine. Economic life was concentrated in the neighborhood that had sprung up next to the *castellum*. Over time that neighborhood became home to hundreds— possibly even several thousand—traders and artisans. There are indications that many foreign merchants were also active in Utrecht. They traded predominantly with, on the one hand, the area around Cologne and, on the other, northern Germany, Scandinavia, and the region bordering the Baltic Sea. Indeed, many coins minted in Utrecht in this period have been found in what are now known as the Baltic States, in particular, as well as in southern and central Finland. Fish, salt, and bricks were exported to the Baltic, while grain especially, but also timber, was traded in the opposite direction. Craftsmen, on the other hand, were mainly oriented toward the local market. In addition to the usual service occupations of tailor, brewer, and so on, the producers of luxury items are particularly noticeable. For them, the episcopal court, the nobility, and the churches were the main clientele. The ambitious program of church building of this period illustrates the significant demand originating from these environments.

The dominant presence of the Church in city life naturally had a significant effect on mutual relations, especially after first merchants and then craftsmen began to organize themselves in guilds. The first mention of jointly operating Utrecht craft guilds dates from 1267. That is remarkably early; craft guilds in other northern Dutch cities developed later, mainly in the following century. Important trading families in Utrecht were represented at an early stage in the city council. However, the merchant government met resistance, and in 1274 the first revolution by the guilds led to the overthrow of the merchants. The ruling families were expelled from the city and, subsequently, the guild administrators took it upon themselves to govern the city. Although this revolution was temporary, in 1304 a second guild revolution led to a more permanent change in the balance of power. A new constitution for the city, known as the "Guild Letter," established the dominance of the guilds in the city's government.[40] Until 1528, the members of Utrecht's city council would be appointed by representatives of the twenty-one "main" guilds. The guilds also took responsibility for the defense of the city: each guild maintained a portion of the city wall, and guild members could be conscripted into military service.

Zutphen and its surrounding countryside was already inhabited in Roman times. Later, with the arrival of the Franks, a small trading post was established on the headland formed by the confluence of the rivers Berkel and IJssel. The site eventually became the location for the court of the counts of Zutphen, who over the years built, among other things, a great hall within the circular ramparts (embankments) that were constructed around 900 to protect the settlement against attackers. In the eleventh century, the wooden hall was replaced by one of stone, which was part of a fortified complex of buildings that also included a church dedicated to Saint Walburgis. The attractiveness of Zutphen for merchants and the strength of the local economy were mainly due to the better navigability of the IJssel. This tributary of the Rhine had deepened in previous centuries through natural erosion and had, as a result, developed into an attractive part of the trade route between the Rhine Valley and northern Germany. This trade route was itself part of a network of trading towns that during this exact period united into an extensive and very successful commercial network: the Hanseatic League. The league was not formally established until 1356, but it was preceded by more than a century of informal cooperation.

In the fourteenth century, Zutphen benefited from north–south trade via the Zuiderzee, the IJssel, and the Rhine. It had become a member of the Hanseatic League early in that century.[41] In addition to the Rhineland and Baltic Sea, Zutphen merchants also traded in England and Flanders. Trade with Cologne and other German cities largely involved wine. Much grain, which came from the Baltic Sea, was sent upstream.[42]

In comparison with trade, local industry remained relatively underdeveloped, and because industry created much more employment this automatically limited the population size of the city. At the end of the fifteenth century, the first point for which there are reliable measurements, Zutphen had approximately 3,700 inhabitants. At this time, Zutphen was still one of the largest cities in the Duchy of Gelre, together with Nijmegen, Roermond, and Venlo, while Gelre itself was in turn one of the most urbanized areas of the Low Countries. Its first guild, that of the cobblers, was founded in 1377, much later than in Utrecht.[43]

Amsterdam was in its entirety the result of the reclamation of the peat bogs described earlier in this chapter. Although in 1275 the privilege to levy tolls was granted to *homines manentes apud Amestelledamme* (people living at the Amsteldam—incidentally, also the oldest mention of Amsterdam), the settlement at that time displayed no urban characteristics.[44] Amsterdam's first buildings were erected along the eastern bank of the Amstel, near where the city's Dam Square is now situated. Its first residents lived from agriculture and fishing, enduring not only subsidence of the land but also the advance of the sea. Indeed, in the twelfth century they probably had to restart from scratch several times after their settlement was washed away by floods. To improve water management, a dam was constructed in the mouth of the Amstel in the second half of the thirteenth century; this was the dam to which the toll privilege of 1275 applied. The dam connected a total of five settlements that had arisen around the mouth of the Amstel. There were now around 250 families (about a thousand people) living there.[45]

A number of things around this time point to urban development. Although Amsterdam was not yet an independent parish, it possessed a church, dedicated to Saint Nicholas. That church, nowadays known as the

Oude Kerk, was renovated and expanded in the first half of the fourteenth century.[46] An even more extensive structure was the brick castle that was built on the west bank of the Amstel probably by the Count of Holland, Floris V, shortly before 1300. Precisely at that time, the bishop of Utrecht and the Count of Holland were competing for supremacy in the region, and the people of Amsterdam thought they could benefit by constantly changing sides. It was with his castle that Floris intended to put an end to this practice. Indeed, in 1285 Amstelland—and thereby also Amsterdam—was definitively subsumed into the County of Holland.

In economic terms, Amsterdam had little to offer in 1275.[47] True, its residents were exempted from paying tolls in the County of Holland in that year, but that privilege was also enjoyed in numerous other places. Excavations have revealed several artisanal workshops that date back to the thirteenth century, but they probably catered to only local customers. At the end of the thirteenth century—the exact year is unknown—Amsterdam also acquired market rights. There are, however, no indications of international trade until 1323, when Count William III instituted a beer toll on Hamburg beer landed at Medemblik and Amsterdam. Ships carrying beer from the "east" had to sail to one of these two places to pay their toll. It appears that in 1435, Enkhuizen, Monnickendam, and Edam also had a beer toll, although in that year it was only the tolls paid in Amsterdam that yielded significant income for the count. Apparently, Amsterdam's trade with northeastern Europe had begun to outstrip that of its competitors. In the years 1352–54, some thirty thousand barrels of beer were registered in Amsterdam; ten years later this had risen to forty thousand barrels.

Amsterdam was attractively situated for this trade. Merchants tried to avoid the route over the open sea as much as possible. Instead, they used a network of waterways that led from the Zuiderzee via Amsterdam and Haarlem over the Haarlemmermeer to Gouda, and then further via the islands of southern Holland and Zeeland to the prosperous cities of Brabant and Flanders. Initially, Amsterdam merchants probably benefited only slightly from this trade, which was largely in the hands of Hamburg merchants and others in the Hanseatic League. Nevertheless, we can safely assume that in this way important contacts were made on the northern coast of Germany and further, in the region of the Baltic Sea. It is not difficult to discern here the seeds of the crucial trade relations that grew between those regions and Amsterdam in the sixteenth and seventeenth centuries.

Slowly but surely, the cities emerged as economic communities with a self-confident administrative elite. Throughout the period, one sees that urban administrations were prepared to spend money—often a lot of money—to enable the extension of local privileges. The fact that time after time, century after century, cities were prepared to make a significant financial outlay to acquire more freedom says something about its perceived value and importance. Simultaneously, the internal distribution of power became more contested. As urban societies became more complex, more administrative functions arose, and with them opportunities to influence the course of affairs in the city. Throughout the Middle Ages, this provided ample matter for conflict.

In Leiden, where the administrative history has been studied in great depth, the city charter, which dates from 1266, mentions both aldermen and sworn judges (*jurati*), probably referring to the same function.[48] Their presence in the charter seems to indicate some form of representation of the citizens of the city. The eight aldermen or sworn judges were almost certainly representatives of the four quarters into which the city was divided. Their representative role is reflected not only in their number but also in the requirement that they could not take office unless they had been a *poorter* (citizen) for at least four years. In 1299 mention is also made of four councilors, also known as mayors. The aldermen had a primarily legal role, the mayors a more administrative one.

There is no evidence, however, that these representatives were elected by the citizens of the city, and here we immediately see the seeds of much conflict in the urban community, between the supposedly representative function on the one hand and, on the other, the socially exclusive nature of the group of people who actually played this role. At the same time we must note that, in economic terms, at least, the fate of these city officials was closely intertwined with that of the city as a whole. Although the nobility played a role in Leiden's city council, and despite the fact that many leading families had invested in land, their primary economic interest was in trade and industry—that is, in the urban economy.[49]

It is therefore no coincidence that in the city charter of 's-Hertogenbosch (known in short as Den Bosch), dating from 1184, a place populated from the outset by merchants, much attention was paid to the regulation of matters important for trade.[50] In particular, this concerned the legal certainty that traders needed to complete a transaction. The charter also laid down in detail the procedures for a fair trial. For example, a citizen of Den Bosch had the right, in the first instance, to answer for his actions to the city's council of aldermen—in other words, his fellow citizens. Disturbances of the peace were to be severely punished by the council. Special attention was also given to the running of hostels, where many commercial transactions were concluded. The charter regulated the inheritance of goods. Finally, attention was paid to the position of *extranei*—foreign merchants who came to do business in Den Bosch. These arrangements were important not only in Den Bosch: they inspired those drafting Haarlem's city charter, and from there they were adopted by many other cities in Holland. In all these cities, merchants and their interests therefore took priority in city law.

With this overall picture in mind, for the period up to 1350 a number of conclusions can be drawn about the cities in the region that would later become the Netherlands (see map 3.1). First of all, none of these cities had a population size that was particularly large for Europe. Major cities could be found elsewhere: in Italy of course, close by in Flanders (Bruges, Ghent), and along the Rhine (Cologne), and London and Paris were also much larger than any city in the northern Netherlands. Second, most cities in the Netherlands were relatively new, having in just the previous few centuries developed from villages to become places with various urban features. Their growth in status was in large part due to their central function for the surrounding countryside, often in combination with location on long-distance trading routes. The relative importance of this trade often determined the opportunities for growth of these towns. During this period, urban populations began to organize themselves and were also able to realize a certain degree of political autonomy for their communities. That autonomy was, however, restricted by the duke or count, who made sure that the cities could not exercise too much influence over the countryside. In this, the lands in the north differed from those in Italy and Flanders, where the cities did dominate the countryside. Initially, these Italian and Flemish cities reaped the economic benefits of this situation, but in the longer term the relationship turned out to be counterproductive. The balance between urban and rural areas in the northern Netherlands would ultimately turn out to be more beneficial to both, facilitated as it was by the fairly even distribution of the urban population over a large number of urban centers. Much of this would become significant only after 1350.

The Ecclesiastical "Civilizing Offensive"

In addition to that of farmers and citizens, the role of the Church deserves special attention. The Church was a factor in urban development: the growth of the city of Utrecht would have been inconceivable without the bishop and the episcopal institutions that sprang up around the cathedral. For the other

MAP 3.1. Map of the northern Netherlands in the late Middle Ages.

city that provides the necessary continuity with the Roman era, Maastricht, a similar story can be told. There, too, ecclesiastical institutions—situated around the tomb of Saint Servaas—played a central role in urban continuity.

We have already described the role the bishop of Utrecht in the large-scale reclamations of the peat bogs of Holland and Utrecht, and similarly his position as territorial lord of Drenthe (beside Groningen and Overijssel). But that is only a rough sketch of the influence of the Church. More importantly, the Church launched a "civilizing offensive" around the year 1000, through which it would have a fundamental influence on the type of society that was to develop in centuries to come.

It may have started with the rise of Islam in the seventh and eighth centuries.[51] Islam has been called the first modern religion, because it directly links a system of rules of life to belief in a god. The Catholic Church had in that respect done much less, for the most part conforming to the morals found in, for example, the Roman Empire of the first centuries CE. The issue of slavery—could one as a Christian enslave one's Christian brethren, or keep them as slaves?—illustrates the essential difference: the Catholic Church had, perhaps with some reluctance, conceded that this practice was unacceptable but was actually lukewarm in its condemnation of slavery. Islam, on the other hand, rejected the practice outright; Muslims were not supposed to enslave other Muslims. Both religions had begun from the principle that all believers were "equal before God," but attached different consequences to it. As a result, with the booming economy of the Arab world in the eighth and ninth centuries following the Arab conquest of the Middle East, North Africa, and Spain, the growing demand for slaves in the Mediterranean region was satisfied mainly by Christians, who enslaved one another.

In the eighth and ninth centuries, enslaved people were perhaps the most important export product of western Europe. The Catholic Church witnessed this situation with great sorrow and revived the dormant doctrine that Christians should not enslave one another, and began actively opposing the enslavement of Christians.[52] Incidentally, many slaves were also taken from the east of the European subcontinent, where the population had not then been Christianized. But the Church's campaign was successful: in the ninth and tenth centuries, slavery decreased sharply.

While slavery among Christians declined, it was to some extent replaced by feudal serfdom, although a serf was bound to the land, could not be sold, and had some rights, such as the right to protection by his lord. Non-Christians could still be enslaved—and this was especially practiced in eastern Europe—but the numbers of slaves brought in from outside Europe remained fairly small in the late Middle Ages. Western Europe, and certainly the Netherlands, where the import of slaves practically ceased after about 1100, became free of slavery—at that time, uniquely in world history.

The Church's stand against slavery of the ninth and tenth centuries was just the beginning of its civilizing offensive. The position of the Church, and especially that of Rome, was further strengthened after 900 by the reform of the monasteries (beginning in Cluny), by which they fell under the supreme authority of the papacy in Rome (before 900 monasteries had often been autonomous). All across Europe, land ownership by churches and monasteries increased strongly during this period, while the feudal transformation—the emergence of stronger state alliances—made it possible to skim off larger portions of surplus profits.

In the eleventh century, strong popes fought secular rulers—in particular the emperors of the Holy Roman Empire—for the right to, among other things, appoint bishops; this became known as the Investiture Controversy. The popes demanded that crucial parts of civil law fall under canon law, which was determined by the Church. Marriage, for example, as a sacrament of the Church thus had to be regulated by the Church. Furthermore, law concerning inheritance and, by extension, all property and contract law—which directly affected the Church, as an owner of large tracts of land—was claimed by the Church to be subject to canon law.[53]

The disintegration of the Carolingian Empire resulted a highly fragmented collection of smaller and somewhat larger states. In response, the Church was able to expand its influence, thus compensating for the power vacuum that evolved, as well as attempting to counter the impending political chaos. The Peace and Truce of God (*Pax et treuga Dei*) movement of the tenth and eleventh centuries is the best example of the Church's efforts in this area.

Political and religious power in western Europe were divided between the state and the Church, each keeping the other more or less in balance. However, the frequent conflict between state and Church also created opportunities for other actors to establish their own power base. Cities in particular benefited from this. Communes in Italy, the Rhineland, and the Low Countries were the first to gain greater independence, thus creating the western European tradition of "power sharing." This matched the feudal balance of power, in which the landlord also had to maintain a delicate balance with his vassals by give and take.

The strong position of the Church gave it a great deal of ideological influence. In the matter of family law, for example, a Church doctrine developed during the eleventh and twelfth centuries that marriage should be based on mutual consent; it became one of the foundations for the development of marriage customs in Europe in the centuries that followed. The idea was simple: marriage was a sacrament (confirmed by the Lateran Council in 1215) in which no believer could be forced to take part. In addition, theologians believed that forced marriages were more likely to fail. Marriage was, thus, essentially reduced to the consent of the two partners and thereby removed from the influence of the father (or parents in general), who in most "traditional" societies decided on matters like this.[54] More generally, and as argued by Goody, the Church seems to have favored nuclear families and aimed at weakening family ties.[55]

The Investiture Controversy eventually led to a compromise between Pope and emperor. In the Roman Empire, as in many "classical" empires elsewhere in the world (e.g., China, Japan, India, the Ottoman Empire, Byzantium), power was "one and indivisible" and ultimately derived from the emperor's "mandate from heaven." In western Europe, power became—thanks to feudal tradition and the way in which Church and state shared power—divisible, and subsequently negotiable. Monarchs—again an essential part of the western European tradition that emerged—became subservient to the law, as were their subjects, and could, if they developed into tyrants, be deposed and even disposed of, as the philosopher of law and constitutional theorist John of Salisbury argued in the twelfth century.[56] In many cases, elections became the means of appointing bearers of authority: the Pope was elected by the archbishops; councils of these same bishops determined ecclesiastical doctrine. Even the choice of the emperor of the Holy Roman Empire became the subject of such a selection process. Large meetings of dignitaries were an essential element in these procedures. Monarchs had always been in the habit of surrounding themselves with their vassals and seeking advice from the ecclesiastical authorities. In the twelfth century, many such meetings developed a more stable format, especially when official representatives of the cities were also invited to attend. The first "modern" parliament met in 1188 in Leon (northern Spain); the parliamentary movement spread throughout Europe in the centuries that followed.[57]

Similar developments also took place in the Netherlands, of which the local assembly that could be found in Drenthe in the thirteenth century is an example. The count of Holland was advised by a council, which included not only his nobles and vassals but also other "good people," among them senior officials and sometimes other citizens. Especially when financial issues were at stake, a count would appeal to representatives of the cities, who in this way could influence policy.

Monasteries often possessed great wealth and, therefore, wielded significant power. To defend their rights—no easy task in a world ruled by knights—monasteries began recording in written charters their possessions and the gifts they received. This gradually led to the norm that rights laid down on paper were considered authentic and deserved protection, a norm that, of course, mainly benefited the Church, as guardian of "the Word." In a certain sense, this also changed actual property rights: feudal lords had in the past almost casually granted property to vassals or ecclesiastical institutions; by recording such gifts in charters, property rights actually became frozen in time and the lord could no longer easily reclaim them.

Two developments that were essential for western European institutional development were set in motion in this way. Feudal property rights, under which various social groups had claims on part of the proceeds of the land, and on actual or alleged ownership thereof, developed—partly helped by the rediscovery of Roman law—toward the modern, unambiguous property rights that we know today. And at least as important was that the written word became central to the developing legal system. While in other societies (such as Islamic ones) people's memory was considered more reliable than the written word (so oral testimonies were always needed to settle a dispute), in Europe a tradition of trust in charters and other documents, which were after all objective, emerged, especially if they were signed by those involved. Feudal lords and, at a later stage, towns and villages began hiring monastic clerks (the word "clerk" being derived from cleric or clergy) to advise them and draw up the necessary documents.

In time, others with no specific ecclesiastical experience also discovered the importance of becoming proficient in writing and arithmetic: in the rapidly growing cities, groups of merchants emerged for whom writing and numeracy were indispensable skills. Indeed, merchant networks were maintained by letter writing, and cities and guilds had their rights recorded in charters—documents that were cherished as a sort of constitution of the city (or guild). The production of charters, manuscripts, and other forms of the written word increased rapidly, and the number of people who could read and write increased accordingly. In the cities, schools for primary and secondary education were established—sometimes funded by the city itself, sometimes by its wealthier citizenry. In short, Europe had taken its first steps on the march toward a "knowledge economy."[58]

Clearly, in many ways the Church played a crucial role in the development of society and state—even in the Netherlands, despite its location on the margins of feudal Europe, where the influence of the Church was perhaps less than it was at the center. It is still an open question as to whether there was a link between the doctrines of the Church and the great wave of institution building that we have described in this chapter. Schulz and colleagues have demonstrated that Catholicism had a large impact on family structures and furthered the rise of the nuclear family.[59] More tentatively, Richardson and McBride have speculated that the cooperative behavior manifest in the lasting partnerships of the guilds derived its stability from the concept of purgatory as a means of disciplining the populace: living a life in accord with ecclesiastical doctrine would shorten a person's stay there.[60]

Laying the Foundations of Capitalism

We will not speculate further about "deep" connections between religion, institutions, and economic development, but merely note that a variety of influences and developments in the High Middle Ages gave rise to a new institutional structure with some striking features. Some of those features were pan-European. To begin with, this was a strong civil society: around 1300, the Netherlands already knew more or less autonomous cities, guilds, villages, *marken*, drainage boards, and at least one count's council, all of which were broadly comparable institutions. Meetings were already fairly commonplace, and elections were held. In northwestern Europe, this bottom-up movement peaked shortly after 1300. The Flemish Battle of the Golden Spurs (1302)—an uprising of the Flemish cities against the French king that ended in a resounding victory for the cities—led to a revolutionary outburst. The guilds seized power in the cities of Flanders; like all true revolutionaries, they also wanted to export their model, which led to a conflict with Holland and Utrecht. In 1304 Flemish troops appeared before the city walls of Utrecht and, thanks to the cooperation of its citizens (who wanted to shake off the authority of the bishop), were admitted to the city. This eventually culminated in the Guild Letter of 1304, in which the guilds took control of Utrecht's city council—after the Flemish model—a situation that remained unchanged until 1528. This revolutionary mutation in the north occurred only in Utrecht: elsewhere the guilds were not yet strong enough, on their own, to fight their way to power.

This robust civil society, with numerous bottom-up institutions, arose quite naturally, alongside other feudal institutions. This was probably due to the fact that feudalism was also a system based on reciprocity between lord and vassal, one that was relatively flexible and able to adapt to new demands. In other words, cities and merchant guilds could carve out a position for themselves within this system, provided they could offer something in return, as was expected from other vassals. The oath of allegiance—modeled on feudalism—played a central role in the newly formed institutions: the urban commune was essentially an "oath-bound society," and we have seen how the people's assembly in Drenthe was considered as such.

We have also seen how feudalism created the preconditions for a striking growth in population and agricultural production. At the same time, conditions were created to enable a greater degree of extraction of surpluses. The inhabitants of Drenthe, who around the year 700 did not pay anything to a central authority, were forced by their new lords to contribute money and produce; but their agricultural production seems to have increased at least as strongly owing to their incorporation into the feudal system, until the revolt of 1227 freed them of feudal exploitation. It was these developments that laid the foundation for the population explosion of 950–1300. Providing flexibility, feudal institutions were also able to effectively manage the large-scale exploitation of the Utrecht–Holland peat bogs: a system was created linking entrepreneurs, subcontractors, and free farmers (as "buyers"), which made this gigantic operation a great success.

Feudalism, often regarded as static and hierarchical, thus appears to have been anything but a brake on social development in these centuries. Moreover, it created, following the fragmentation of the Carolingian Empire into more compact, controllable units, the foundations for the process of state formation. Finally, it concentrated relatively large incomes in the hands of a small elite of nobles and ecclesiastical office holders whose demand for luxury goods from faraway places created new markets and thereby boosted the growth of international trade. The "free" north of the country actually lacked many of these developments, and eventually lagged behind the west and south, where the growth-boosting effects of a development started by feudalism became more apparent. Although in the ninth and tenth centuries the Frisian lands did not in many respects lag behind those south of the Rhine—there was much more money circulating then, presumably because there was more trade—during the eleventh to thirteenth centuries this changed and the south and west of the country developed relatively more favorably (this will be discussed in more detail in chapter 4). The trade of the "free Frisians" hardly, if at all, led to the new patterns of division of labor and urbanization that were characteristic of the areas south of the IJ sea arm and river IJssel. This comparison shows how feudalism was the engine of early European growth, and that it is no coincidence that Flanders, part of the feudal core area, became one of the most dynamic parts of medieval Europe.

Most interesting, given later developments, was the mixture of feudal and "free" structures that crystallized in Holland, with its free farmers and a gradually developing feudal state emerging from the fragments of the Carolingian Empire that acquired (semi-)independence. This mixture seems to be something specific to the Netherlands—or, rather, Holland—but in the period before 1350 this unusual combination was a mere variation on a European pattern. Its potential would only emerge in the centuries that followed.

The Church played a major role in these developments. It ensured European unity in values and norms—within certain limits, of course—and tried to take the edge off some of the harsh consequences of political disintegration. It was, moreover, an economic factor of importance, as the great wave in church building demonstrates. In this respect, it is and remains something of a miracle that a rather underdeveloped western European economy was able to successfully complete such a large number of massive construction projects as demonstrated by the great reclamations of the peat bogs and the Romanesque and Gothic churches. Such an achievement required strong institutional cooperation, to which the Church made an important contribution.

In 1015 the Netherlands was way behind—Alpert of Metz was visiting a peripheral region in a Europe that itself was marginal to the world economy—but in the years that followed, particularly after 1350, it gained momentum and underwent relatively rapid development, to which we turn in the next chapter.

4

Capitalism and Civil Society in Late Medieval Holland, 1350–1566

On August 29, 1514, a committee of five senior officials traveled from The Hague to Haarlem to begin a carefully prepared investigation of the towns and villages of the County of Holland. The committee, consisting of Roelant le Fevre, Jan Carondelet, Guillaume de Margues, Floris van Wijngaerden, and Vincent Cornelissing, all senior financial officials of the Habsburg court, had the task of investigating the economic and financial situation of the cities and villages to determine a fair distribution of the land tax called *verponding*, the most important tax paid to the central authorities in Brussels. The committee came well prepared: a detailed list of the questions to be asked had been drawn up. How many communicants and hearths (how many inhabitants and houses) were there? What were the main sources of income? How much tax was levied and on which goods? How much debt were the cities carrying? In the case of villages, how much land was in use, and who owned the land (the villagers themselves, or townspeople and monasteries)? And so on. In addition, the committee wanted to know how things had developed over the past ten to fifteen years. Had industry increased or decreased? Had the population grown? To what extent had people suffered from the war with Gelre, or Gelderland (which had been raging since 1502)?

The committee began with great enthusiasm—after establishing itself in the Haarlem town hall and presenting its credentials to the mayors and aldermen. The first to be questioned was the city's treasurer, Frederick Deyman, who provided full details of its finances over the previous fifteen years. He was followed by Reynier Wynant, priest to the parish of Haarlem for more than thirty years, who informed the committee of the numbers of communicants in recent years. Next, the city's wealth-tax *zetters* (local officials in charge of the tax) were interviewed, such as "Jacob Hendricxz, *wantsnijder* [textile merchant] aged 62 years; Pieter Hermanszoon, *brouwer* [brewer] aged 46 years, Willem Dirkzoon, *wantsnijder* aged 46 years." Various occupational groups followed, such as ships' masters, millers, and brewers, all of whom were called upon to testify about the economic development of the city and their trade. The result was an exhaustive overview of local economic activity, full of precise figures, even presented here and there in the form of something resembling a table.

It took the committee until April 11, 1515, to complete its task, visiting city after city and village after village, finishing in the village of Hoogmade, where it spoke with "Lord Gerrit van Poelgeest, knight and lord of Hoichtmaede, aged 54; Huge Aelwijnszoon, local bailiff, aged 56 and Jacob Jacobszoon, village elder, aged 46."[1] The report documenting the committee's findings, the *Informacie*, is one of our most important sources for the socioeconomic and political history of Holland in this period. Some five hundred years after Alpert of Metz wrote his chronicles, we find a completely different kind of society emerging.

The reason behind the committee's survey was itself a complex one, but what it ultimately came down to was that the central government in Brussels wanted to levy land taxes, and that a means for distributing the tax burden fairly among towns and villages had to be found. Clearly, this was directly related to the state-building process of this period. Because they had incurred large debts, often to the benefit of the central government, a number of cities had run into financial problems in the 1490s. This financial crisis had serious consequences for Holland's economy: if cities could no longer meet their obligations, then merchants from these cities could no longer count on receiving credit elsewhere, and abroad they could even be placed under arrest by their city's creditors.

An additional issue, as is so often the case, was disagreement about the distribution of the tax burden. In particular, the city of Dordrecht, pointing to privileges gained in earlier days, disputed the amount it was expected to contribute to tax revenues. To address the issue, details on population size and the prosperity of urban and rural areas had to be established. At the time, Holland was part of the Habsburg Empire, ruled over by Maximilian of Austria and his grandson Charles V, who were therefore mentioned in the preamble of the *Informacie*. The States of Holland functioned as the intermediary between Brussels—the seat of the central government of the Low Countries—and the towns and villages of Holland, with the States attempting to fix the fairest possible amount of tax to be paid, based on the income and wealth of the towns and villages. It was the committee's task to establish quantitative indicators of that income and wealth. The whole thing has a very modern feel about it.

The *Informacie* is also important because it describes the kind of society Holland had become by the early sixteenth century. Based on numbers of hearths (houses) and communicants (people taking communion—i.e., almost all adults), it has been estimated that there were about 275,000 people living in Holland at the time of the survey, of which no fewer than 124,000 (i.e., almost half) lived in urban communities.[2] Around 1500, Holland was one of the most urbanized areas in the world, perhaps even the most urbanized. The economy, as can be seen from the occupations and business activities mentioned in the *Informacie*, possessed a very modern structure (table 4.1). Only a quarter of the working population was active in the agricultural sector, while the rest worked in fisheries, industry, and services. Even in rural areas, nonagricultural activities were just as important as agriculture: spinning for the textile industry, large-scale peat digging, fishing and merchant shipping, and more.[3] In an economic and social sense, Holland had therefore become a modern society. Moreover, the citizens of Haarlem and Beverwijk (and the other places in Holland) are represented in the *Informacie*; only seldom were invitations issued to a pastor or the Lord of Poelgeest to testify before the committee of inquiry. The survey was carried out on behalf of the States of Holland by capable officials, some of whom were directly connected to the Habsburg court in Brussels.[4] Particularly in the cities, they would interview officials who held positions comparable to their own—for example, treasurer or secretary. The existence of such a capable group of officials was of great importance for the process of state formation during this period.

This chapter looks into the question of how the County of Holland became a society of cities, citizens, and civil officials, of figures and tables, of finance and economics, during the relatively short period between 1350 and 1500. How, in other words, it was transformed from a feudal into a capitalist economy and society. From 1500 onward, Holland became the undisputed center of the Netherlands, at least economically and sociopolitically. This in no way means that the other parts of the Low Countries stood still

TABLE 4.1. The Occupational Structure of the Workforce of Holland in 1514 (in percent)

	Countryside	Cities	Total
PRIMARY SECTOR			
Agriculture	41	1	24
Fisheries	20	2	12
Peat digging	6	—	3
Total	**67**	**3**	**39**
INDUSTRY			
Construction/dikes and dams	4	6	5
Woodworking/metal industry	4	16	9
Leather working	—	2	1
Textiles	9	14	11
Clothing	1	10	5
Brewing	—	8	3
Other food industry	1	9	4
Total	**19**	**65**	**38**
SERVICES			
Trade	2	16	8
Transport	13	5	9
Other services	1	10	5
Total	**16**	**31**	**22**
Total	100	100	100

Source: Zanden 2002b.

during this "crisis of the late Middle Ages."[5] Simultaneously, in the south, in the equally dynamic region of Brabant, an urban system was developing in and around Antwerp that flourished between 1500 and 1570. In the region along the River IJssel, the Hanseatic centers of Deventer, Zutphen, Kampen, and Zwolle were also evolving into trading hubs, albeit of a different scale than the metropolis of Antwerp. During much of this period, Deventer was the intellectual center of the northern Netherlands, responsible, for example, for the lion's share of books published at the time. The big difference between Holland and the rest of what was to become the Netherlands was not so much to be found in the growth and prosperity of the cities—that took place everywhere in the Low Countries—but rather in the far-reaching transformation of its entire society that was taking shape throughout these centuries, including in its countryside—perhaps especially its countryside.

Holland's Growth Spurt from 1350 to 1500: The Birth of Dutch Capitalism

Before 1250, the western regions of the Low Countries were economically marginal. There was hardly any international trade, and what there was was in the hands of foreigners, such as merchants from Hamburg. At that time, Holland was still so focused on agricultural expansion, on completing the reclamation of the peat areas, that little attention was paid to other activities. That began to change between 1250 and 1300. In this, the "welfare policies" of the counts of Holland, who liberally granted new city rights in the hope of benefiting from this themselves, were a driving force. Often a count also responded positively to "bottom-up" initiatives by citizens who wished to strengthen the position of their town. Another example of such policies was the construction of the lock at Spaarndam in 1253, mentioned in the previous chapter. Floris V (1256–96), one of the county's more consequential rulers, combined welfare policies with the systematic pursuit of expansion of his county borders and consolidation of his internal power.

One of the drivers of the transformation process that began during this period was transportation along Holland's waterways. Earlier trading cities—Dorestad, Tiel, and (later) especially Utrecht—were dependent on the large flow of trade from northern Europe to the south and, to a lesser extent, from the Rhineland to England. Up until the twelfth century, the major flows of north–south traffic bypassed Holland, because the route via Utrecht (following the Vecht, the Rijnse Vaart, and the Lek) offered more advantages. Waterworks (such as the construction of the Gouwe canal) to simplify the waterways in this area had already been carried out in Holland around 1200, because the route via Utrecht required the frequent passing of dams and locks. Thanks in part to the lock at Spaarndam, an efficient waterway for shipping traffic from IJ to Merwede was created. The Rhineland Drainage Board, which was created just for this purpose, became a body that not only had to reconcile supra-local interests related to water management for agriculture, at the same time it also had to consider needs of trade and traffic of the emerging cities.[6]

The first phase of growth finished around 1300. At that time, Holland possessed quite a few smaller cities, of which Dordrecht was probably the largest, still with no more than about five thousand inhabitants. Other towns, defined as communities with urban charters, were much smaller, but all told urbanization was already at around 14%, which is high by European standards of the time. Up to this point the growth had really amounted to catching up, and fitted fully within the overall dynamics of the European economy during the "big boom" of the Middle Ages. The fact that the growth of cities and nonagricultural activities continued after 1350, which led to the economic structure that was investigated in 1514 through the compilation of the *Informacie* of that year, made Holland (and the western Netherlands as a whole) special.

The cause of this Dutch *Sonderweg*—its own special path—has to be sought in the way in which its society and economy reacted to two external shocks: the Black Death of 1348 (and the many "echo epidemics" that followed) and the environmental crisis of the late fourteenth and, especially, fifteenth centuries. The sociopolitical and economic structure that had developed in Holland in the late Middle Ages was put under great pressure by these two crises, but it emerged much stronger from them.

The first shock, the Black Death, which spread throughout western Europe in 1347–49, resulted in a death rate of between one-third and two-thirds of its inhabitants, bringing the big boom of the Middle Ages to a halt. Elsewhere in Europe, this massive number of deaths had been preceded by the Great Famine of 1315–17, which created a hunger crisis that is often seen as the real breaking point in the growth of population.[7] In the Netherlands, there is only limited evidence that this food crisis was severe. The Black Death probably struck less savagely than in Italy or England, but this too cannot be precisely estimated owing to insufficient sources.[8] Nevertheless, it is clear that despite the more or less regular occurrence of echo epidemics, over the long term their effects were far less dramatic than elsewhere, as shown by the growth in population numbers: in the year 1300 cities in Holland counted 30,000 citizens; in 1400, 69,000 citizens; and in 1514 a total of 124,000—45% of the entire population.[9] Van Bavel has tentatively linked the divergent responses to the Black Death to differences in social property relations, but the debate about the Black Death and its impact is still undecided.[10] What is striking is that there were no attempts to control wages and suppress the consequences of the acute shortage in the labor market. In England, for example, a strict regulation of the labor market was introduced in the immediate wake of the pandemic, the Ordinance of Labourers, to freeze wages at their pre-1348 level.[11] No city or provincial government in the Netherlands tried to do anything similar, and the Dutch labor market was and remained basically free.

The evolution toward this exceptionally high degree of urbanization is the clearest evidence that something special was going on in Holland between 1340 and 1500.[12] In addition, the size of cities was unusually well balanced: no megacities, such as those in Flanders, with more than 50,000 inhabitants, but quite a few medium-sized ones, such as Leiden, Haarlem, Amsterdam, and Dordrecht, all with 10–15,000 inhabitants, followed closely by cities that fell just short of these numbers, such as Rotterdam, Delft, Gouda, The Hague, Alkmaar, Enkhuizen, and Hoorn, plus a whole swarm of even smaller cities and towns, from Schoonhoven in the south to Medemblik and Schagen in the north.

This process of urbanization was accompanied by strong growth in GDP per capita. According to the tentative estimates presented in chapter 2, GDP per capita increased by about 40% between 1347 and 1400; at the time the *Informacie* was being drawn up (1514) it was about 70% higher than it had been just before the Black Death. International literature shows that the Black Death affected individual countries in different ways. In Spain and Sweden—relatively sparsely populated parts of Europe—the population decline caused markets to shrink, commercialization to decline, and GDP per capita to fall. In Italy—Europe's most developed economy at the time— there was initially an increase in GDP per capita, but by the fifteenth century decline had set in. Only in the North Sea region do we see a sharp increase in GDP per capita as a result of the population decline of the plague, followed by a stabilization of per capita income at a much higher level in England and even more growth in the Netherlands.[13]

In principle, this was the "normal" response, at least according to classical Malthusian thinking that population pressure is an important factor in premodern economies. Due to the sharp decline in population, after 1348 more land and capital per capita were available, so that—assuming other conditions remained the same—a higher level of production could be achieved. This does, however, presuppose the presence of a mechanism for converting the post-1348 scarcity of labor and the abundance of agricultural land and capital into a different mix of factors of production. We know from numerous studies on the development of prices and wages in western Europe during this period that markets indeed managed to make the necessary adjustments: everywhere real wages rose owing to the declining population; everywhere the premium on education decreased and the reward for human capital declined; and interest rates fell almost everywhere.[14]

Only in England and the Low Countries did these radical changes in relative prices cause a systematic climb to a higher income level (in other words, an economy that used less labor and more capital). Everywhere in western Europe, experiments were conducted with new, more capital-intensive production techniques, such as cranes for unloading and loading freight in ports and, even more dramatically, the printing press (as a substitute for copying manuscripts by hand). But the evidence of the various projects to reconstruct the development of GDP per capita in this period strongly suggests that only in northwestern Europe did this lead to a structural increase in income levels and set in motion the slow, but sustained growth described in chapter 2.[15] Álvarez-Nogal and Prados de la Escosura have, for example, argued that the absence of such a response in the Spanish case—where GDP per capita by contrast fell after 1348—was due to the "frontier" character of the Spanish economy, where markets were more marginal and unable to function as well after 1348 owing to the decline of the population. Epstein has made the point that institutional rigidities and the exploitation of the countryside by the cities hindered economic transformation in Tuscany.[16] The sharp increase in GDP per capita found in the North Sea area was clearly not universal in Europe and can be seen as evidence that these economies reacted to the population decline as market economies are supposed to do. This successful adaptation to the new balance of factors after 1348, therefore, is proof of the emergence of a market economy—the breakthrough of the market as a central economic mechanism—in the Netherlands (and in England). In other words, after 1348 the breakthrough of capitalism took place in the Low Countries, and in particular in Holland. As Bas van Bavel has shown, an estimated 40%–60% of the population depended partly or entirely on wage labor for its living—and this was perhaps even more so in rural areas than in cities (where many craftsmen were something between an entrepreneur and an employed worker).[17]

In the Netherlands, land had also become a highly commercialized commodity and was widely traded and commercially leased. The capital market was, certainly by the standards of the day, and despite the Church's reservations about charging interest, well developed and quite accessible—even to small savers, including women.[18] Interest rates had fallen from around 12% to 5%–6% annually, exactly as you would expect from a market economy of which the population has declined strongly. New financial instruments made it possible to invest in ships, shipyards, farmland, and so on. The reaction of Holland's economy to the Black Death thus indicates that it not only had the external characteristics of a market economy (wage laborers among the working population, development of land and capital markets) but also behaved as a market economy (by adjusting decisions on production and consumption to relative scarcity).

The second shock that hit Holland, the decline of arable farming due to subsidence of reclaimed peat bogs, provides an even more dramatic example of market-driven adjustment processes. As we described in the previous chapter, the peat bogs of the western Netherlands were reclaimed between 950 and 1300, which enabled the agricultural area and the population that depended on it to grow strongly. The surface levels of the peat areas were originally relatively high, so the bogs could be drained with channels and ditches without much effort. However, as soon as water is extracted, peat settles and erodes (oxidizing in air); farming on reclaimed peatlands is like living on top of a ticking time bomb. To stay ahead of the subsidence and erosion, drainage had to be intensified, and even then it was only partially successful. Quite early on, it became necessary to intervene more actively in water management. Beginning in the twelfth century, dams and locks began to appear everywhere in Holland, as is evident from the numerous place names from this period that end with the suffix *dam* or *sluis*. Nevertheless, several catastrophes occurred after 1350, the major ones having consequences for the agricultural sector. Around 1374, and again around 1420, extended wet periods combined with storm surges caused major flooding, the most notorious being the Saint Elisabeth's flood of 1421. The effects of such disasters were huge drops in arable production and large-scale abandonment of the land, such as in the Riederwaard in 1373–75 and the Grote Waard in 1421, both near Dordrecht (see figure 4.1).[19]

Farmers in the peatlands also found it increasingly difficult to grow cereals: the soil had become too moist, forcing some farmers to switch to keeping livestock—producing cheese, butter, and fattened oxen—or to concentrate crop production on smaller areas that could deliver high yields from the cultivation of industrial crops such as flax or hemp. In large parts of Europe, farmers worked first to feed their own families and second to supply the market, but this strategy became impossible in the west of the Netherlands owing to the environmental shock occurring in the peat areas. Concentration on animal husbandry—the most commonly chosen approach—meant that butter and cheese were produced for the market, and that farmers had to buy bread grain for their own household on the same market. This implies almost complete dependence on the market. Since there was not enough grain available in Holland, it had to be imported from elsewhere—from northern France, for example, and, increasingly, from the Baltic region, where grain was produced in abundance and at low prices. For this strategy to succeed, there also had to be demand for "luxury" agricultural products such as butter, cheese, and meat. In that respect, the times were advantageous: during the "crisis of the late Middle Ages," real wages everywhere rose sharply, owing to the sharp decline in the population, and the demand

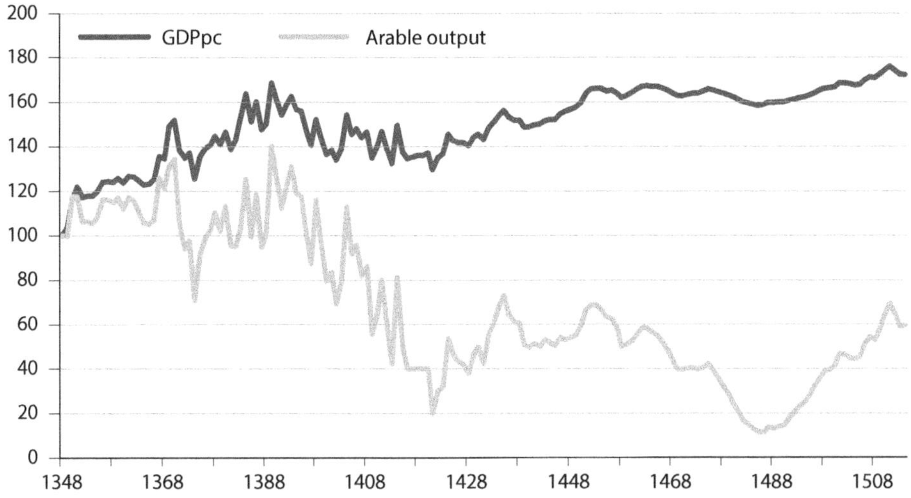

FIGURE 4.1. Index of the development of GDP per capita (GDPpc) and arable output (according to tithe data) in Holland, 1348 = 100.
Source: Zanden and Van Leeuwen 2012.

for luxury agricultural products grew, particularly in the cities. Holland's agriculture benefited from this. However, as livestock farming was less labor-intensive than arable farming, many people working in agriculture became redundant, and so they moved to the towns and cities. The strong urbanization experienced in Holland in that period has to be largely explained by this development.[20]

The accelerated commercialization of the countryside is also reflected in the increase in the number of organized markets (fairs) and rural facilities such as weighhouses. This can be seen in the increase in the number of specialized horse fairs being run from the late fourteenth century onwards. Furthermore, while sources for earlier centuries suggest that most markets were held in the coastal strip directly behind the dunes, from the fourteenth century they were mainly held in peat regions. Many of these new markets and fairs were used for trading dairy products.[21] Cities were hardly able to prevent—if they had wanted to—these rural markets springing up. Although in 1350 Holland was still at the same level as England in terms of market orientation, and lagged far behind Flanders, by around 1500 these roles had reversed.[22] The same picture of a thoroughly commercialized countryside emerges from the *Informacie* of 1514, from which it appears that in rural areas farmers had developed numerous secondary activities. The rural population had started spinning for Leiden's textile industry, cutting peat to meet urban demand for fuel, fishing and catching birds at the increasingly larger peat lakes, working on dikes and excavations in the water management projects that had to be maintained, providing transport services, and, finally, crewing for the herring fleet and on merchant ships. In 1514, when this process was in full swing, about half of the occupational activities in Holland's countryside turned out to be nonagricultural (as we saw in table 4.1).

The crisis in arable farming that began in 1373 set in motion a number of developments that resulted in the countryside of the western Netherlands becoming fundamentally different from that elsewhere in Europe. Wage labor was becoming quite normal. Already in 1514 more than half of the work done was performed by wage laborers: in the fishing sector, the merchant fleet, textiles, peat digging, and water management.[23] The link between city and countryside became stronger. In, for example, Vlaardingen and Zaandam, where nonagricultural activities predominated, the economic difference between countryside and city in occupational structure had all but disappeared. How could an agricultural crisis have such positive effects in the long run? How were farmers able to adapt so well to such new circumstances?

One important reason was trust in markets. The alternative—to withdraw to small-scale production for self-sufficiency—was not chosen; the Dutch apparently dared to put their fate in the hands of the market. We can measure that trust in the market economy to some degree by looking at the capital market, and in particular the interest rates that were being charged there. Douglass North has argued that the rate of interest is perhaps the best measure of the quality of institutions.[24] If a creditor cannot count on receiving future interest and repayment of debt, very high interest must be charged to compensate for the risk, which explains why interest rates of tens of percent are often still charged in developing countries today. In Holland, during the period 1350–1450, the fall in the interest rate was remarkably steep, from around 12% to 6%.[25] This drop was due to a European development, sometimes explained by the population decline after the Black Death of 1347–48. The argument is that high rates of mortality caused demand for capital to decrease, which resulted in falling interest rates. In Holland, however, population decline between 1347 and 1400 amounted to about 10% at the most, and was followed by growth in the fifteenth century.

The halving of the interest rate must therefore be explained by other factors; for example, improvement of property rights (a major concern of Douglass North), increased trust in the markets, and new financial instruments (e.g., annuities and bonds) may all have played a role in this. Even so, an interest rate of 6% is historically low—in fact, the rate of interest on the capital market fell barely any further between 1450 and 2000. (Only the very unusual monetary policy pursued in response to the global financial crisis of 2008 produced even further decline.) This demonstrates, if we follow North's reasoning, that the institutions regulating Holland's financial markets were apparently efficient and instilled confidence.

Property rights in Holland were well organized and protected thanks to the institutional structure that had arisen there. The farmers active in peat-bog reclamation were free farmers, who to a large degree had a business relationship with the government: they paid taxes, fulfilled their military obligations (collective military service) as good citizens, but they were not, like serfs, personally subordinate to a lord. They were free to defend their rights and they did so. One of the striking features of the Dutch countryside is that the villages were not subordinated to nearby cities but were given plenty of room to develop their own economic activities. Elsewhere—for example, in Flanders—cities and their guilds tended to monopolize all non-agricultural activities. In Holland this was much less the case, since the cities were much younger. As a result, they were less able to resist any plans or activities of the nobility, who had large interests in the countryside. Only with the Reconciliation of Delft of 1428—a peace treaty intended to end the protracted civil war known as the Hook and Cod wars—did cities gain a strong position in the States of Holland, which was then established. Moreover, no one city was able to dominate the entire region; rather, the many small and medium-sized cities kept one another in check. Only through mutual coordination and cooperation, such as in negotiations with the count and later his successors, the dukes of Burgundy, could the cities effectively promote their interests.[26]

In 1345 Count William of Holland was in great need of money because of two wars he was waging simultaneously, one against the bishop of Utrecht and the other against the Frisians. He called the representatives of Dordrecht, Haarlem, Delft, Leiden, Middelburg, and Zierikzee to his camp near Utrecht and demanded that they guarantee a loan of 300 pounds that he wanted to take. The cities agreed and signed a pledge to assist one another in both word and action to ensure that they would get the principal back. A century and a half later, the system had developed to such an extent that Maximilian of Habsburg and his son Philip the Handsome (Philip I of Castile) could saddle Holland's cities with debt that brought them to the brink of bankruptcy. Unintentionally, however, this system of collective responsibility for the county's debt also strengthened mutual relations and interests between the cities.[27] The fact that the count resided in the village of The Hague—and not in one of the main cities, such as Delft or Leiden—further contributed to balance the system: the cities were not tempted to see the count's decisions as him handing out favors to rival cities. The well-developed capital market mentioned earlier was thus supported by an equitable political economy.

The structure of the economy of Holland changed radically as a result of these developments. In 1350, 55%–60% of regional income came from agricultural activities, with the rest spread more or less equally between industry and services. By 1514, however, the share of agriculture had shrunk to less than 20%, produced by a quarter of the workforce; 38% of the workforce worked in industry and 22% in the service sector, while the remaining 15% was active in fishing and peat cutting. Another sign of the efficiency of the market economy was that the relative productivity of agriculture was close to that of the rest of the economy, whereas traditional peasant economies are characterized by large productivity gaps. In that period, more than 80% of income was thus earned from nonagricultural activities, the industrial sector was twice the size of agriculture, and the service sector was half its size.[28] Such a radical change was possible only because of the expansion of the urban sector.

Large export industries emerged in these years: the Leiden wool and Haarlem linen industries contributed greatly to exports, but above all it was the export of beer from Delft, Haarlem, and Gouda (especially to the Southern Netherlands) that dominated. Peat was also exported to the south on a large scale, as were fish. The dense network of waterways that had been created dramatically lowered transport costs and facilitated market exchange. Shipping was an important source of foreign currency; in addition to its dominance in the Baltic, Dutch shipping also began to gain importance on other routes. This illustrates the transformation that had taken place within agriculture, because the biggest import was grain—especially rye—from the Baltic countries, necessary to compensate for Holland's lack of its own bread grains.[29]

The expansion of these export industries was not the result of low labor costs, as has been previously assumed. In fact, around 1300 Holland was still a kind of "frontier" economy, where (just as in the United States during the nineteenth century) a lot of land was available. Around 1340, wages were therefore relatively high—higher than elsewhere in northwestern Europe. Apparently this did not hinder the growth of industry or the service sector, although the wage gap between Holland and the rest of the region (Flanders, England) narrowed in the period between 1350 and 1450, because elsewhere—owing to the population decline after the Black Death in 1347—wages also rose sharply.[30] Nevertheless, it seems that industries in Holland had to deal with high wages early on and were therefore better prepared for the situation that arose everywhere after 1347. This may have also contributed to the Dutch economic success of this period. Elsewhere in western Europe, we also see real incomes rising after 1347, although that usually coincided with a sharp decline in the population. What made Holland special was that its population decline was less pronounced—although possibly more pronounced than was previously thought—yet income nevertheless increased sharply, and the economy changed in structure.[31] What emerged was a market economy in which almost all production—as well as labor, capital, and agricultural land—was highly commercialized.

Switch from North–South to West–East

Holland's growth spurt in the period 1350–1500 changed the economic geography of the Netherlands. Until 1300, the differences between the "free" north and the "feudal" south predominated. Although the Frisian north started from a strong position, given the importance of Frisian trade in the centuries spanning the turn of the millennium, to an increasing degree the north was overtaken by the favorable long-term effects of feudalism and state formation in the south. There, in intensely feudalized Flanders, to be precise, the economic center of northwest Europe was located: the large cities of Bruges, Ghent, and Ypres dominated the industry (especially textiles) and international trade of the region. Next to Flanders, Brabant also developed into a center of trade and industry—medieval cities such as Malines, Louvain, Antwerp, and Brussels had no equivalent north of the major rivers. Internationally, in the late Middle Ages, the regional economies of the southern Low Countries were much more prominent than those of the north.[32]

The rise of Holland broke this pattern, although this was not so clear at first. Looking at the current territory of the Netherlands, by 1500 the County of Holland had already become the dynamic center of economic and sociopolitical progress, where the average income level—based on the wages paid—was probably about 30%–50% higher than in the east and north of the country.[33] In the century following 1500 this pattern would crystalize even further, such that during the Dutch Revolt against Spain it was almost inevitable that Holland, being the economic powerhouse, would become the center of resistance. From that moment on, the dominant axis in Dutch history became that between "the west" (i.e., Holland and Zeeland) and "the rest." The economic basis for this reversal had been laid during Holland's growth spurt in the late Middle Ages.

That did not mean that "the rest" stood still in the centuries after 1350. By European standards, other parts of the northern Netherlands also developed rapidly. This whole area, which until 1100 was on the periphery of Europe, now became increasingly integrated into the European economic landscape, to which the strong growth of trade along the River IJssel and flourishing cities such as Deventer, Zutphen, Kampen, and Zwolle testify. The prosperity of these cities is linked to the growth of the Hanseatic League, of which they, in contrast to the cities of Holland, were members. Deventer is without doubt the most striking example of a prospering Hanseatic city. In fact, it controlled two trade flows: that between Holland and Germany—insofar that the Rhine was not used, but overland routes instead—and trade between the north and the Rhineland, where Cologne was the main hub. Deventer attracted a lot of trade owing to the large fairs that were organized there four times a year; the city had obtained the privilege to do so from the bishop of Utrecht in 1344. In the fifteenth century Deventer's fairs became important for the export of Holland's butter, cheese, and textiles. The involvement of the city of Deventer in this trade went so far that in 1444 it issued regulations concerning the quality and packaging of the butter to be sold there, informing the cities and villages of Holland by letter of the rules with which they had to comply. Holland subsequently complained about the tolls levied by the city and called for a boycott of the Deventer fairs. Merchants had to move to nearby Zutphen, where the Count of Gelre attempted to establish a rival market. The "butter war" that ensued lasted ten years, from 1463 to 1473, after which Holland's merchants finally returned to Deventer.[34]

The Hanseatic League was originally an alliance of traders, a continuation of the merchant guild of Tiel, mentioned at the beginning of the previous chapter. What started in part as an informal coalition of merchants from different cities grew in the mid-fourteenth century into an alliance of autonomous cities that identified themselves with the interests of "their" merchants. The typical medieval instrument of a meeting of representatives of the member cities was used to unite their interests: the first *Hansetag*, commonly regarded as the foundational meeting of the Hanseatic League, was held in Lübeck in 1356. It was precisely in this period that Deventer joined the Hanseatic League. Initially, the city of Kampen tried to make agreements outside the Hanseatic cartel—for example, with Norway's King Valdemar.[35] Later—between 1407 and 1441, when it also regularly participated in the

Hanseatic meetings—Kampen continued to follow a fairly opportunistic strategy in dealing with the League.[36]

The example of Kampen illustrates the weakness of such an alliance: cities that for opportunistic reasons deviated from the official policy could not actually be compelled to conform, especially if they were beyond the political sphere of influence of Lübeck. The free-rider problem could therefore be addressed only to a limited extent. Up until the mid-fifteenth century, merchants from Holland were rarely involved in this practice, which demonstrates once again the late arrival of the region in the arena of economic development in western Europe.

Instead of joining, Amsterdam and the other cities of Holland became the main rivals of the Hanseatic League. As so often during this period, trade was inextricably linked to the exercise of power; the rise of Amsterdam would soon have ended had it not been accompanied by effective action in military—especially maritime—conflicts. The Dutch-Hanseatic war of 1438–41 was the first example of this, with more to come in the centuries to follow. But when it suited them, the Hollanders also made agreements with the Hanseatic League, such as in the period 1467–70, when Holland cooperated with the League against the Danish king, Christian I. In such international conflicts, it became increasingly important that Holland could count on powerful partners and be part of the growing Burgundian empire, which could play a decisive role in conflicts with Lübeck and Denmark, or any of the other Baltic cities and states. The long-term effect of this maneuvering was that the trade and merchant fleet of the Hanseatic League was forced to give ground in the face of the competition from Holland's cities. This shift occurred also at the expense of the position of Kampen, Deventer, and Zwolle (the last began to establish itself as an active trading city only around 1450). Although they were by the standards of the time large cities, and much larger than the towns in the northern part of the country, over the period 1450–1550 the eastern towns were overshadowed by Amsterdam.

The economic boom that took place in the eastern Netherlands in the fourteenth and fifteenth centuries was largely the result of successful international trade. An important difference with the economy of Holland was that Deventer, Zutphen, Kampen, and Zwolle did not develop significant export industries of their own. The lack of export-producing activities also meant that these cities relatively quickly reached their growth ceilings of five to six thousand inhabitants. Another striking difference was that relations with the surrounding countryside were not anywhere near as strong as in

Holland. Most farmers in the eastern Netherlands continued to produce primarily for their own use and concentrated on cultivating the same crops as in previous centuries—rye, barley, and oats—in combination with small-scale animal husbandry.

During their heyday, the eastern Netherlands took the lead in the areas of religious and educational innovation. In Deventer, Geert Grote founded the movement of the Brothers of the Common Life—also known as Modern Devotion—a lay movement that focused on spiritual development through independent reading (in the words of Thomas à Kempis: "met een boekske in een hoekske," or "tucked away in a corner with a book"), distributing books (copying manuscripts and, later, printing), providing education, translating books (including the Bible in the vernacular), and, of course, by preaching the "correct" doctrine, one in which personal experience of faith and following the example of Christ were central. Brothers and sisters in faith lived together in independent communities, as the early Christians would have done, fully focused on further spiritual development. Their reformed system of education was influential beyond their own community, and was an important source of inspiration for Church reformers in the fifteenth and, especially, sixteenth centuries. Erasmus, for example, was educated at a Latin school run by the movement, and he can be seen as the most important link between the Brothers of the Common Life and the Reformation of the sixteenth century, although eventually he chose to remain in the Catholic Church.[37]

The cities of the eastern Netherlands developed, owing in part to the Modern Devotion movement, into centers of knowledge and learning—perhaps even more so than the strongly economically oriented cities in the west of the country. This is also evident from the spread of the printing press in the northern Netherlands in the decades following its invention by Gutenberg. Thanks partly to its close contacts with the Rhineland, Deventer benefited from the first wave in the spread of the technology that arose in the 1470s, as printers from central Germany spread throughout Europe. The city quickly grew into the leading publishing center of the Netherlands. In the European ranking of the printing of *incunabula* (pre-1500 books) between 1452 and 1500, the city holds thirteenth place, having produced approximately 610 titles—well behind the 3,641 books published by leader Venice, but far ahead of all other cities in the Low Countries. The much larger city of Antwerp, which in the sixteenth century would become the center of new industry in the Low Countries, managed to publish only 445 titles (fifteenth place) between 1450 and 1500. In the eastern Netherlands, more than twice as many books were produced as in Holland. So, thanks to the Brothers of the Common Life, Deventer had become an intellectual center of note, to a significantly greater extent than the much larger Utrecht, for example, which was officially the religious center of the northern Netherlands, but was much less dynamic.[38]

State Formation

To understand what was simultaneously happening to the state, and therefore to the institutional context provided by the state, we need to step back in time. With the decline of the Carolingian Empire and its subsequent fragmentation during the ninth and tenth centuries, the political consolidation in the centuries that followed was at least as profound as the rise of markets and trade. It started with relatively small units—counties, dioceses, "free" cities—that were still embedded in the Holy Roman Empire but were already fairly independent. Regional sovereigns attempted to form coalitions or, through the strategic choice of marriage partners, to unite several areas under one family. Blunt power politics was also used: through conquest, or annexation, smaller, less-powerful entities were subsumed. As we have seen, between 1000 and 1300 the counts of Holland gradually expanded their territory to encompass the current provinces of North and South Holland, at the expense of many minor lords, as well as the bishops of Utrecht in the east and the free Frisians in the north. A trace of the latter's history remained visible in the name of the region, which until the end of the eighteenth century was called Holland and West Friesland. In time, Zeeland was also brought under the authority of the counts of Holland, although formally it continued to be an independent entity.

The counts of Holland had been successful in bringing a cohesive area under their control. In a similar manner, the counts of Gelderland (or Gelre, for short)—from 1339 onwards the dukes of Gelre—built a state in the center of the Netherlands, although Gelre continued to consist of four more or less autonomous regions: the Veluwe, the County of Zutphen (today also known as the Achterhoek), the quarter of Nijmegen, and, finally, the Overkwartier, the area around Venlo. The impetus for "modern" state building was provided by Count Reinoud I of Gelre (1271–1318) after 1290, when he was forced to offer his county's main sources of income as collateral to the Italian banker Tadeo Cavazzone, who in turn resold them to the Count of Flanders, Reinoud's father-in-law. For the funds he needed to buy back his county, Reinoud became dependent on the cities of the region, which were the financially most powerful parties at that time. Nijmegen, the largest city in Gelderland, was the leader of Gelderland's cities; it even claimed for itself the status of an autonomous free imperial city answering directly to the emperor of the Holy Roman Empire. Reinoud's predicament led to a typical medieval compromise: in exchange for their support, the cities of Gelderland were given a say in the decision-making processes of the count. This led in 1318 to the first meeting of what would later become the States of Gelderland, in which the cities occupied a position equal to that of the nobility as advisors to Reinoud. During the Flemish intermezzo, modern techniques of financial administration and official financial control were introduced to Gelre and contributed greatly to the further development of the county. For example, official tax collectors and auditors were instated, and the first general accounts of Gelre were drawn up in 1294/95.[39] Administrative innovations like these played an important role in Gelderland's development into one of the most powerful states of the region, so powerful that the county managed to maintain its independence up until 1543.

Nevertheless, state formation in Gelderland increasingly took place in the shadow of a new political unit that was forming in the south: the Burgundian proto-state. It is called a proto-state because the dukes of Burgundy never succeeded in actually forging their territories into a single entity. Indeed, Burgundy itself remained formally subordinate to the king of France, but the steps it took toward realizing its ideal of unity were to have a decisive influence on Dutch history. Without the Burgundians, the Netherlands and Belgium would probably never have become the independent states we know today. In 1477, the last male duke of the house of Burgundy died, and Burgundy's political legacy passed to Maximilian of Habsburg, already the most powerful European ruler of the time—making him even more powerful.

The combined tax revenues of Burgundy's territories were comparable to those of England and Castile, two other substantial powers at the time in Europe. But Burgundy also found itself at a crossroads. Burgundian politics was a ruthless combination of deception and conquest. By granting regions their own institutions, Philip the Good (1419–67) had allowed the elites in those regions a degree of political independence, while at the same time keeping them bound to himself. Through the creation of a number of new institutions, he attempted to simultaneously bring unity to the administration of his territories: in 1444 he appointed a treasurer (something like a minister of finance) with jurisdiction over all his lands. Between 1435 and 1445 a new high court of law gradually evolved, the Great Council of Mechelen (Grote Raad van Mechelen), which became the supreme court of appeal for all courts in the Burgundian territories and brought greater unity in leg-islation and regulations. And perhaps most importantly, in January 1464 representatives of all Burgundian lands met for the first time in a formal assembly of the States General. That assembly had been preceded by several preliminary developments. For example, as early as 1427 representatives of several of Burgundy's territories were invited to meet jointly with the duke. In 1464, however, representatives of *all* territories were invited to meet. This assembly was, moreover, not just a one-off event, but the first of regular meetings to come: the States General became a real "parliament," where common issues could be discussed according to set procedures.

Medieval parliaments such as the States General were based on a deal: in exchange for greater participation, representatives of the various social classes and—in particular—cities were pressured to pay more tax. There was an inevitable tension between the aims of the two sides. The distribution of the tax burden shows that the concessions were real. The inhabitants of Flanders and Brabant paid much less tax per capita than those of Holland, undoubtedly because the large—and wealthy—cities in the south were able to force the duke to be more lenient. The cities of Holland were forced deep into debt to meet their financial obligations. (Later, under Maximilian I of Habsburg, that would lead to a genuine financial and economic crisis.) In 1477 the cities in Holland protested loudly—against all the obligations with which the Burgundian state had saddled them in the previous decades. But it was in the southern regions of the Low Countries that resistance was greatest, and, to be more precise, mostly in the large towns and cities there. This led to major confrontations between the duke and the inhabitants of the towns and cities. Ghent, for example, rebelled against the authorities in 1337, 1379, and 1449, with the bone of contention being the balance of power between city and sovereign.[40] The citizens of Ghent demanded greater autonomy and a count (later duke) whose political interests would be determined by those of the city, instead of the other way around.

These conflicts intensified during the reign of Charles the Bold (1465/67–77). It was Charles's ambition to ensure a permanent place for Burgundy among the predominant states of Europe. Charles no longer negotiated taxes with his individual territories, but rather in the States General, with every-one at once. And instead of seeing it as a request for monies, he considered his budget as a command to his territories to collect the money. Already with his ascendance to power in 1467, unrest had broken out in various cities, triggered by recent increases in excise duties. His councilors advised him to have Mechelen razed to the ground, a proposal that Charles ignored.[41]

Nevertheless, a year later that was more or less what he did in Liège, after the city rebelled for a second time. His soldiers were given free rein to plunder the city, and they did so with enthusiasm.[42] Ghent also had its turn. The city's magistrates were summoned to Brussels, where they were made to wait outside for hours, bareheaded, in the snow—a public humiliation—only to learn that the provisions of the Treaty of Gavere of 1453, under which the city had had to surrender almost all independence, would continue to be enforced. It is no wonder that in 1477, directly after Charles's death on the battlefield, uprisings erupted everywhere.

Maximilian I of Habsburg continued the policy of the Burgundians. In 1515 he was succeeded in the Low Countries by his grandson Charles V. Even more so than Maximilian, Charles was a true European monarch, with territories in Germany, Italy, and Spain. In addition to his interests in the Low Countries, where he was born (in 1500, in Ghent) and grew up, Charles also had to take into account all the other territories under his rule. Everyone had to pay for the costs of maintaining his empire. And it was during this period that these costs began to rise sharply, in particular to fund military innovations.[43] Instead of occasionally requesting contributions for the government of their kingdoms, rulers found themselves obliged to levy taxes on a regular basis. And to do that effectively, the administrative apparatus also had to be streamlined; only then would it be possible to carry out complex operations such as tax reform based on real estimates of residents' income and wealth (e.g., the *Informacie* with which we began this chapter).

From the 1530s, Charles began to centralize government administration of the Low Countries in Brussels. In 1531 three new administrative institutions were established there to replace the royal advisory council: the Council of State (political), the Secret Council (judiciary), and the Council of Finances. In that same year, the local governor, whose position as Charles's deputy had existed since the late fifteenth century, became a sort of viceroy, with his own authority. These institutional innovations created greater unity in the government of the Low Countries—or, in any case, that was the intention. Charles concluded this process—for the time being, at least—first in 1548 by gaining recognition of the Low Countries as a separate administrative unit within the Holy Roman Empire and subsequently in 1549 by establishing that his seventeen territories in the Low Countries were not to be divided up by his successors, but should always remain under the same ruler (pragmatic sanction).

Despite these institutional changes, major regional disparities persisted. Most of the lands of the northern Netherlands were more or less independent states in 1550; Gelderland had been added to Charles's empire only in September 1543, with Friesland, Groningen, Overijssel, and Utrecht having been subsumed nearly twenty-five years earlier. The differences in formal organization and administrative culture between these regions were therefore significant. The pressure of Charles's politics was palpable. In Holland, which had for some time been possessed by the Burgundians and later the Habsburgs, the tax burden increased rapidly. In the mid-sixteenth century, Holland was paying ten to fifteen times as much into Charles's war coffers as it had done thirty years before. These were very substantial efforts, the benefits of which were sometimes immediately visible—such as campaigns against Gelre's scavenging raids in the 1520s—but just as often they funded distant campaigns that could not immediately count on enthusiastic backing among the Hollanders. In order to get all that money to Brussels on time, the urban elites in Holland were forced to develop new financial instruments and to collaborate more than ever before: Charles's centralization policies unintentionally also strengthened regional solidarity.[44]

The process of state formation was initiated by monarchs but met constant opposition from those with vested interests. These interests were institutionally well anchored in the Low Countries. Originally, the finances of the monarch and his court coincided with those of the state. But gradually the idea was gaining ground that the state was a separate body, distinct from the person of the monarch, with its own rights and obligations and thus its own income and expenditure. So if, for example, the cities were expected to help finance a war, they could also make their own demands: "no taxation without representation." The medieval instrument of a parliament—often called "States" in the Netherlands—developed from about 1400 in Burgundy, Holland, and Gelderland into a powerful institution that guarded the interests of nobility, Church, and, especially, urban citizens. The northern Netherlands were relatively late in this development: comparable institutions had already arisen in southern Europe around 1200. Nevertheless, in the 1420s they broke through in Holland and Zeeland, presumably for the most part because of their inclusion in the Burgundian state, and in Utrecht and Gelre owing to more or less autonomous developments there.[45] Once institutionalized, the states' assemblies assumed greater powers. In Utrecht they often met dozens of times a year, and in Holland and Zeeland a similar frequency of meetings eventually became normal.[46] This was almost comparable to Flanders and Brabant, whose states often met about thirty times each year, much more often than elsewhere in western Europe, where such meetings usually took place no more than once or twice annually. Frequent meetings were made possible by the relatively small size of polities in the Low Countries and their high population density; the costs of travelling to these gatherings were therefore much lower than in large states.[47]

The state-building process was not a path without obstacles and challenges, however. Burgundy's central administrators tried to establish more unity in the way government functioned and the application of its legal system. The Grote Raad van Mechelen was established as a court of law in the Burgundian Low Countries that could review, and even overturn, the rulings of the highest courts of law of the various subordinate regions (such as the county court of Holland). Greater certainty in legal matters throughout the state's territories was expected to also benefit the economy: tax harmonization might even create a large free trade area, and uniformly levied taxes could yield much more revenue if all kinds of local privileges no longer stood in the way. Yet this pursuit of unity was at odds with precisely these urban and regional privileges. The "freedoms," as they were called, which had been acquired over the centuries with great effort and often only after payment of large sums of money, formed the basis for the urban community. Legal jurisdiction over one's own citizens protected the property rights of those citizens, and a local tax system could be carefully attuned to local economic interests.

Whenever a political crisis arose, the cities tried to strengthen their claims for autonomy. In 1477, during the crisis of succession following the sudden death of the Burgundian duke Charles the Bold, the cities managed to obtain the Great Privilege from his successor, Duchess Mary of Burgundy. At the time—the country was in turmoil and the French army was assembled at the border—she was in no position to refuse anything. The states demanded, for example, that the merger of the audit offices of Holland and Brabant be reversed, and with it the financial centralization that threatened to arise.[48] The Great Privilege was ignored by Burgundy's central administration as soon as Mary had consolidated her position, although the cities of course continued to invoke it. This regularly resulted in conflict between the central administration and the cities—especially the very large cities in the Southern Netherlands. The tension between centralism and particularism in large part also underpinned the Dutch Revolt, which would erupt in 1566.

The process of state formation was thus accompanied by a realignment of the institutional relations by which the power of cities and their citizens became increasingly prominent. The states of the individual territories and the Burgundian and Habsburg states as a whole were instruments by which the growing economic power of the cities could be translated into political influence, whether or not through control over the finances of the state. Representatives of the cities usually wanted a stable currency (whereas lords could often not resist the temptation to manipulate its value), limitations on spending on warfare and royal consumption, but also support in commercial conflicts with other cities or states.[49] The growing importance of cities was reflected in shifts in the structure of the economy: commercial and industrial activities became increasingly important, at the expense of agriculture. In this sense, political-institutional relations adapted to changes in the economic structure, although in the eyes of many cities and their citizens this may not have been fast enough nor radical enough. Against this backdrop, Charles V pursued a policy of unification that could bring major benefits to the economy and the state, albeit at the same time undermining the "freedoms" of the cities and territories.

A common feature of state formation and economic development was that in both processes competitive pressures stimulated all participants to become increasingly efficient. Each process was dependent on the other: the state benefited from any economic boom enjoyed by its inhabitants, and, as the story of the Hanseatic League and trade in the Baltic Sea has shown, entrepreneurs and cities needed states to protect them from competitors from other states. Once more, a special variant of this relationship between trade and warfare evolved in the Low Countries. While in many countries rulers managed, slowly but surely, to subdue vested local and regional interests, the Burgundians and Habsburgs in the Low Countries faced fierce opposition. This opposition was concentrated in the south, where the cities of Flanders in particular were, owing to their large size and economic superiority, also dominant politically. Cities such as Bruges and Ghent revolted about once every generation, and the rulers were unable to put a permanent end to this. Meanwhile, the northern regions, which for the most part remained outside the Burgundian state complex, were developing their own institutions. As they were one by one subsumed by Maximilian and Charles, this strengthened the position of those demanding "freedoms." As a result, in the Low Countries an unusually strong level of organization at the local level was present that could not only offer opposition to rulers but also provide an alternative organizational model for society as a whole. That organizational model derived its strength, on the one hand, from its broad base and high participation rate and, on the other hand, of course, from the economic growth that had been achieved. In the second half of the sixteenth century, the model would be tested to the extreme in what became nothing less than a life-and-death struggle against the sovereign and his military might.

The process of state formation and the associated economies of scale did not, therefore, undermine civil society in the Low Countries. This differed in the long term from developments in Italy, where communes first emerged. During the High Middle Ages, those communes had played a central role in the political economy of the Italy's patchwork of city-states. Yet precisely because city and state coincided there, many of those Italian city-states had gradually evolved into regional states. In Tuscany, for example, Florence had conquered and subjugated neighboring cities such as Volterra and Pisa, after which their communal power was curtailed or even entirely subordinated to that of Florence. The number of active communes gradually declined, and the few that remained fell prey to the ambitions of "noble" families such as the Medicis and the Sforzas. In the Low Countries, no city could dominate the process of consolidation into larger political units in this way: cities had to maintain and strengthen their local privileges through cooperation.

On the one hand, the process of state formation as manifested in the late Middle Ages led to greater law and order, a more systematic administrative culture—as demonstrated by the *Informacie* in 1514—and more effective promotion of the international interests of merchants. These were all developments that could benefit economic development. On the other hand, such a new, strong state had its own rationality and developed its own sphere of power by introducing new taxes, building up a (still modest) civil service, and developing a professional army, whereby this power—in the person of a monarch with "absolutist" ambitions—could also be used to break away from and, if necessary, turn against "civil society."

Integration: The Impact of Antwerp's Economy

The sixteenth century was the "Century of Antwerp."[50] Around 1500, the city took over the position of Bruges as the center of international trade in the Low Countries, further developing to become the center of the western European economy in the period up to 1566. This had important consequences for the northern Netherlands, which benefited much more than previously from the renewed dynamism of the south. In Brabant, 's-Hertogenbosch and Bergen-op-Zoom were satellite cities of greater Antwerp, and they shared in Antwerp's prosperity. This applied to an even greater extent to Amsterdam, which developed into a sort of satellite port of Antwerp. The Southern Netherlands imported grain on a large scale, which came increasingly from the Baltic countries. Amsterdam merchants were crucial in this trade, albeit without completely excluding Hanseatic merchants, or traders from the south.

The grain trade was one of the many links that brought Holland and the economy of Antwerp closer together.[51] In the south of the Netherlands, local peat reserves were running out, and more and more fuel had to be imported, first from northern Brabant and later from Holland and Utrecht. In the mid-sixteenth century, Antwerp merchants, led by entrepreneur Gilbert van Schoonbeke, started a company dedicated to peat cutting in the peat bogs east of Utrecht (around Veenendaal); at that time peat was being exported on a large scale from Holland to Antwerp and its surrounding areas.

During the fifteenth century Holland's largest export industry, brewing, had become dependent on exports to the south. In the Southern Netherlands, however, brewers were very successful in imitating the beer from Haarlem, Gouda, or Delft, putting this export product under increasing pressure. Similar pressures on textile exports from Holland emanated from the light drapery of the Flemish Hondschoote, where much lighter and therefore cheaper woolen fabrics were manufactured, resulting in decreasing production in cities such as Leiden and Amsterdam. The closer links with the south therefore turned out to be worse for industry than for trade. The primary sector, on the other hand, blossomed, with Holland's and Zeeland's herring fisheries flourishing as never before. While this industry had in the thirteenth and fourteenth centuries been concentrated in Flanders, from the fifteenth century onward its center of gravity shifted increasingly to the north—to Zeeland and the Meuse estuary, where Brielle became the most important fishing center. In the course of the sixteenth century this shift continued, with North Holland becoming increasingly important. Thanks to the growing trend of gibbing (partial gutting) and salting of herring and the development of the *buis*—an almost industrial-scale fishing vessel, where the catch was processed on board and prepared for consumption—herring fishing developed into one of the pillars of Holland's economy.[52]

An unintended side-effect of the fishing industry was the training it provided for seafarers of the merchant fleet. In the sixteenth century much shipping was used alternately for commerce, fishing, and, also, warfare. Shipping increasingly became a specialty of the northern coastal regions, especially in Holland and Zeeland. The size of the Dutch merchant fleet around 1500 was equal to that of the Hanseatic cities combined. The Southern Netherlands, on the other hand, did not have a significant fleet of its own and became more and more dependent on Holland's and Zeeland's merchant vessels. The trading fleets of these two provinces grew dramatically in the 1500s, from about 60,000 tons in 1500 to 230,000 tons in 1560. Around that time, Holland's fleet amounted to more than 1,800 seaworthy vessels; Amsterdam alone accounted for about 500 of these. Together, Holland's and Zeeland's fleets employed 16,500 seamen.[53] Thanks to this fleet, during the sixteenth century Holland became not only a significant commercial power but also a formidable naval one.

The increased commercialization and urbanization also started to transform the countryside. Gradually, the water management problems faced by agriculture were brought under control. This was absolutely essential because—especially to the north of the IJ—a patchwork of rivers and lakes had arisen that expanded with each storm, causing a continual reduction in the area available to agriculture. The first experiments using a new drainage technique had already been carried out in Alkmaar in 1407: polder drainage by means of a windmill. The windmill had been in use from about 1200, but almost exclusively for grinding grain into flour. Its application in water management encountered both technical and institutional problems, which hindered its spread. Around 1500 there were no more than two hundred windmills being used for drainage; together they kept 10%–20% of agricultural land dry.[54] However, the sharp rise in agricultural prices after 1530 made it increasingly attractive to reclaim land, or at least to halt reduction of its area, through investing in wind-powered drainage. Several major projects, such as the reclamation of the Zijpe, were put out to tender in the mid-sixteenth century—a development that would not really progress until after the Dutch Revolt.

These sorts of projects were especially attractive when the required capital could be borrowed at a reasonable rate of interest. The capital markets of the northern and southern Netherlands had been integrated since the thirteenth century: the "big money" was made in the south, and cities in the north tried to finance their deficits by borrowing money in Flanders.[55] This had great advantages—in this way the north benefited from the low interest rates that were already common in Flanders around 1300—but sometimes there were also disadvantages: if a city had difficulties repaying a loan, the lenders were entitled to detain the citizens of that city until the arrears were paid. In this way, a crisis in public finances, which several Dutch cities experienced after 1490, threatened to become an general crisis in trade and industry. It took many years—the *Informacie* of 1514 is a silent witness to this—for such a "capitalist" crisis to be resolved and confidence restored.

The instruments that had been developed to finance public debt, annuities and interest-bearing loans (*lijfrenten* and *losrenten*), evolved during this period into general instruments of credit, used by rich and poor alike to obtain credit or invest savings, and designed in such a way that they evaded the official ban on interest by the Church.[56] These sorts of capital market transactions could even be concluded between close relatives. For example, parents who wanted to transfer their farm or business to their children or other relatives could do so in exchange for an annuity, the proceeds of which would be paid from the farm or business income. The annuity was in fact a pension provision. Similarly, brothers and sisters sometimes distributed an inheritance with these instruments: if one of them entered a monastery or a beguinage, for example, a personal annuity could be arranged for them. In due course, moreover, the custom developed of dividing ownership of a house, ship, or mill into smaller units—called parts, or shares—that could be traded separately. One could invest savings in one-eighth of a merchant ship, and thus take advantage of profits that were made. These parts could be divided into very small shares—1/256th and sometimes even smaller—so that barriers to participation were correspondingly low. Someone could be a co-owner of all kinds of assets and, if the need was high, redeem them or use them as collateral for a loan. From detailed data provided by the town of Edam and the neighboring rural district Zeevang, we know that the wealthy were not the only ones active in the capital market: except those without any property, it seems that almost everyone was involved—and women were almost as active as men.[57]

Of course, those who wanted to actively carry out transactions in money and goods had to have at least rudimentary counting skills. Many sources confirm that the "human capital" of the northern (and southern) Netherlands had already in the sixteenth century reached a high level. The Italian traveler Lodovico Guicciardini, in his *Descrittione di tutti i Paesi Bassi* (published in 1567), noted that levels of literacy were remarkably high in Holland and that differences between men and women and between city dwellers and rural inhabitants were strikingly small. Recent research confirms this picture. The fact that people were also—perhaps even especially—familiar with large numbers can be concluded from the phenomenon of age heaping. Already in 1514 in Haarlem, the list of citizens interviewed for the compilation of the *Informacie* shows that everyone gave an exact age rather than rounding up or down to multiples of five or ten, as people who are not used to working with larger numbers tend to do. Fortunately, age heaping can be measured: the results indicate that this phenomenon was on the decline in the Low Countries, and was much less common than in, for example, northern Italy or England.[58]

Many of the Dutch were able to read, count, and write; in other words, they were relatively highly educated. The popularity of movements such as Modern Devotion was closely related to this and, of course, also reinforced the process of education. It is not surprising, therefore, that the Reformation was embraced early on in the Netherlands. As early as the 1520s, donations to ecclesiastical—Catholic—institutions declined dramatically, a sign that Luther's message was gaining supporters. Luther was especially popular in the south. The first inhabitants of the Low Countries to be put to death for their "heretical" views were two monks from an Augustinian monastery in Antwerp; they died at the stake in Brussels on July 1, 1523. But Luther's popularity was soon eclipsed by even more radical movements, such as the Anabaptists, an almost anarchist group without a hierarchical organization that was particularly popular in Friesland and Groningen. In the mid-1530s they were able to mobilize thousands of people, but also, for example, in Amsterdam among the city's craftsmen and even its elite. Indeed, there was a persistent rumor that mayors Cornelis Benninck and Pieter Colijn were "infected with heresy," and Amsterdam's bailiff Jan Huybrechts, was also suspect. It was known that he had read the works of Philip Melanchton, one of Luther's collaborators, and that he had shielded the reformists from prosecution.[59] Just as in several German regions, the reformists' ideas were for a number of reasons well received in urban societies at this time. Shortly beforehand, thanks to the invention of the printing press, printed texts had dropped spectacularly in price. Craftsmen and shopkeepers could now read the Bible without the intervention of a priest or other servant of the Church, and they did so with dedication. The elite, which could only groan under the increasing demands of the central government, saw in the Reformation an opportunity to gain more control over religious life among their own congregation. All were appalled at the ruthless repression that had been practiced by the central government since the 1520s against anyone suspected of dissenting views.

For the administrators of the cities, who always had to take their constituency into account, a policy of complete intolerance toward the reformed was difficult to accept, even if they themselves had no sympathies in that direction. Many cities in the north depended on international trade, including—and often especially—with parts of northern Germany and Scandinavia, which had officially embraced Lutheranism. The tolerance of the Dutch (for which they would later become famous) that arose during this period had, therefore, also a materialistic basis: one had to respect the beliefs of the merchants with whom one regularly did business.

The Rise of Capitalism—Curse or Blessing?

Between 1350 and 1566, the Netherlands moved rapidly from the margins to the economic center of western Europe. Indeed, after 1590 Amsterdam would even rise to become the main hub of European trade. Bas van Bavel, whose research on the rise of capitalism is often the basis for our views, has expressed the challenging view that, taking everything into account, the breakthrough of the market economy after 1550 had a negative impact on broad sections of the population. He points out that, among other things, archaeological data on the height of the Dutch indicate a decline in their health. It is undoubtedly true that the process of urbanization, which Van Bavel sees as the main culprit, took its toll, because cities were relatively unhealthy places in which to live. The spread of all sorts of endemic diseases will also have had a negative impact on the physical development of the Dutch: they were no longer said to be "long and strong," as the Hollanders and Frisians of the High Middle Ages were.[60] Nevertheless, there were also a considerable number of trends that had a much more favorable impact. We have already pointed to the strong growth in GDP per capita in precisely that part of the Netherlands where capitalism first broke through; an increase of about 70% in 170 years is a significant achievement for a premodern economy (chapter 2). As we have seen, the qualitative data on the development of Holland between 1350 and 1560 closely mirror this increase.

Holland's urbanization created an exceptionally dynamic region, which also translated into the relatively favorable development of real wages. An international comparative study by Robert Allen has shown that almost everywhere in Europe real wages fell sharply between 1450 and 1600. The Low Countries (data mainly for Amsterdam and Antwerp) and England were the exception in this, however. It is precisely in these locations—which were to become the centers of capitalism—that long-term real wages stabilized at a high level, despite alternating favorable and unfavorable years.[61] In particular, the prosperous years after the integration of Holland into Burgundy by Philip the Good in 1433 stand out, just as do the bad years at the end of the fifteenth century, when the Burgundian state experienced a period of violent political instability. The years of civil war between 1417 and 1425 also stand out negatively in all respects. It is reassuring that both data sets—GDP per capita and real wages of an unskilled construction worker—show roughly the same fluctuations between 1340 and 1510 (figure 4.2). The long-term trends are different, however. The very high levels of real wages directly after the 1348 pandemic (sometimes called the Black Death bonus)

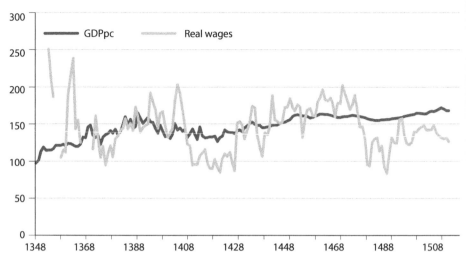

FIGURE 4.2. Estimates of GDP per capita (GDPpc) and real wages of an unskilled laborer in Holland, 1348–1514 (1348 = 100).
Source: Zanden and Van Leeuwen 2012.

were no longer achievable in the fifteenth century, whereas GDP per capita saw a strongly rising trend.

In terms of the nonmaterial dimensions of well-being, there also seems to be some reason for optimism. In the Human Development Index (the multidimensional measure of well-being, inspired by Amartya Sen), the development of education is one of its three composite indicators (GDP per capita and life expectancy are the other two). There is no doubt that the development of human capital in Holland was decidedly positive during this period, although the first robust data available (including the literacy rate of Amsterdam's inhabitants) are of a somewhat later date. Another indicator of the gradual increase in human capital is the size of the literacy gap between men and women in the Low Countries, which was quite small. In other words, women's personal development was relatively strong, which was presumably related to the European marriage pattern that became established during this period: marriage in the Low Countries was based on the consent of both partners.[62] Such consensus-based marriage meant that "family" and "household" took on a very different character than in more patriarchal societies, in which the pater familias dominated. The fact that under the European marriage pattern newlyweds set up their own household and did not move in with the husband's (or wife's) family was an important dimension of the "agency" they had over these types of decisions.[63]

Similar trends held sway at the political level. The dense civil society of medieval western Europe made it possible to exert influence on labor, production, and consumption (through the guilds, for example); charity (through all kinds of institutions affiliated with the Church); the way agriculture was organized (through commons); and, in general, on the living conditions of the—predominantly urban—bourgeoisie (through urban communes and comparable rural institutions). There are no indications that these institutions, founded in the High Middle Ages, came under pressure in Holland or elsewhere as a result of the process of economic development. On the contrary, the data we have on the numbers of guilds in various parts of the Low Countries show in most regions a doubling per capita of these organizations between 1400 and 1560.[64] The number of places with city rights also increased sharply during this period, although this mainly concerned the smaller urban concentrations: the bigger cities had acquired these rights much earlier. As we have seen, the establishment of regional and "national" parliaments concluded these developments, bringing with it further increases in bottom-up influence.

To summarize, capitalism appears to have originated in a society that was relatively egalitarian, with a strong and continually developing civil society that was characterized by a balance between bottom-up influences and top-down institutions. It was not an orgy of violence, as Marx maintained, a forceful expropriation of the means of production by the newly emerging capitalist class, that gave birth to capitalism. Of course, there was a lot of violence in late medieval society—warfare was a regular feature, interpersonal violence was quite normal (as we saw in chapter 2)—but this was not the kind of violence directed at a specific social class to rob it of its means of subsistence. As we will see, after 1600 this was going to change, at least in the colonies and overseas settlements. But Dutch capitalism, as such, was the result of a relatively peaceful transition, in which people more or less voluntarily became more dependent on the market. The involuntary aspect was that the environmental crisis in the peat districts of Holland and Utrecht pushed farmers into the marketplace, but they could have developed more subsistence-oriented strategies instead. It was probably, as we saw in the previous chapter, no coincidence that the capitalist engine became most dynamic in the border region between feudalism and freedom. Yet, there was an orgy of violence in the Netherlands in this period; the Revolt against the Spanish overlord that began in 1566 has rightly been described as a civil war. But was it also a "capitalist revolution"?

5

A Capitalist Revolution?

THE DUTCH REVOLT, 1566–1609

On June 9, 1584, a heated discussion took place among the aldermen of Amsterdam's city council. Before them was a proposal to appoint Prince William of Orange as count of Holland and Zeeland. The position had become vacant after these counties and other regions in the Low Countries had rebelled against the authority of their lord and ruler, Philip II, King of Spain. Three years earlier, in 1581, the rebellious regions had officially declared their independence in the Placard of Abjuration, relieving Philip of his status as their sovereign. Yet the nature of political relations and the imperial ethos of the period made it inconceivable not to be ruled by a sovereign monarch. A proposal in 1581 to invite the French Duke of Anjou to replace Philip as sovereign had from the outset never appealed to the Dutch, and ultimately the whole thing fell through. Now, the proposal before Amsterdam's city council was to proclaim William (once Philip's governor, or stadtholder, in the Netherlands) count of Holland.

Not everyone thought this to be a good idea. We know this because—extraordinarily—the notes for a speech that one of the members of the Amsterdam city council gave on that occasion were saved. (Minutes of council meetings recorded only decisions, never preliminary discussions.) The speaker was Cornelis Pieterszoon Hooft, who today is best known as the father of one of the literary greats and early historians of the Netherlands.[1]

Hooft was a man who was highly respected. Although his family was from the Zaan area, Hooft's father and two of his brothers lived in Amsterdam in

1566, when the iconoclastic Beeldenstorm raged throughout the city. This would prove to be the first stage of what became known as the Dutch Revolt, an uprising that would end in the establishment of the Dutch Republic. However, Amsterdam as a city remained loyal to Philip until 1578, while the rest of Holland sided with the Revolt from 1572. The Hooft brothers, all three active in the grain trade with the Baltic region, had, in contrast, joined the rebels early on and were forced to flee the city. For some time, Cornelis Pieterszoon Hooft probably lived in Danzig (Gdańsk), the main port for the export of Baltic grain. He later returned to Amsterdam, when it was safe again for Protestants like himself, and he was soon elected to the city council. All his life Hooft prided himself on being one of the original "*geuzen*" (literally, beggars; sing. *geus*), one of the first generation of Protestants.

Although Hooft was a Protestant, he was no friend of pastors, and although he was a *geus*, he did not support the idea that the leader of the "beggars," Prince William of Orange, should become his lord. In his speech, Hooft revealed himself as an unadulterated republican and even a democrat.[2] He firmly rejected the argument that a prince would be better able to represent Holland abroad than a council such as the States of Holland. Indeed, he predicted that "many prominent citizens" would rather leave Holland than be ruled by a prince or a count. He also believed that many towns would have thought twice about joining the Revolt if they had known that it would result in the replacement of one prince by another. Hooft demanded, therefore, that the proposal to appoint William should be not only discussed in the council but also submitted to the officers of the local militia, who could speak on behalf of the citizens and the city districts of Amsterdam, of "all other citizens" and even "seafaring folk," who had risked their lives in the cause of freedom. In fact, he argued that these groups were "the strength" of Amsterdam. Hooft was a keen supporter of the idea that authority should rest with local administrators and the representatives of ordinary citizens. He opposed strong central authority, especially when succession to that authority was a hereditary right. In Hooft's speech these two models of government were presented as being diametrically opposed to each other.

This discussion took place during one of the most dramatic episodes of the Dutch Revolt. In 1566 the Dutch provinces were part of the global empire of the Habsburg dynasty, yet only fifteen years later, in 1581, these same provinces established themselves as an independent state. That did not take place without a struggle, and the outcome of their uprising—revolution would be a better word—was by no means certain. Barely a month after the discussion in the Amsterdam council, William of Orange was murdered, thus settling the dispute. But the questions discussed in the council meeting in Amsterdam—who should govern, and how—continued to haunt the Republic of the Seven United Netherlands, as the new state was to be called. Hooft's point of view, in which Protestantism, republicanism, and a very broad definition of citizenship were intertwined, was one extreme of a wide spectrum of political ideas. At the other end of the spectrum were those who wanted to turn the new state into an "ordinary" monarchy.

The example of Cornelis Pieterszoon Hooft also tells us something about the social roots of these ideas. Hooft was a wealthy merchant, who had amassed his wealth through the grain trade with the Baltic region, the famous "mother of all trades" that flourished in these years.[3] One of the reasons for this was growing demand for grain in the Mediterranean region, where in previous decades of the sixteenth century population growth had outstripped agricultural yields, resulting in dramatically rising prices. Only one region in all of Europe was producing large grain surpluses: the regions bordering the Baltic Sea, and in particular Poland, with Gdańsk as the main port of export. This grain trade had been dominated by the Dutch for some time, and in particular by Amsterdam's merchants, who specialized in supplying cheap grain to the Low Countries (Holland, Zeeland, and Flanders). Suddenly they were confronted with highly profitable demand from Portugal, Spain, and Italy, regions that largely belonged to the Habsburg Empire, of which their archenemy Philip II was monarch. Indirectly—through high demand for grain—profits from the grain trade made it possible to finance the first phase of the Revolt. It was the ability of the new state that emerged out of this rebellion to finance a war, and thus the willingness of merchants like Hooft to actually contribute to it, that was largely responsible for its eventual success.

The reasons for merchants like Hooft to advocate such a "free" form of government can be reconstructed. The merchant community was extremely international in character, and merchants of widely differing convictions and backgrounds gathered and lived in cities such as Amsterdam, Middelburg, and Antwerp. In addition, many of these merchants came from countries with differing official religions (many German regions and all of Scandinavia had become Lutheran, England had its own version of Protestantism, and so on). As a result, the merchant community was also pre-eminently multireligious, and almost every merchant traded with someone who held different religious beliefs. It was, therefore, virtually impossible for large trading cities to enforce religious uniformity, as Philip II demanded on behalf of the Catholic Church. More generally, people like Hooft had learned to mistrust crowned heads of state: the absolute power claimed by monarchs like Philip II was at odds with the economic and political interests of an urban community such as Amsterdam.

The two themes of this chapter come together in the person of Hooft: the new state that emerged from the Revolt and the simultaneous economic boom that arose, partly by chance and partly by the "freedom" the Republic offered its citizens and immigrants. The Dutch Revolt, also known as the Eighty Years' War, was actually a "Revolt of the Low Countries." At first, this uprising took place just as much in the south, the future Belgium, as in the north, the future Netherlands. In the south, where many merchants shared Hooft's views, the cities were closer to the Spanish army's lines of supply and were unable to find protection behind expanses of water, as could cities in the north. As a result, the southern provinces were brought back under Habsburg rule, while the northern provinces stayed independent. At the beginning of the twentieth century Pirenne and Weber identified the important role of autonomous towns and cities, and their elites, in the emergence of the capitalist economy.[4] The problem with their interpretation is that we find such autonomous towns everywhere in Europe, but capitalism emerged only in some regions.[5] One element that stands out is levels of urbanization: capitalism emerged in regions with high urban densities. These were first reached in medieval Italy. However, as Epstein has demonstrated, the independence of the major Italian cities was such that, instead of providing the institutional space for markets to flourish, they became predators in their own right, creating a negative interaction with the countryside.[6] Moreover, they were engaged in endless rounds of internecine conflict, which undermined their popular constitutions as well as their economic advantages. Italian city-states were also handicapped by their size; Florence, for example, was a large city, but Tuscany was still a small state. The Dutch Republic created a federal state that was big enough to make an impact on the international stage. It was a state in which the towns determined policy, but no single town was large enough to dominate the others; a state that, for precisely this reason, had to coordinate between various interests. And it was a state that, through the competition between towns, and between towns and countryside, could benefit from the advantages offered by urban markets. A state, in short, where capitalism could flourish.

The Dutch Revolt (1566–1609)

The reasons for the Revolt were identical in both the north and south of the Low Countries. The centralizing policies of Charles V and Philip II, coupled with their bitter opposition to Protestantism, met with stiff resistance everywhere.[7] Major cities such as Bruges and Ghent in Flanders, and Antwerp and Brussels in Brabant, had through rebellious movements regularly asserted their urge for political autonomy and demand for participation.[8] Since the early fourteenth century, these cities had been governed through a pact between the elite and the middle classes, the latter through their guilds, represented in city councils. The cities themselves set the tone in the meetings of the regional States, where they were constantly negotiating with their respective lords. The urban middle classes in the metropolises of the south became politicized through this direct participation in local government and their indirect involvement in the administration of their provinces.[9]

Since then, the problem had only become more acute. Charles V's successive annexation of Friesland, Groningen, Utrecht, Overijssel, and, finally, Gelderland between 1498 and 1543 had increased the numbers of the "particularist" camp—supporters of the idea that regions, cities, towns, and villages should be able to decide for themselves on internal matters. Meanwhile, the forces in favor of centralization had, under Charles V, also gained strength. In the summer of 1566 this tension erupted spectacularly in the iconoclastic Beeldenstorm, which from Flanders boiled over into a large number of provinces. Statues of saints and other holy images were smashed to pieces, while churches were desecrated. To a pious man like Philip II it was blasphemy of the most extreme kind. Ghent, which had rebelled unsuccessfully in 1540, was one of the first cities where the Beeldenstorm raged in full force. The eruption was partly orchestrated and partly a spontaneous expression of political and religious resistance. The perpetrators were not all Protestants, nor was their intention in any way to unleash a revolution, let alone establish an independent state. That this is what happened was in part because of the reactions of the authorities themselves.

After much deliberation, Philip's court in Madrid decided to send the most outspoken proponent of the "hard line," the Duke of Alba, to the Netherlands to restore order. To achieve this, Alba was given an army of more than ten thousand men; these would be supplemented by men recruited in the Low Countries. Immediately upon his arrival in the Low Countries, in August 1567, Alba took a number of measures. He set up a special court, the Council of Troubles, to try the participants of the Beeldenstorm. And, without consulting the regional states' assemblies, he introduced a number of new taxes to pay for his army. Both measures ran counter to the regular political processes of decision-making that Alba's sovereign, Philip II, had promised to respect at his accession to his various lordships in the Low Countries. Alba's actions confirmed the impression that Philip's intention was to place his personal authority above that of the people's representatives, rather than rule jointly with them. That impression was reinforced by the brutal manner in which Alba used his troops to restore Philip's authority. Cartoons of the day depicted Alba on a throne, suggesting that the duke was behaving as if he were a king. In one, seventeen virgins in chains knelt before him, symbolizing the plight of the seventeen provinces, with the gallows, where the victims of his reign of terror met their unfortunate end, visible in the background.

Such portrayals of the government in Brussels were confirmed by the way Alba and his soldiers went to work. They hardly made any distinction between those who had supported the Beeldenstorm and those who had not been involved: both loyal and rebellious towns and cities were treated harshly; in the eyes of the Spanish soldiers and their commanders, all inhabitants of the Low Countries were heretics. The soldiers, who were billeted in ordinary people's homes, were paid only after long delays and so behaved like hungry locusts, taking whatever they wanted. The resentment this caused made them immensely unpopular, which became all too apparent by the spring of 1572.

By then the rebels had been reduced to a handful of armed groups, dealing out pinpricks to the Spanish government with guerrilla raids from the sea and attacks along the eastern border. On April 1, 1572, the rebels, attacking from the sea, captured the isolated seaport of Den Briel. To their surprise, the "Sea Beggars," as they were called, found that they were welcomed elsewhere in the delta. The conditions in the delta worked strongly to the Sea Beggars' advantage. On land, the well-trained Spanish troops reigned supreme, but at sea the odds were far more even, thanks especially to Holland's long naval tradition. In the cat-and-mouse game that played out in the waters of Zeeland over the following months the small, flexible flotillas of the Sea Beggars turned out to be most effective adversaries, assisted by, on the Spanish side, indecisive administrators and, on the side of the rebels, resolute citizens.[10]

In Middelburg and Amsterdam, the city councils unanimously—and successfully—defied the demands of the Sea Beggars to open the city gates. But elsewhere local authorities hesitated, officials divided as to whether they should meet these demands. In such situations, citizens were able to play a decisive role. Unsure of what to do, city functionaries often asked guild officials or local militia officers for their opinion.[11] In this way the guilds and militia were able to act as spokesmen for the bourgeoisie. The militia also had an important role in keeping the peace, but they were often reluctant to take action against fellow citizens. Thanks to favorable physical geography, general support among the population, and inadequate response by the authorities, the rebels managed to capture a significant proportion of the water-rich western regions of the Netherlands.

To keep Alba and his troops at bay, the rebels had to achieve two things: the raising and then maintenance of their own army, and the creation of a new political order. The connection between these two tasks was that to recruit troops you needed money, and the taxes needed to get that money could be levied only if there was a degree of civil order. Remarkably, despite the chaos of war the institutions of public administration did not collapse. On the contrary, soon after 1572, proceeds of the "common means"—that is, excise revenue, which was the backbone of the Dutch tax system—were higher than they had been in the years preceding the Revolt. And although interest rates had risen to astronomical heights—the States during the most difficult phase of the Revolt, were paying at least 30%—jointly the cities were still able to raise substantial sums of money on the capital market.[12] The money came mainly from merchants and small savers, suggesting that the revolutionary regime enjoyed a degree of popularity.

On July 15, 1572, the States of Holland gathered in Dordrecht for the first time without the prior permission of their lord, King Philip II of Spain.[13] This was a revolutionary act, because in this meeting the States established themselves as an alternative authority to Philip. They didn't say that in so many words, of course, but during the meeting they did instruct William of Orange to take charge of their war efforts. In addition to the States' traditional members—representatives of the provincial college of nobles (*ridderschap*) and of four of the six major cities of Holland (Dordrecht, Haarlem, Leiden, and Gouda)—delegations from Gorinchem, Oudewater, Alkmaar, Hoorn, Enkhuizen, Medemblik, Edam, and Monnickendam were also invited. Rotterdam would join the Revolt two days later and thereafter also attended the States' meetings.[14] Ultimately, in addition to the six major cities that had always participated in the meetings, twelve more towns and cities would acquire a permanent place in the States of Holland. This meant that political support for the Revolt was particularly widespread in Holland, and that it had taken on an especially urban character.

Political autonomy was an item high on the agenda, as was demonstrated by the Union of Utrecht, which was signed in January 1579. In order for their revolution to be successful, the rebellious provinces joined together in this treaty "as if they constituted only a single province." However, in the same (first) article of the treaty, those provinces also stated that their unity would not affect each member's "special and particular privileges, franchises, exemptions, rights, statutes, laudable and long practiced customs, usages and all its rights"; in other words, the numerous privileges that the cities and provinces had traditionally enjoyed.[15] The difference between the number of words devoted to the topic of unity and that discussing diversity speaks volumes as to where the hearts of the rebels lay: unity was a necessary evil, the crux of the matter was provincial and urban autonomy. It has often been suggested—with good reason—that the Union of 1579 is the written foundation of the modern-day Netherlands. Nonetheless, it should be remembered that, in addition to the representatives of Holland, Zeeland, Utrecht, Gelderland, Friesland, and Groningen, the signatories in 1579 also included the Flemish and Brabant cities of Ypres, Antwerp, Bruges, Lier, and, of course, Ghent.

The Union of Utrecht was a collection of agreements between rebel cities and provinces aimed at fighting those governing in the name of the Spanish king. Even so, in those agreements the contours of a new state were visible. The arrangements included raising an army and setting up a standardized system of taxation to pay for that army; in keeping with the spirit of regional autonomy, however, nothing came of the idea to standardize taxes. The process of state formation reached its logical conclusion on July 22, 1581, when the rebellious States General officially revoked its obedience to Philip II in the Act of Abjuration; Holland and Zeeland had already done so a year earlier.

During the whole process it was never completely clear who exactly was in charge. Initially it looked like William of Orange might be appointed head of state, but there is every indication that, above all, the States of Holland saw itself as the highest authority. In 1587 that was confirmed in so many words when it adopted the *Corte verthoninghe*—we would call it a policy memorandum—written by François Vranck, Gouda's legal advocate and advisor, in which the supreme authority of the States of Holland was demonstrated by numerous examples. That authority was, however, in turn based on that of the cities. It is significant that despite the difficult circumstances, revenues from general taxation (imposts on consumption, services, and possessions) followed an upward trend, largely owing to a far-reaching decentralization of Holland's taxation system.[16] In 1579 each city had, for example, won the right to appoint its own receiver of taxes—the official to whom all tax collectors had to hand over their money. When Amsterdam joined the Revolt in 1578, it had already stipulated that the receiver had to be a citizen of the city.[17]

The causes of the Revolt are easier to explain than its outcome. In the century preceding the Beeldenstorm, the Low Countries had been increasingly restricted by a political straitjacket imposed on them by their lord and his governors. The incorporation of the northern regions into the Habsburg Empire was a relatively recent event, and there the memory of independence was still alive. When the Spanish court responded to the Beeldenstorm with harsh repression, it forced those who protested to take a more radical course. After hostilities broke out, the demands the protestors made, like those of Cornelis Pieterszoon Hooft, could no longer be reconciled with a monarchy. Hooft and his companions wanted a return to the old situation: autonomous cities, towns, and villages that worked together in a relatively loose coalition, if necessary under the leadership of a tolerant prince such as William of Orange, but not a religious fanatic like Philip II.

But all this was by no means a guarantee for success. Elsewhere in Europe, for starters in Flanders and Brabant, the same formula was tried, but achieved a very different outcome. So the insurgents also needed a bit of luck. In part, that luck was determined by the strategic obligations that Philip (and his successors) had in other territories. In the 1590s the struggle for the French throne became more important than the conflict in the Low Countries. As a result, many Spanish troops were redirected to France. That luck was in part also due to the somewhat marginal location of the northern Netherlands, and the problems that the Spanish troops had to contend with while waging war in its watery terrain. The Spanish military efforts first focused on the most prosperous regions, Flanders and Brabant. In the meantime, the northern regions were able to strengthen their defenses. That was important because the Revolt would never have been a success without the enterprising attitude of many city officials. Their experience in raising funds also came in handy. The rebels quickly managed to get their economies up and running, while also maintaining support from the urban citizens.

Economy and Revolution, 1585–1609

Wars, especially when fought on one's own soil, are usually bad for the economy. Valuable human capital is lost, capital goods are destroyed on a large scale, land may be flooded (especially if flooding is used as a means of defense), and scarcity, famine, and disease arise. The Revolt was no exception to this at first: during the period 1566–74, as well as famine, a deep economic crisis arose, partly because the Sea Beggars were blockading the Baltic trade. The tide turned, however, in the mid-1570s, and after 1578, when Amsterdam joined the Revolt, economic recovery set in—albeit with some fluctuations—developing into strong growth. Until 1609 (and again after 1621), this economic boom took place in a society engaged in a life-and-death struggle with a much larger and more powerful enemy. To understand this paradox, we need to dig deeper into the causes of the amazing growth experienced in these years.

For a start, the new republic did not suffer the population decline after 1578 that might have been expected during this time of turmoil and widespread violence, as a massive migratory movement sprang up from the south. The war in the (southern part of the) Low Countries was a "push" factor, and the more the theater of war moved specifically to the southern regions, the more strongly its "push" effects were felt there. Yet migrants who leave hearth and home because of hostilities, or for religious or other reasons, usually have a variety of destinations to choose from. That was also the case during this period, and migrant communities sprang up, as well as in the northern Netherlands, along the borders with Germany and in England. The migrants also benefited from the fact that the core provinces Holland and Zeeland had become militarily secure from approximately 1590, after which the war was confined mainly to the landlocked regions along the eastern and southern borders.[18]

In the mid-1580s, two abrupt changes occurred in this migration pattern. First, it grew strongly in magnitude. This was directly related to the fall of Antwerp to Spanish forces in 1585 and the simultaneous blockade of Antwerp's port by the rebels. The blockade forced shipments for Antwerp to be transferred to smaller vessels at great expense, in effect forcing merchants to seek out cheaper options. The blockade was lifted only in 1795, after French troops overran all of the Low Countries. Many Netherlanders in the south concluded from this change in Antwerp's fortunes that the Revolt was doomed to fail in their region. The second change was that these emigrants from the south no longer spread out in all directions but traveled en masse northward, in particular to the cities of Holland and Zeeland. Apparently they thought they would be safe enough there.

Historians have long debated about the contribution of these immigrants to the Dutch Golden Age. The key question was (and is) whether or not the prosperity of the seventeenth century was due to their resettlement in the north. One school of thought points to the foundations that were laid, mainly in Holland, in the period prior to their arrival, while the other points to the acceleration experienced in the economy of Holland exactly during this period.[19] The discussion may have become unnecessarily complicated owing to poor distinction between cause and effect and between long- and short-term effects. So it is time to first look at some bare facts. Between 1586 and 1595, more than half of men getting married in Leiden came from regions in the south. And more than two-thirds of immigrants from the Southern Netherlands came from the Flemish southwest corner around Ypres, where a flourishing export trade in textiles had developed in previous decades.[20] In 1572, just before the Spaniards besieged the city, Haarlem had about 18,000 inhabitants. No doubt many of these died in the six months of hunger and deprivation that followed. Nevertheless, by the year 1600 Haarlem probably numbered about 30,000 inhabitants, while two decades later, in 1622, when for fiscal reasons a count took place, they numbered almost 40,000. It is estimated that half of those inhabitants were from regions in the south.[21] In Amsterdam, the increase was if anything even more spectacular. In 1560 Amsterdam had 30,000 inhabitants, but in 1622 some 105,000 people were counted. This growth factor of more than three in sixty-two years was entirely due to immigrants. By the end of the first quarter of the seventeenth century at least half of the population of Amsterdam had been born outside the Dutch Republic and another third came from places elsewhere in the Republic.[22] The total size of the migration from south to north cannot be determined with certainty, but estimates place it at approximately 100,000 people, an increase of at least 10% in the population of the north.[23] Due to the positive selection bias among migrants, many of whom were well educated, this amounted to a substantial windfall in human capital, benefiting the struggling urban textile sector in various towns in Holland,[24] as well as many newly established industries. Because, moreover, the vast majority settled in a handful of cities in the west of the Netherlands, the impact there was many times greater.

Alongside the push factor experienced by migrants there were also "pull" factors, two of which played a major role in the concentration of immigrants in the west. First, there was the abundance of economic opportunities to be found in the cities there. Holland's economy had blossomed in the previous two centuries: an international trade network had emerged and export industries had developed. Both had, of course, suffered from the turmoil and uncertainty that were a direct result of the Revolt, but knowledge and experience were available in Holland's cities. Amsterdam, for example, had, as Antwerp's satellite port, developed into a hub for trade with the northern coast of Germany and the Baltic Sea region. Amsterdam's import-export data for 1580 to 1584 clearly show that these destinations dominated trading in Amsterdam at the time.[25] The data also show that Antwerp was, nevertheless, still by far the most important center of trade in the Low Countries at this point. But, as has already been mentioned, Amsterdam's grain trade had surged ahead on international demand for grain, in particular from the Mediterranean region. Partly because of this, in the space of a few years the roles of Antwerp and Amsterdam were reversed. In the five years after 1585, when Antwerp fell to Spanish troops, about 150 merchants from the southern regions of the Low Countries settled in Amsterdam, with over a 100 more following in the next five years. Some migrated directly to the north, others had first settled elsewhere in Europe—usually in Germany. Shortly before 1585, Protestant merchants originally from Amsterdam, but who had often lived abroad in voluntary exile for many years, also returned home. Together with the migrants from Antwerp and its surrounding areas they now set off for new destinations, such as the Mediterranean and—soon—Asia and the New World.[26]

The second pull factor was the aggressive policies of Holland's cities to attract the newcomers from the south. This can best be illustrated by the treatment of the Spanish and Portuguese Jews who wanted to settle in Holland. Although nominally Christian—Jews from southern Europe who had converted to Christianity to avoid the inquisition—these immigrants were viewed with suspicion. However, they brought with them valuable trading contacts, especially in South America, a source of precious metals, sugar, and salt. Cities competed with one another in offering attractive conditions for Portuguese Jews to settle. In 1598 Amsterdam offered them the citizenship of their city, "trusting that they are Christians." Alkmaar was also keen to attract Jewish merchants, and in 1604 its city council formally opened the way for them to move there; later, Rotterdam also made attractive offers. In the following year, Haarlem made its intentions plainly clear when it tried to persuade Jewish merchants ("some merchants from Portugal, called Jews") to move from Amsterdam to Haarlem.[27] By then, they were not even pretending to be Christians anymore. Conditions for these immigrants to settle in Holland were ideal.

The synergy that arose between the local inhabitants and the newcomers—the next factor that helps explain the economic boom of the early Golden Age—led to numerous new initiatives in an astonishingly short period of time.[28] In 1589, a ship from Holland loaded with grain, financed by merchants in the south, sailed for the first time to the Mediterranean, where there were major food shortages. In no time, some two to three hundred ships were sailing this route annually, initially loaded with mainly Baltic grain, later increasingly with textiles from Holland. Their return freight brought a huge expansion in the range of products that Amsterdam's merchants could offer their customers. In 1599 the first Dutch ships sailed to the Caribbean to buy salt. In June 1594, an expedition set off from Texel's roadstead for northern Russia, to find a northeastern passage to Asia. The following year, merchants from Holland and Brabant financed a fleet of four ships to sail to Asia via the southern route, around the Cape of Good Hope. Although only one of the four returned, the profit was large enough to cover the costs. More importantly, that one ship showed that direct trade between Holland and Asia was possible.

In those same years, several major technological breakthroughs took place—for example, in marine architecture and shipbuilding. In 1595 the first *fluyt* was launched from a shipyard in Hoorn. The *fluyt*'s design was the end result of two centuries of modifications to Holland's freight-carrying vessels.[29] Other cargo vessels could not compete with these ships, which achieved considerable cost savings owing to their large loading space and a small crew. Thanks to the *fluyt*, ships from Holland and Friesland were able to acquire a significant slice of the international transport market during the seventeenth century. Of course, this strong position in the transport market also gave merchants in Holland a great advantage. Another revolutionary invention from these years—the sawmill—ensured that ships could be built cheaply in Holland. In 1593 and again in 1597, Cornelis Corneliszoon van Uitgeest patented the essential components of a sawmill. Until then, rough timber was fashioned into usable objects with axes and handsaws. The invention of the sawmill meant that these manual processes could be mechanized. The crux of the improvement was the conversion of the circular motion of a windmill's sails into the up-and-down motion of a saw. In an era when just about all rigid structures were made of wood (if not stone), a sawmill was a significant improvement.[30]

The new immigrants also started new enterprises that were previously unknown in Holland. The first paper manufacturers in Holland were probably from Flanders and Brabant. From 1586, wind energy was used in Alkmaar for papermaking, a fine example of local technology combined with imported knowledge.[31] In 1577, two residents of Antwerp made a proposal to Leiden city council to open a sugar refinery in that city. This would have been the first in Holland, but the plan fell through. Around 1590, other entrepreneurs from Antwerp had more success: they set up sugar refineries in Amsterdam and Rotterdam. In 1597 three or four such companies were active in Amsterdam, probably all run by entrepreneurs from the south.[32] Other immigrants from the southern regions brought knowledge about the manufacture of new, light, and cheap fabrics, with which they had already had great success in the south. The textile industries of Leiden (wool) and Haarlem (linen) were now able to profit from their success.[33] In the field of art, Holland's famous school of painting likewise profited greatly from innovations brought by immigrants from Flanders and Brabant.[34] Frans Hals, for example, had fled Antwerp with his parents as a child, and Johannes Vermeer's ancestors had also fled from the south to Holland around this period. The richness of the scenes of everyday life for which Holland's school became famous would have been inconceivable without the sixteenth-century skills and ideas brought from Antwerp.[35]

Immigrants thus played an essential role in the economic dynamics that arose between 1585 and 1609. However, the speed with which their activities were incorporated into existing economic structures can be explained only by developments that had been going on for much longer. Holland's merchants already had 150 years of experience in international trade. Although this experience was limited to the North Sea, the northern German coast, and Baltic Sea regions, these merchants had acquired the knowledge necessary for doing international business, and they had also set up the institutions necessary to support it. City councils, typically dominated by merchants and entrepreneurs, were sensitive to the interests of business and pursued probusiness policies aimed at attracting new initiatives. Important preconditions were also in place for industrial activity, such as an innovative approach to shipbuilding and an export-oriented textile industry. And, finally, the institutional context they had to work with in their new home towns was already familiar, because it resembled in many aspects the institutional situation in Brabant and Flanders. The important role of the local benches of aldermen in the facilitation of credit, for example, was identical north and south of the border.[36] Likewise, guilds were a major feature of urban life in both regions of the Low Countries. On top of that, towns in Holland like Amsterdam did not give separate legal, corporative status to foreign merchants, thus further lowering the barriers for both permanent and short-stay settlement.[37]

The interactions between Hollanders and immigrants, and between entrepreneurs and government, could not be better demonstrated than in the establishment of the Verenigde Oost-Indische Compagnie (VOC, or Dutch East India Company) in 1602. The VOC was a merger of several companies that had sprung up after the first successful journey to Asia in 1595. Such expeditions were for Holland's and Brabant's merchants a step into unexplored territory. Antwerp had always relied on the Portuguese for the supply of Asian spices, but now ships from Zeeland (where many of Antwerp's traders had settled) and from various ports in Holland were setting sail for the East. In 1601, four companies sent a total of twenty ships to the East. In terms of sheer numbers, the Dutch had already surpassed the Portuguese.[38] Yet this enormous expansion created its own problems. Owing to increasing demand, purchasing prices rose in Asia, while the increasing volume of Eastern goods being supplied in the Netherlands actually led to a fall in selling prices. On the initiative of the advocate of Holland (prime minister), Johan van Oldenbarnevelt, Holland's merchants attempted to coordinate their trading activities. To involve the inhabitants of Zeeland, the States General was notified, which made the collaboration attractive by granting the VOC partnership a charter that gave the company sole trading rights in all regions east of the Cape of Good Hope (see chapter 6).

Beside the business interest, the Republic's government also had a military interest in establishing the VOC. After all, this could substantially damage Spanish and Portuguese interests—the same monarch now ruled over both countries—in Asia. Older companies were closed down and merged with the VOC, which had operating companies (called chambers) in ports from which the original companies traded. In this manner, local merchants and the authorities were all able to keep a finger firmly in the pie. The VOC's largest chamber was that of Amsterdam, where about half its working capital was held.[39] Almost half of the initial 3.6 million guilders raised in Amsterdam came from immigrants from the Southern Netherlands.[40] Among those first investors, in Amsterdam at least, merchants from southern and northern regions kept each other in perfect balance.

Although the Revolt created a lot of unrest and insecurity, and in the early stages definitely also damaged the economy, the core area of Holland not only bounced back remarkably quickly but at the same time experienced a wholesale economic transformation. Capitalism was accelerating. International trade networks were expanded, within and outside Europe. With the support of the state, a company was launched, funded with private capital but chartered by the state, that would very quickly establish a foothold in Asia. In Holland numerous new industries were founded, and both they and existing industries were propelled forward with the help of technical innovations. In a handful of decades the Dutch Republic emerged as the new leader in the capitalist world order.[41]

Institutions

The Revolt divided the Low Countries in two: the predominantly Protestant north, and the Catholic south, which had been reconquered by the Spanish. The boundaries were fairly arbitrary—determined by the vagaries of the battlefield and the strategic needs of both sides—but this was true for every premodern state. Moreover, in 1609 those boundaries were not yet definitive; that would be the case only after the Treaty of Münster, which in 1648 brought an end to the armed conflict between the Spanish Habsburgs and their former subjects in the Low Countries. Nevertheless, in 1609 there was a general impression that a new country had appeared on the European map, and the Republic of the Seven United Netherlands (also commonly referred to as the Dutch Republic) was recognized as such by other powers. The new state was in need of an institutional structure. This structure was made up of existing elements, although these elements were assigned new roles.

The separation between north and south creates an interesting natural experiment for our topic. In the Southern Netherlands the Habsburg dynasty remained in charge. It shared power with nobles and towns, but the Habsburg Netherlands would be a monarchical society with power structures supported by the Catholic Church. The Protestants could either leave or convert to Catholicism; religious diversity was suppressed by the state. The new state that emerged in the north had no clearly identified political center and gave a lot of political agency to local and regional institutions. The power structures in the Dutch Republic were poorly defined. Nonetheless—or perhaps because of this—it turned out to be the ideal environment for this acceleration phase of capitalism. How did that work?

At a national level, the States General became the most important institution: it decided foreign policy and therefore also matters concerning the army and the naval fleet. Each of the seven provinces had one vote, and the States General's presidency rotated weekly among the provinces. Despite considerable inequalities in population numbers, economic size, and contributions to the shared treasury, formally all provinces in the States General were equals. Decision-making was preferably by unanimous vote or by acclamation. Internal affairs, on the other hand, were the domain of the provinces, each of which had its own political system and laws, as well as its own system of taxation; nothing had come of plans to standardize taxation.[42] At a provincial level, each state assembly comprised representatives of the nobility (*ridderschap*) and the cities.

The organization of the States of Holland was essential to the success of the Revolt. In Holland, six cities had already had a voice in decision-making for some time, and from 1572 that number was gradually expanded—at first only informally and temporarily, later permanently and formally—to eighteen cities. The States of Holland was above all an organ through which the major cities of the province coordinated their affairs. As the States of Holland and the States General were housed in the same building complex in The Hague, Holland's representatives in the States General could easily coordinate with their principals in the States of Holland and ensure that they were always present when the States General was making decisions that affected Holland's interests. In this way, Holland's cities also had a major impact on the Republic's foreign policy.[43]

As a result, a great deal of influence lay with city councils. The political upheavals of the 1580s and the economic upsurge that also began during this period had a direct impact on the composition of councils. In Amsterdam, of the seventy-four members appointed to the city council in the period 1578–99, only three were the son of someone who had helped run the city before the so-called Alteration of Amsterdam in 1578, when the Catholic city council was replaced by a Protestant one. The business community dominated the Amsterdam council. During the first quarter of the seventeenth century, out of the forty-one newly appointed members, thirty-one were merchants or industrial entrepreneurs. Of the thirty-six councilors who were active in 1602, sixteen were among the first investors in the VOC.[44] What these new administrators also had in common was that almost without exception they came from indigenous Amsterdam families; there appears to have been no room for immigrants at the highest administrative level.[45] We see a similar pattern elsewhere. In Leiden, only six of the eighty-nine administrators appointed between 1574 and 1618 originally came from elsewhere. The share of industrial entrepreneurs rose from a third before 1574 to half after that date.[46] In Rotterdam, 80% of the councilors appointed between 1572 and 1609 were active as merchants or industrial entrepreneurs.[47] First-generation foreign immigrants, however, found themselves excluded from these town councils.[48] Nonetheless, urban institutions in Holland displayed very little interest in excluding migrants from participation in economic activities.[49]

These new administrators had the task of giving direction to the rapid changes unfolding in these years. Roughly speaking, this boiled down to carrying out strongly focused economic policies and delegating the smooth management of social change to other institutions. The main concern of many city councils in the western Netherlands was to benefit from the rapid economic developments taking place, which was the reason why they often offered immigrants attractive conditions under which they could establish their businesses. To facilitate business, city councils also set up new institutions, as did Amsterdam by creating an *assurantiekamer* (chamber of insurance) in 1598, the Wisselbank (Bank of Exchange) in 1609, a *bank van lening* (city credit bank) in 1614, and the College van Zeezaken (Tribunal for Merchant Marine Trading) in 1641. In addition, cities actively attempted to poach entrepreneurs from one another, again by offering attractive conditions for the establishment of their businesses.[50]

Thanks to its local origins, the Revolt was firmly rooted in Holland's society. Nevertheless, it would have ended badly for the rebels if they had not been able to find an effective form of cooperation among themselves. From 1572, Holland and Zeeland took the lead in mobilizing funds for the Revolt, and to this end a quota for determining the relative contributions of each province to overall tax revenues was agreed. However, taxation remained primarily under the control of the provinces; the States General had no budget to speak of. The funds needed to finance the army were therefore to be raised by the provinces individually. Such an agreement had the potential to become a major source of friction, and to prevent the likelihood of this occurring, in 1583 the advocate of Holland, Johan van Oldenbarnevelt, proposed using the quota system introduced in the time of Charles V.[51] Under that system, Holland's contribution was to be half that of Brabant, Zeeland's was one-quarter that of Holland, Friesland's was one-fifth of Holland's, and Utrecht's one-tenth. Groningen paid half the amount of Friesland's contribution, making it, like that of Utrecht, one-tenth of Holland's. In the years that followed some adjustments were made, but from 1610 onward the quotas were fixed. Once the total budget of the States General was agreed, everyone could calculate how much they had to contribute, thus providing a great deal of clarity. The large share provided by Holland also contributed to this: it accounted for almost two-thirds of the Republic's budget and Holland regularly intervened when there were shortfalls, or if other provinces were unable or unwilling to pay their full share. In the seventeenth century, most of the Republic's debt was raised by the States of Holland, which was much more creditworthy than any other province or the States General. Even though Holland became the Republic's "lender of last resort" only in the final decades of the seventeenth century, it was in fact from the beginning the financial cork that kept the entire Revolt afloat.[52]

Ultimately, however, cooperation in this form could succeed only if all provinces, not just Holland and Zeeland, were prepared to carry their fair share of the burden. As long as a uniform taxation system across the entire Republic was not an option, the other provinces had to introduce taxation that made it possible for them to indeed meet their obligations, preferably with taxes that were identical or comparable to the numerous indirect taxes that formed the backbone of the taxation systems of Holland and Zeeland.[53] New research provides a picture of the extent to which the provinces succeeded in this and, thus, in keeping to the agreements made. Figure 5.1 compares tax revenues per capita of four of the seven provinces comprising the Dutch Republic between 1572 and 1794 (the original seven provinces plus Drenthe). Rich, commercially active Holland and Zeeland paid relatively greater amounts from the beginning; the landlocked, more agricultural provinces of Overijssel and Drenthe considerably less; the other provinces were somewhere in between.

We can also capture the development of tax revenues in the seven provinces in a graph (figure 5.2) of the spread of the variability relative to the mean (i.e., the standard deviation divided by the mean). Also known as the coefficient of variation, this can be seen as an indicator of the level of the cooperation among the provinces: if the spread is low, all provinces contribute about the same amount (per capita); if the spread is high, the tax burden is unevenly distributed. The curve begins in 1572, when Holland alone financed the Revolt and the rest did not contribute at all. The line falls until about 1610, which indicates increasing collaboration, followed by a long period of stability (small fluctuations in spread). Although in times of crisis this stability was disrupted—when primarily Holland was financing the war against Spain or France—the system proved to be most successful, remaining stable for more than a century and a half.

While the Spanish crown was constantly plagued by financial worries, making its armies unreliable, the Dutch Republic managed, thanks to its stable financial system, to form and maintain a disciplined fighting machine.[54] The Republic's army consisted of mercenaries (the majority of them foreigners), and since they fought for their living, regular pay was of the utmost importance. In addition to tax revenues, the States relied increasingly on loans. Holland already had a lot of experience from its Habsburg period in acquiring loans, and that experience came in handy now. Money could be borrowed on the credit of Holland to close the gaps that arose when provinces were behind in their contributions or were unable to pay the full amount. The hostilities on the Republic's borders were such that these situations were anything but imaginary. Nevertheless, despite a growing debt

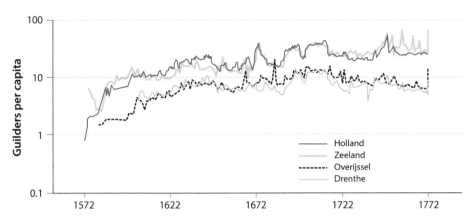

FIGURE 5.1. Tax revenues (guilders) per capita in four provinces, 1572–1794.
Sources: Population estimates: Paping 2014, 15–17; tax revenues: Fritschy 2017.

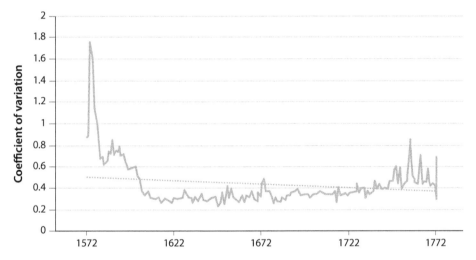

FIGURE 5.2. Spread of variability of tax revenues (guilders) per capita relative to the mean for the seven provinces comprising the Dutch Republic, 1572–1794.
Sources: Population estimates: Paping 2014, 15–17; tax revenues: Fritschy 2017.

burden the States of Holland paid increasingly lower interest rates. In difficult years these rates sometimes rose to well above 20%, yet in the 1580s the going rate for the States of Holland was only 12%. In 1597 it paid only 8% interest, and by 1611 the rate had dropped further to 6.25%. Substantial private savings were, obviously, crucial for driving down the interest rate.[55] However, this necessary condition was probably not sufficient; the public had to be persuaded that the government could be trusted with their money.

A stable tax base gave investors growing confidence in the Republic's ability to meet its commitments. That confidence, however, still had to be regularly reinforced with a firm hand by the authorities: "forced loans" were used, whereby the impost was involuntary but interest on the "loan" was still paid. And taxpayers were rewarded for their contributions with an army whose behavior off the battlefield was civilized. Discipline was considered of paramount importance and was bought by regular payment. While in other countries civilians tended to view their own army as a plague, many cities in the Republic requested the stationing of a garrison in their midst because they were happy with the soldiers' patronage in their businesses. In this way the Dutch Republic managed to limit the costs of war.[56]

From the Dutch Revolt a state emerged that put the "bourgeoisie" square in the middle. This happened in a multistage manner from the institutions in which they had been in charge for centuries: the urban governments. In the Republic, the towns were, through the regional States of Holland, a dominant influence in the States General. Holland was the Republic's most important financial contributor, and because the States General and the States of Holland shared the same buildings in The Hague, coordination between the two institutions was relatively straightforward. The balance between the central state and the provinces was stabilized by a division of labor that gave the States General responsibility for foreign affairs and the military, whereas the provinces had a final say and much room for variation in their domestic affairs. The financial contribution of each province in military operations had been fixated, allowing a seemingly poorly coordinated army to grow into a fearsome fighting force, capable of supporting and furthering the economic interests of Dutch capitalists.

The Dutch Republic's constitution was seen by contemporaries as an example of *res publica mixta*—depending on the political theory one preferred, a combination of two or three different elements. Certainly the aristocratic and the popular (or democratic) should be included, the former in the shape of the provincial states' assemblies and their overarching States General, the latter in the form of the town governments. Those who were looking for the third element could see the Orange stadtholders as the embodiment of monarchy; they were princes, after all.[57] The challenge in a "mixed republic" is to maintain a balance between the two or three elements. In the modern literature on state formation and economic performance this third element has usually been overlooked. In his penetrating analysis of the topic, S. R. Epstein contrasts monarchies and republics, as does David Stasavage, who calls them city-states and territorial states. The point about the Dutch Republic is that it was both at the same time. What makes these authors' analyses worthwhile is that they compare the strengths and weaknesses of the two types, whereas many others tend to see only strengths in one and weaknesses in the other. In a nutshell, centralized states or monarchies are strong on returns to scale but carry the risk of the sort of predatory behavior by rulers that contemporary republicans were always so anxious about. Epstein thinks that centralized states were more fragmented than the ideology of absolutism would acknowledge, and therefore that this risk was, in practice, not so great. Republics benefited from high information densities due to their small size, but were predators of their own hinterlands, a risk usually overlooked. The presumed economic advantages of republics were often wiped out by the rent seeking of privileged groups.[58]

This sort of analysis, however, overlooks the role of citizens, by concentrating too much on the institutions of the state. In most early modern monarchies, citizens tended to be constrained in their political expression and representation—unless the monarch was prepared to strike a deal with a parliament. Since the fifteenth century, parliaments had been in decline in many European countries.[59] During the Middle Ages urban citizens had enjoyed a substantial amount of self-rule, but under the increasing power of centralized states these liberties came under growing pressure. The Dutch Revolt managed to produce a state form that combined the advantages of local autonomy with the those of centralization. The stadtholders had a limited political brief but were given much leeway in their military roles. Under the leadership of the province of Holland, where experiments of urban collaboration had a long history and none of the towns could dominate the rest, the Dutch Republic managed to balance local and regional interests.[60] These balances served the Republic's citizens very well during the seventeenth century.

Calvinism and Capitalism in the Dutch Revolt

When Hooft objected in Amsterdam's council meeting to the elevation of William of Orange to the position of count of Holland, he advocated consultation of officers of the local militia and "seafaring people," because these were "our strength," by which he probably meant that they had supplied most of the combatants during the Revolt. This coalition between the radical Sea Beggars (sailors, fishermen, dike laborers, and all kinds of other unskilled "proletarians"), middle-class citizens who made up the militia, and the urban elite to which Hooft belonged represented the social backbone of the Revolt. In this coalition, religion was an important binding agent. The Revolt was not just about maintaining a certain degree of political autonomy but also about the defense of religious freedom and in particular the variant of the Reformation that had (or was to get) the most support in the Netherlands: Calvinism.

Since Max Weber published his book in 1905 about the "Protestant ethic," there has been much debate about the connection between Protestantism and capitalism.[61] Weber observed that both were flourishing at the same time in the same regions of Europe. The Dutch Republic fits this argument perfectly, but simultaneity is not causality. So we still need to ask: What connected the two? Initially, the debate focused on predestination, and the question who would be saved and who would burn in hell. This idea was supposed to encourage Protestants to go the extra mile, because economic success might be interpreted as a sign of God's approval. In recent debates, the emphasis has shifted to "discipline." Protestant Churches, and especially the Reformed Church, may have engendered changes in behavior that made people more receptive to market incentives. Think of the substantial decrease in the number of holy days in Protestant areas, after the veneration of saints was abolished. The extra income generated from the extra working days could be spent on luxury goods that were out of reach for previous generations.[62] Discipline, according to the recent literature, was enforced by the state: Protestant Churches were instruments of what was at heart a political program.[63] However, in the Dutch Republic the state lacked the authority and the capacity to do this. This weakness on the part of the state made it easier for followers of different religions to live together, but also to trade together, and in this way removed religious barriers to the development of capitalism.

For Luther, the Reformation was based on the idea that every Christian had, or could have, his own, autonomous relationship with God. This perception of faith was supported, independently of the Church, by the reading of the Bible in one's own language, which, thanks to the Modern Devotion movement and the relatively high level of literacy, was not unusual in the Low Countries. But Lutheranism took on the form of a state religion, and the institutional structure of the Lutheran Church remained hierarchical. In England, the Reformation of Henry VIII was initiated from the throne, which in no way satisfied the desire in the Low Countries for more autonomy in religious matters. Anabaptism, which enjoyed great popularity in the most "capitalist" coastal provinces, where the socioeconomic group of craftsmen and laborers was large, did not recognize any religious authority. In the "New Jerusalem," proclaimed by Anabaptists during the Münster rebellion in 1535, many followers came from the Low Countries. Indeed, its leaders were a baker from Haarlem and a tailor from Leiden. But this anarchist variant was too unstructured and certainly not considered by the merchant elite as a viable alternative.[64]

Calvin's intellectual position lay somewhere between the hierarchy of Lutheranism and the anarchy of the Anabaptists. Calvin was one of the few reformers who had paid much attention to the organizational needs of the new Church. His ideas on this, described in his magnum opus *Institutio Christianæ religionis*, were developed from the context of autonomous cities— Basel, Strasbourg, and, especially, Geneva. Calvin emphasized the autonomy of local churches, each to be led by a college—a church council of elected laymen (elders, deacons). These local congregations would work together within the overarching structure of the *classis* (the organization of several local churches), and all *classes* together would form a synod, the national organization of the Church. In principle, local churches were autonomous, but they were embedded in a larger structure—via representation—that ultimately defined faith and practice. In the Republic, this balanced structure of "bottom-up" and "top-down" elements was integrated into urban society because members of the city councils were often also elected members of the church councils.[65]

The fact that Calvinism in the Republic fitted well with the institutional structures of the provinces did not mean that everyone joined the Calvinists and their Reformed Church.[66] Although the Calvinists became the largest Church in the Republic over the course of the seventeenth century, 20%–25% of the population was still Catholic. Other Protestant movements, including Anabaptism, also remained popular. The result was an ambivalent stance of the Reformed Church and a considerable degree of tolerance. As elsewhere in sixteenth-century Europe, the Dutch authorities struggled with the problem of religious diversity. They could try to suppress it with violence or the threat of violence, but this was by no means possible everywhere, leaving aside the question whether it was at all desirable. So compromises were made. A fairly generous and successful variant of this was the arrangements that were developed on the basis of the Union of Utrecht.[67] The thirteenth article of this treaty stipulated that all provinces were allowed to decide their own religious affairs.[68] At the same time, it was decided that there would be individual freedom of conscience, and that no one could be held accountable by the authorities for his or her faith. In this way, the rebels created a situation of religious pluralism and offered all residents room to privately follow their own faith.

Nevertheless, over time restrictions were imposed on those who professed other religions. High offices of the state and membership of urban councils were accessible only to Calvinists. Only members of the Reformed Church (i.e., Calvinists) were allowed to perform their rites in public. They were given possession of all buildings previously owned by the Catholic Church, and the funds of Catholic institutions were also made available to them. Other faiths had to conduct their religious activities behind closed doors. This is how the phenomenon of the "hidden church" arose, which Catholics frequently made use of: a church that was not identifiable as a church from its architectural form. Local authorities were free to exercise flexibility or apply the rules strictly.[69]

Amsterdam was very flexible in its approach to freedom of worship: in the seventeenth century, not only did it allow the existence of approximately thirty hidden churches for Catholics, it also offered Lutherans and Jews the opportunity to erect two places of worship each that were even clearly recognizable as such. When the Portuguese-Jewish synagogue was officially opened on August 2, 1675, members of the city's council were prominent guests at the festivities.[70] The word "tolerance" would be misplaced in this situation, because very few people subscribed to a principle of tolerance. Still, in reality it was widely practiced.[71] Insofar as there had been religious barriers to the development of capitalism, these disappeared in seventeenth-century Holland.[72]

We can only speculate about the size of the windfall in resources that the Reformation produced for local economies, in buildings that lost their religious purpose and were converted into hospitals and universities, for example, and more generally the funds no longer destined for the maintenance of altars and the saying of mass.[73] In Holland, for example, the local guilds were ordered in 1572 to redirect such funding "toward common causes," in practice often welfare for their members.[74] From the very outset, the Calvinists actively strengthened local community-support structures. They also had their own separate organization for community care, the *diaconia*, which was an integral part of the Reformed Church organization. Reformed *diaconias* collected a great deal of money for this purpose, which they distributed among their followers. Over time, this ecclesiastical care for the poor was integrated with other local bodies offering social support. In some places this even led to people other than Reformed worshippers being supported by *diaconias*, which in effect had then become a municipal facility.[75] At the same time, Reformed Church councils and *diaconias* provided a source of training for acquiring administrative skills, which could be put to good use serving the local community.[76]

The Revolt saw an increased interest in schooling, also stimulated by the idea that everybody should be able to read the Bible. The growth of cities and the desire to enhance religious conformity induced local governments to increase investment in public education, including for the poor.[77] In the cities schooling was already well organized, but the continuous rise in levels of literacy among both men and women demonstrates that the initiatives to increase the supply of education were also reaching beyond the city borders. The predominantly Catholic regions in the south were the exception to this rule; there, the schooling system was organized by a Protestant government distrusted by the locals, which may help to explain why literacy remained much lower in those parts of the country (see chapter 8).[78]

Education is only one of the many public goods that urban governments supplied. Via the regulation of the guilds, many markets—from bakeries to health services (hospitals, the licensing of medical personnel)—became "organized." Cities regulated shipping services between them, and would from 1618 develop a complex system of barges for passenger transportation (elegantly analyzed by Jan de Vries).[79] In chapter 7 we will argue that due to these policies the Dutch economy can be characterized as a "coordinated market economy" avant la lettre.

Another role of city councils was to maintain a stable balance between the different religious movements. In Haarlem, the Reformed congregation enjoyed all sorts of privileges, such as the use of Church buildings and access to municipal subsidies, but the city council did not allow Reformed norms to be imposed on the entire urban community. Indeed, the city's Latin school, which provided preparatory education for university studies, retained its Catholic rector. In general, complaints from the Reformed Church's council about Catholics were ignored, and Haarlem's city council promoted a neutral religious urban identity that was based mainly on the shared, nonreligious aspects of the city's history.[80]

Conclusion

Within a single generation, from 1579 to 1609, a fundamental political revolution had taken place in the Netherlands. In 1579 the rebels were fighting against the supreme military might of the Spanish empire of Philip II with a courage born of despair. The war was over how much authority should be retained by the government in Brussels and Madrid and how much the provinces and cities should be allowed to regulate themselves. In that year, the Union of Utrecht laid the foundations for a state in which the principle of local and regional autonomy was clearly established, but, at the same time, a state whose chances of survival had to be estimated as poor. Nevertheless, by 1609, the first year of the Twelve Years' Truce with Spain, the rebels had managed to establish a state that was recognized by virtually all European powers of the day. That same state had, moreover, adopted a political structure that contradicted just about all prevailing thought on good governance. Instead of the centralization and administrative uniformity that monarchs elsewhere in Europe tried to implement, the rebels cleared the way for local government and any variation associated with it. Entrepreneurs were happy with the outcome: Hooft's vision—with which this chapter opened—consisted of an amalgamation of republicanism, tolerance, moderate Protestantism, and citizenship, while allowing room for entrepreneurs and skilled craftsmen to create opportunities for further economic expansion.

Can the Dutch Revolt be considered a capitalist revolution? That is usually understood to mean a revolution by which the capitalist class—the bourgeoisie—takes control of the state at the expense of a precapitalist elite—for example, the feudal nobility. In the Low Countries, in many respects the merchant class was already dominant before 1572. However, this dominant position came under pressure owing to the emergence of the centralized state, as promoted by Charles V and Philip II, and that began to affect the property rights of the bourgeoisie. Alba's brutal military actions and new taxation were a clear demonstration of this. For the opposition, more important still was the issue of the autonomy of urban institutions—the local institutional instruments through which the urban citizens could exercise direct control. This clash also occurred elsewhere in Europe—and most of the time the representative bodies, rooted in the "corporatism" of the Middle Ages, were the losers, because the newly emerging autocratic monarch had more effective means of force at his or her disposal. In other words, the Revolt was rooted in a conflict over control of the state. In the past, feudal authority had been compatible with local autonomy, but in the sixteenth century that balance was disrupted. The Dutch merchant class did not want power over the state, rather they were defending local "freedoms." That they nevertheless acquired that power is a fine example of unintended consequences.

The urban elites did not act alone, however. Their revolt would never have been successful without broad support from middle-class city dwellers, from citizens organized in local militias, from members of guilds, and from the councils of the Reformed Church.[81] And alongside them, of course, were the Sea Beggars, mostly made up of wage laborers and the lower middle class, who earned their living from the merchant and fishing fleets. All these coalitions were unified around the notion of "freedom." In this, their first thoughts about freedom were closely linked to the privileges bestowed on cities as a whole or their corporative organizations. They also increasingly associated it with freedom from foreign domination. And as an alternative to the imperial authority of Philip II and his successors, the rebels saw it as a means for achieving the freedom associated with a republican form of government. Furthermore, certainly as long as the Calvinists were in the minority, they could also accept the principle of freedom of religion, albeit with reluctance.

We can now also draw some conclusions about the connection between capitalism and Reformation—at least as far the Low Countries are concerned. We saw in the previous chapter that there are good reasons to believe that capitalism (as it is commonly defined)—the market economy in combination with large-scale wage labor—was emerging as early as the fourteenth and fifteenth centuries, thus long before the Reformation. The Dutch Revolt in 1572 and the struggle for the recognition of Calvinism were primarily carried by the two usual protagonists of capitalist society; namely, capital (the bourgeoisie, especially the merchant community) and labor (the wage laborers who manned the Sea Beggars' fleet). In other words, Protestantism broke through thanks to the capitalist society that was already present in 1517, when Luther initiated the movement. The outcome during this acceleration stage was twofold, from a religious point of view. On the one hand, the Reformed Church was given special privileges as the "public Church"—that is, the Church supported by the state. On the other hand, Calvinism was not imposed as a state religion; there was room for other creeds, often characterized as "tolerance" even if the principle of tolerance had very few supporters. This double outcome was no coincidence. Merchants-cum-burgomasters like Hooft, with whom we began this chapter, supported the Calvinists but were reluctant to hand Reformed ministers a monopoly over the religious life of their fellow citizens.

6

New Capitalism at Home and Overseas

In February 1609, on the eve of the Twelve Years' Truce with Spain and during what could be said to be the most dynamic period in the economic history of the Netherlands, the city council of Amsterdam issued an ordinance for the establishment of a bank of exchange (the Wisselbank) in the city. The ordinance began with a powerful argument:

> To prevent speculation with the guilder and exchange rates, and to assist merchants, the aldermen, with the consent of the States and upon advice of the council of this city, have considered it essential that order be created concerning currency exchange and everything related to it by establishing a bank of exchange. To this end, the aldermen have decreed that, for the convenience of all, a bank for currency exchange be established in this city, to which everyone can bring such coins if he wants.[1]

The rest of the ordinance shows that "if he wants" should not be taken literally: anyone who wanted to transfer amounts greater than 300 guilders had to do so through an account with the Wisselbank; the City of Amsterdam stood as guarantor for the bank.

The establishment of the Wisselbank is widely regarded as one of the most important institutional innovations of this period. As we will see, this was the response of Amsterdam's council and merchants to the new phase that capitalism had entered at the time. But where did this innovation come from? And why did Amsterdam decide to regulate the flow of money so strictly—in fact, to monopolize it?

To clarify this, it is useful to distinguish two different concepts of capitalism, that of Marx and that of Braudel. As we saw in chapter 1, for Marx, capitalism was about the commodification of labor; as part of the same process, markets for other factors of production are also created. That type of capitalism had flourished in the Netherlands in the late Middle Ages: wage labor became very common, a capital market with relatively low interest rates emerged, and the market for land flourished. In short, according to all Marx's criteria the Netherlands—in particular its western parts—had become a capitalist market economy from the fourteenth or fifteenth century. According to Braudel's definition, however, one could not (yet) speak of Dutch capitalism.[2] For him, capitalism was about global economic centers, the hubs through which great flows of money coursed to keep the world economy going; it was about big banks and big financiers.

Braudel's capitalism is essentially hierarchical: there is always one clearly identifiable center where the world's financial flows converge. By contrast, Marx's capitalism could in principle be duplicated in any part of the world. In Braudel's view, the essential dynamics of his type of capitalism originated in northern Italy in the late Middle Ages, where banks from Florence and Genoa set the trend. There were connections with the Low Countries, especially Bruges in the fourteenth and fifteenth centuries, but there, too, the Italian bankers and financiers often dominated. Around 1500 this center moved to Antwerp, and new financial practices and instruments emerged that made the capital market more flexible, but they also brought the risk of speculation and—as an inevitable downside of this—financial instability. In 1559, with Antwerp facing an economic crisis related to mounting tensions with Spain, the financial hub moved to Genoa, which took on a central role in the money flows linked, within the Habsburg Empire, to the influx of silver and gold from the Spanish Americas and the financing of Philip II's military campaign in the Low Countries. This phase of dominance by the bankers of Genoa came to an end around 1627, when (again, according to Braudel) the central hub of capitalism moved to Amsterdam. In Braudel's view, the transformation the Netherlands underwent around 1600 can be seen as both cause and effect of the new role that Amsterdam, in particular, played in the world economy at that time. New ideas and financial instruments came from Antwerp to booming Holland in the persons of cashiers and money changers, who lived off "monetary fluctuations and confusion," as the ordinance of 1609 described it.[3]

The arrival of financial capitalism was evidently experienced by Dutch merchants as a mixed blessing, because in 1606 they turned to Amsterdam's city council with the request to set up a bank of exchange similar to the one in Venice. As things went, and to this day continue to go in the Netherlands, a committee was set up that same year to investigate the desirability of such a bank. To this end, the "national" monetary authorities—the mint masters (who guarded the quality and stability of the Republic's coinage)—were consulted, which, after the necessary discussion, led to the ordinance of 1609.[4] At the same time, an earlier decision, made in 1604, to ban the establishment of cashier businesses, small-scale banks that focused on monetary transactions—and thereby block the introduction of the new financial services—was reaffirmed.[5]

In many ways, this situation is reminiscent of the recent global financial crisis of 2008 and the years that followed. In 2008 the world economy was plunged into crisis owing to unrestrained speculation, which led to the collapse of the international banking system. One of the key problems was (and is) that banks were (are) indispensable for national and international money flows, making it not merely a crisis in "just any industry," but shaking the entire global economy to its foundations. The lesson learned in the 1930s, that the two primary functions of banks, money supply and meeting the demand for risk-bearing credit, should be kept separate from each other—a lesson forgotten again in the 1990s—had already been recognized some three centuries earlier. Ingeniously, the ordinance in 1609 was aimed at providing an alternative to a system in which money transactions were left completely to the market, because that led, according to the aldermen of the city, to speculation and turmoil. The proposed Wisselbank had to deliver a public good "for the pleasure and security of everyone in the city," which was possible only because the City of Amsterdam operated as its regulator and guaranteed its stability. The Wisselbank did not aim to suppress all risk-taking activities, but was focused on payments only. It was also decided that the Wisselbank would not be allowed to provide credit on the basis of deposits it held. Full, 100% coverage from cash on hand became the norm, and the bank was set up as a nonprofit entity, part of the city administration, housed in the city hall.[6]

Another, separate institution, the Bank van Lening (Amsterdam Credit Bank), was established in Amsterdam a few years later, in 1614, to fulfill the second function of the monetary system—meeting demand for risk-bearing credit. The dream of many a radical economist who has analyzed the causes and consequences of the global financial crisis of 2008 had already been realized in Amsterdam in the early seventeenth century! Amsterdam's city fathers had, moreover, decided to curtail financial capitalism before a financial crisis ever had a chance of breaking out. The Banco di Rialto, founded in Venice in 1587, was the product of the reflection that followed a deep financial crisis, and this has remained a familiar pattern to the present day, with the 1930s as the best recent example. In 1609 there was no question of a financial crisis, although the creation and development of the Dutch East India Company did place increasing strain on money and capital markets.[7]

And so the new form of capitalism just starting in the Netherlands began with strict regulation of the money market: speculative transactions and the companies that facilitated and organized them—the cashiers—were forbidden. If there is such a thing as a symbol for capitalism then it has to be money, yet instead of creating room for the pursuit of unlimited profit, the financial sector was in fact curtailed and in a sense even nationalized. The City of Amsterdam played a crucial role in this: there, the merchants who distrusted the appearance of new financial instruments found a ready ear, and it was Amsterdam's city council that, after consultation and in collaboration with the States General, took the lead and established the city's Wisselbank. Other cities—such as Rotterdam, Middelburg, and Delft—would follow this example, but their banks of exchange were of much smaller size and significance. The conservative policy (100% coverage) instituted in 1609 meant that the Wisselbank provided no extra economic stimulus—no extra money was created (at least, not as long as this policy was adhered to). It led to growing confidence in the bank, especially after it passed a stress test with flying colors during the crisis of 1672. In the long run, this made the bank an ideal clearing house for facilitating national and international money flows, which contributed greatly to Amsterdam's position as a financial center. Paradoxically, the reliability of the Wisselbank—an answer to the mistrust arising from "fluctuations and confusion"—was an important factor in the attractiveness of Amsterdam and the growth of international capital flows through it that would eventually destabilize its financial market, and with it Holland's economy, in the second half of the eighteenth century. Such is the irony of history.[8]

The financial capitalism à la Braudel that arose in Amsterdam around 1620 acquired a specific institutional embedding, which was in part induced by the institutional structure of the Republic and the interests of the dominant group of merchants who sat on the city council. This certainly also applied to that other symbol of the new capitalism, the Dutch East India Company, founded in 1602.

The Dutch East India Company

Even more so than the Wisselbank, the Dutch East India Company (Vereenigde Oostindische Compagnie, or VOC) exemplified the new capitalism that was taking shape around 1600. This capitalism, perhaps for the first time in history, possessed all the characteristics of the capitalism we are familiar with today. For the first time, we see the limited liability company emerging as a new business entity, the trading of company shares, speculation in these shares on a stock exchange, conflicts between shareholders and management over the policy of the new company—all rooted in the "modern" separation between ownership and management of a company. In short, the "excesses" of capitalism as it would fully develop in centuries to come were present at this moment.

The concentration of economic power that was realized is also remarkable. While there were hardly any large enterprises in the Netherlands before 1602, with the establishment of the VOC an early modern megaconcern was created that possessed an unprecedented capacity for making profit and would in time employ tens of thousands of people. This company also dominated a substantial part of the Dutch economy—trade with and within Asia—for almost two hundred years. How did a company like this come about? And was this manifestation of the unlimited pursuit of profit gladly accepted, or were there similar reactions as those to the changes occurring in the money market that led to the establishment of the Wisselbank?

The financial capitalism of the stock market and the "coupon-clipping" shareholder have always been criticized for the pursuit of short-term profit at the expense of stability and long-term growth—the same contradictions seen in 1609 between developments in the money market and the purpose of the Wisselbank. Does similar criticism apply to the VOC? To answer, we first need to take a step back in time. The supply of spices from the Indies was a crucial lifeline for the economy of Antwerp. Prior to 1500 this lucrative trade had flowed via the Middle East through Venice and Genoa to the rest of Europe. When the Portuguese pioneered the sea route to Asia, they established a state monopoly that regulated the trade in spices between Indonesia, India, and Ceylon, on the one hand, and Lisbon, on the other. Antwerp's merchants had managed to gain control over the further distribution from Lisbon of these spices. But the Dutch Revolt of 1572, the annexation of Portugal by the Spanish king in 1580, and the capture of Antwerp by Spanish troops in 1585 all but completely blocked this trade. As a consequence, it became attractive to undertake direct voyages to Indonesia, for which, from

1595, a dozen expeditions from Amsterdam, Middelburg, and other ports were fitted out. Formally, these expeditions were registered (and privileged, with the exclusion of competitors) as one-off ventures, temporary alliances of groups of merchants who pooled resources for a particular expedition and then shared the profits among themselves after the sale of the commodities brought back from the Far East—as had long been the practice for trading ventures within Europe. Anyone could then withdraw from the company, or decide to participate in the following expedition. The companies' directors organized this for a small fee, and the participants were liable only for the money they had invested (here we see the first moves to limit liability).[9]

Two developments forced these groups of merchants to further increase their level of cooperation. To begin with, they quickly discovered that growing competition in the Moluccas (and elsewhere) for the purchase of spices, and their sale in the Netherlands, endangered what had initially been high profit margins. In addition, it turned out to be necessary to set up a network of fortresses and trading settlements throughout the region to protect and stabilize trade, just as the Portuguese had done. Without this, every new arrival of a Dutch trading fleet meant that prices immediately shot up, because everyone knew that it was important for the traders to buy as much as possible as quickly as possible. The alternative, continually building up stocks, had to happen on location, but this could be done only if the accumulating stock was kept under armed protection. In addition, such expeditions and the trade resulting from them also had a distinct military-strategic dimension. After all, these expeditions were meant to undermine Spanish-Portuguese dominance in Asia and, thus, to weaken an enemy with which the Dutch had been at war since 1572. Cooperation among all merchant groups involved had the potential to forge a powerful weapon to use against the enemy.

The private trading companies that had been founded prior to 1602 were in that year forced by the state to merge into a company that was granted the monopoly over all Dutch trade east of the Cape of Good Hope. This was the result of lengthy negotiations in which the leading statesman, the secretary of the States of Holland, Johan van Oldenbarnevelt, brought together all parties—particularly the major merchant cities situated in the west of the country—and managed to draw up a list of compromises that everyone could agree to. The company charter described this process: "after taking into consideration various communications, deliberations, induction and reports, we arrived at a decision after much deliberation."[10] The complex organizational structure that resulted comprised six chambers, located in the towns where the original private companies actually did business. The chamber in Amsterdam was by far the largest, with 50% of the business, with the others (Zeeland, Rotterdam, Delft, Hoorn, and Enkhuizen) together accounting for the other 50%. Each chamber supplied a proportionate number of delegates to sit on the central administrative board (totaling seventeen members, it was known as the Heren XVII, or Gentlemen XVII) that was to direct the new company. In fact Amsterdam supplied only eight members, slightly underweighting its presence on the board, to prevent it from complete domination. The actual commercial management was carried out by the directors (from whom the Heren XVII were selected) of the chambers, who were appointed by the cities and the provincial States where the chambers were located—illustrating once more the interaction between state and market. The biggest and without a doubt most successful company in Dutch history, the VOC, was—perhaps with a little exaggeration—a large, continuous circuit of meetings.[11]

The company's share capital was assigned in the same proportions as given above, whereby the States General, who had granted the VOC its charter, also determined that public expression of interest in the company's share issue had to be facilitated, in order to make these shares accessible "for all residents of the United Provinces who would like to participate," so that they, too, could benefit from the company's profits. The charter stipulated, moreover, that if the share capital was oversubscribed, any reduction of share allocations had to be at the expense of large investors—that is, those who wanted to invest more than 30,000 guilders. Oldenbarnevelt thus emerged as an advocate of popular capitalism, whereby anyone who wished to acquire a share in the new venture had to be able to do so. The issue of shares turned out to be a great success, and from the records it appears that, indeed, slightly less wealthy people from outside the merchant class participated, although this was a small minority, possessing a minimal share of the total issue.

Originally, the VOC's charter was granted for twenty-one years, with an interim assessment after ten years in which the directors were to report the company's results and give investors the option of withdrawing their capital. Although its predecessor companies had paid out generous dividends, initially the VOC hardly did so, except for several payouts in kind of spices, which were not greatly appreciated by shareholders. Virtually all profits were instead reinvested in the company, in particular for the creation of a sizeable, well-armed fleet, the establishment and maintenance of forts and settlements, and pay for the thousands of sailors and soldiers who manned the fleet and trading posts in Asia. Long-term investments to set up a trade network that covered half the globe—from Amsterdam to Japan—outweighed short-term dividend payments to keep shareholders content. Not all shareholders were satisfied with this strategy. Isaac Le Maire, who came from the south, like many other protagonists in this story, and had originally belonged to the "inner circle" of the VOC, expressed this opposition most strongly, and he tried to induce a crisis by "going short" (speculating on a drop in share prices) to force a change in policy. It was the first bearish speculation in history, accompanied, as was to be expected, by rumors, among them that the VOC would become redundant and go into liquidation once a peace treaty was signed with Spain. Here, again, we see another sign pointing to modern capitalist relations. Such speculation was made possible by a flourishing trade in futures of VOC shares, and, given its destabilizing nature, even then there was a plea for banning this form of speculation.[12]

The directors refused to change their policy of long-term investment and continued to allocate resources for the consolidation of the VOC's trading monopoly in the Moluccas and the rest of "the East" by Jan Pieterszoon Coen (governor-general of the "East Indies possessions" from 1617 to 1629).[13] The VOC's performance compared favorably with England's East India Company (EIC), which had been founded in 1600, because the latter lacked the VOC's broad capital base and was continually forced to raise the resources it needed to individually finance each trading fleet setting sail for the East. With the renewal of the VOC's charter in 1621, the argument about the company's investment-profit policies was repeated in intensified form, now with a large number of merchants joining in who felt ignored and unheard; they wanted a higher dividend. To accommodate them to some extent, the revised charter stipulated that dividends should normally be paid (which had become possible thanks to positive developments in the company's profits), and a committee of nine was created with access to the company's annual accounts. In effect this became a supervisory board, and the VOC adopted and developed a "two-tier structure" of governance that would become characteristic of Dutch businesses.[14]

This first business corporation—for that was what the VOC was, in fact—was modelled on the Admiralty boards that governed the Dutch navy.[15] These Admiralty boards were, however, the result of local and regional opposition to attempts of the Burgundian and subsequently Habsburg governments to impose a centralized governance structure on the navy.[16] In this sense, they shared the medieval governance model of many other institutions, originally created to run the affairs of the Catholic Church, but later gradually extended to apply also to cities, guilds, and universities, to name some of the best known examples. The most important feature here was that a legal entity no longer had to be a person (or a family), and an organization could also act as such, whereby its directors carried only limited personal liability. Such corporations could engage in business transactions—for example, acquire debt or buy real estate.[17] What was new was that the VOC was raising capital that would remain under the authority of the company's management for a long time. The monopoly it possessed was one way of reassuring investors. But equally important was the legal structure of the company, which instilled confidence among investors that the state would not at some stage lay claim to part of the company's funds (in effect, a form of entity shielding); after all, the Republic was at war. Even so, in the Republic the possibilities for the commander in chief, Stadtholder Maurice of Nassau, to do so were limited. The States General, which had granted the VOC its charter, was a collective institution, the members of which often owned shares themselves. By way of comparison, in England the king did not let Parliament prescribe law, and in 1601 and 1607 James I also issued charters to direct competitors of the EIC. Only after James's son Charles I was dethroned in 1649 could the EIC adopt the VOC's business model.[18]

The corporation's organizational form allowed the VOC to keep shareholders at arm's length and focus on long-term gain. The organization and development of the VOC shows how an institution originally focused on arranging "one-off" projects or trading transactions was transformed into one with a permanent structure focused on long-term investment and corresponding trade flows. This type of company was not completely unknown in 1602: land reclamation projects—such as those in the Zijpe area in 1597— made it clear from the start that capital would be committed for a lengthy period of time. The fact that shares in new polder-reclamation projects or trading companies could be traded provided the investors with whatever flexibility they needed. The management of the VOC, supported by the States General and the rest of the Republic's political elite, contributed to this transformation of the company. And, just as with the Wisselbank, the emphasis placed on long-term over short-term profit was not at the expense of efficiency or growth. On the contrary, thanks to the company's great financial strength and its long-term view it was able to become the dominant player in Europe-Asia trade and a powerful source of growth for the Republic's economy. Governor-General Coen, mentioned earlier, conquered the Moluccas and established a network of fortresses in southern and southeastern Asia, leaving the company's old competitor, Portugal, and its English neighbor far behind. The Bandanese, however, and other Moluccans paid the price for the company's ascendance.

The VOC Overseas

In the Netherlands, it seems, this new form of capitalism was effectively curbed, or at least the pursuit of short-term profit was channeled by setting up institutions that served long-term goals. The negative consequences of this economic system surfaced mainly in the way the VOC and later the Dutch West India Company (hereafter WIC) dealt with non-European peoples and trade contacts. In general, during this period the Dutch behaved as aggressive overseas colonizers who did not hesitate to oppress other peoples for their own gain. Their conquests in Indonesia—the nadir being the Banda genocide of 1621—are the most striking examples of this, but their treatment of Native Americans in New Amsterdam and Surinam, and the Khoikhoi and San peoples in the Cape Colony, could also be pointed to in this respect, not to mention slavery, no doubt the most shameful stain on the Dutch Golden Age.

A study of Dutch overseas expansion can help us to understand the nature of early modern Dutch society.[19] In previous chapters we have seen that, by the standards of the time, the Netherlands was a fairly egalitarian society, one in which the various sociopolitical groups kept one another more or less in balance. What kept this society together? Was it deeply rooted common values and norms based on Judeo-Christian tradition? Or was it the institutions that had emerged from the High Middle Ages that bound human behavior to a set of rules and ensured a fairly balanced distribution of power? Was this "European cloak" discarded immediately upon arrival abroad, or were the rules of conduct associated with it deeply rooted in the fiber of all involved? How did the Dutch, once overseas, organize their "new" society locally? And what place was there in it for the original inhabitants?

Leaving the issue of slavery aside for now, what for the twentieth- or twenty-first-century observer is one of the most painful features of the colonial societies that emerged in the seventeenth and eighteenth centuries is the structural inequality between Europeans and the indigenous populations. In the Dutch East Indies (for the most part, present-day Indonesia) this evolved during the nineteenth century into a detailed system comprising three classes of citizens: Europeans, indigenous peoples, and "other Asians," the last referring to a collection of inhabitants who were, or were descended from, Asians such as the Chinese, Japanese, or Indians. In some ways this sociopolitical structure is reminiscent of the class society that was common in Europe before 1800.

Before 1789, societies in much of Europe consisted of a number of distinct social groups, each with very different rights and obligations. This had begun with the three basic social classes: nobility, clergy, and commoners, each of which had different privileges (for example, in large parts of Europe nobles and clerics did not pay taxes). The class of commoners was made up of urban burghers, as well as farmers, peasants, and others living in the countryside. Urban communities were further subdivided into separate groups with their own rights; the guilds are a good example, but also religious minorities—like the Sephardic and Ashkenazy Jews—could have some degree of self-government. The council of a city's synagogue, the *ma'amad*, fulfilled various public-judicial functions, mediating between Jewish traders, and more generally watching over the fortunes of Jewish residents. Spinoza's excommunication in 1656 was more than just a religious statement by a synagogue council: it made it impossible for him to continue living in Amsterdam as a Jew. This example of self-government did not emerge in Amsterdam until 1639 (with the official establishment of the Jewish community there), but there are significant parallels with the way the Chinese population was managed in Batavia.[20]

Dutch merchants who settled in other trading settlements in the fifteenth and sixteenth centuries—Gdańsk, Bergen, London, Archangel, and others—often lived in their own districts and tried to safeguard their interests as a group by claiming a separate status. This often concerned legal protection in conflicts with locals (merchants and ordinary citizens), as well as a certain degree of self-government, to be able to resolve internal conflicts themselves, to be exempted from certain taxes, and so on. The Hanseatic League, which was established, among other things, to promote the interests of Baltic and German merchants abroad, is an example of the strong institutionalization of this type of merchant self-rule. Incidentally, in the Netherlands—and certainly in Holland—such privileges were hardly ever granted, perhaps because Dutch merchants were traditionally opposed to the Hanseatic League. It was also characteristic that in Holland Jewish residents did not live in separate, closed ghettos, as they often did elsewhere; they did tend to concentrate voluntarily in certain quarters of cities, but that was not exclusively a Jewish practice.

The specific institutional features that a trading settlement in Asia or the Americas chose depended very much on local circumstances and the balance of power between the Dutch, united in either the VOC or WIC, and local rulers. If one had to operate on the margins of a strong state—such as in Archangel, or in Decima, where the Japanese tolerated the VOC only in an extremely subordinate role, or in Canton (the only port in China open to foreigners in the eighteenth century)—then there was no other option than to adapt to what the authorities would allow.

The intentions of the VOC, and how they turned out in practice, can be clearly illustrated by the example of Batavia, located on the island of Java. The choice of the name "Batavia"—city of the Batavians, the mythical freedom fighters of the Low Countries who opposed the Roman Empire (a myth popular in the seventeenth century because of its obvious parallels with the Revolt against Spain)—is an indication that they wanted to make this a home away from home.[21] The way in which the VOC governed abroad can be illustrated by the decision-making that preceded the establishment of Batavia as the company's central trading hub. From its first voyages to the Indonesian archipelago, the VOC had been active in the important trading port of Banten (or Bantam), which was conveniently located in the center of the archipelago. However, it was also the capital of the Javanese sultanate of the same name, ruled by a *pangeran* (the name of heads of noble Javanese families) in the name of the sultan. This meant that the VOC had to submit to a local legal system that was not its own, including in cases of conflict with other partners, such as Chinese merchants (who had great influence on the local government).

The *pangeran* was the supreme judicial authority in Banten and closely involved in the economic prosperity of the port.[22] The VOC, however, cherished the ambition of establishing a monopoly in the spice trade—cloves, mace, perhaps even pepper—which was, of course, at odds with local interests. This led to constant clashes, and from the moment that Jan Pieterszoon Coen was appointed director general of all VOC offices in the East Indies, a discussion arose around his proposal to move the company's central trading post to Djacarta (also spelled Jacatra; later to become Batavia, and later still, in the twentieth century, renamed Jakarta). Djacarta was ruled by a local prince who was a subordinate of the sultan of Banten, but the latter was not very powerful and his wishes could be by and large ignored. The discussion was conducted by the members of the Council of the Indies, a typically Dutch administrative body, originally (in 1610) comprising four members with extensive local experience.[23] Collective management by councils was the rule throughout the VOC enterprise, and meetings were the most important moments in the company's decision-making processes. When Coen was appointed second-highest official in 1613, his superior,

Governor-General Both, praised him as "a person with a moderate lifestyle, modest, of good character, not a drunkard, not stubborn, *persuasive in meetings*, a skillful trader and bookkeeper" [emphasis added].[24] In short, the most successful "imperialist" in Dutch history excelled at bookkeeping and during meetings.

On March 15, 1618, a meeting of the Council of the Indies was convened, supplemented with the presence of the captains of all Dutch ships in the port of Banten. The captains were invited because this was also a "war council": the possibility of waging war against Banten was to be discussed and it was Dutch custom that ships' captains were always present at such moments—after all, they would have to implement any decision to attack. During the meeting Coen explained his case against the *pangeran* and pleaded for a relocation to Djacarta. Nevertheless, he also insisted that everyone should carefully weigh up the pros and cons, which led to a majority of the thirteen present speaking out against the move. Coen then announced—calling, at such a moment, on his experience and skill in handling meetings—that it was too early to make a definite decision and that the meeting was intended only to gauge opinions.[25]

In fact, Coen had already started expanding the post at Djacarta, where the local prince had reluctantly given permission for the construction of a fortified house and warehouses that also functioned as a fortress. With his increasing presence in Djacarta and by investing large sums in new facilities, including the fortress (now in the face of mounting resistance from the local prince), Coen's proposal was de facto carried out. Indeed, the Council of the Indies held its first meeting in Djacarta at the end of 1618. The strategic vision behind all this was that Coen wanted to develop and manage an Asian trade network from a trading center that the VOC itself could control, enabling the company to make profits sufficient to finance the export of spices and other products to the Netherlands. To do so required a fortified "rendezvous," a company-owned port, where other groups of traders from China or southern India could also settle. After first being forced to leave Djacarta owing to British naval pressure, Coen returned in mid-1619 to capture Djacarta (fortunately the local fortress had remained in Dutch hands) and evict the local prince, so that he was able to establish himself as the highest authority present. For all his actions, Coen consulted with the Council of the Indies, and often also with the captains and officers of the VOC ships in port. That said, he nevertheless implemented his plans with a heavy hand.

When Coen started designing his new trading hub in 1619, after razing Djacarta, he had a copy of a classical Dutch town in mind (just as the

Portuguese built copies of Portuguese towns throughout Asia). The new port, to be named Batavia, however, was a copy of a Dutch city not only in a spatial sense—it did indeed boast city walls, a fortress, a town hall, a harbor, canals, and so on—but also in an institutional sense: it had a *schepenbank* (chamber of aldermen, which functioned both as an administrative council and a court), a bailiff, a civic militia, social institutions for poor relief, an orphanage, a credit bank, a hospital, a school, and, of course, an officially sanctioned Reformed church.[26] At the top of the administrative structure was the Council of the Indies, of which the governor-general was chairman. At the same time, Coen set about appointing a captain of the Chinese community. Su Ming-Kang, called Ben Con in Dutch sources, was chosen by the Chinese and given extensive powers to facilitate the self-government of this community.[27] Ben Con became not only the most powerful official in charge of the Chinese community but also a good friend of Coen, whom he visited many an evening. He was one of the Chinese who participated in the typical Dutch institutions created locally, contributing as an advisory member to Batavia's college of aldermen,[28] and later also as a member of the Boedelkamer (Orphan Chamber), an institution created to administrate estates left to orphans, including those of Chinese origin.

Serious attempts were made to create a typically Dutch city while at the same time accommodating the Chinese community. There were good reasons for doing so. Relations with the Javanese population were tense—the nearby Sultanate of Banten and the powerful Sultanate of Mataram, centered further away in Central Java, were both hostile to the VOC establishment at Batavia. Chinese intermediaries played a pacifying role in conflicts with these neighbors. More importantly, Coen's commercial strategy, to participate in Asian trade and use its profits to finance the export of spices to the Netherlands, could be achieved only by cooperating with Chinese merchants, who were experienced traders in Asia. Coen's strategy depended on attracting these merchants (who received no support from the Chinese empire; until 1683, trade with foreigners was even prohibited) to Batavia, which they turned into a predominantly Chinese trading center.[29] For the Chinese, legal certainty was an important factor, and it is characteristic of these early years that Chinese merchants quickly found their way to the aldermen—sometimes to complain about the corrupt practices of Ben Con. One complaint made in 1620 involved no fewer than forty-seven Chinese timber traders, and although it was declared inadmissible, it was nevertheless seriously investigated; on other occasions complaints against him were declared well-founded. Coen's strategy was successful: the Chinese community grew rapidly from 400 inhabitants in 1619 to 2,390 in 1632,[30] and brought a great deal of trade to Batavia. Another ethnic community was the Mardijkers, of mixed Portuguese/European and Asian blood, descendants of native troops who had converted to Christianity, along with Tamils, Sinhalese, and other peoples from India. This community became the "free citizens" of Batavia, with their own, predominantly Portuguese, church and institutions. Coen encouraged this, too, by giving them civil rights.

Coen thus strove to make Batavia a genuine Dutch settlement, and he argued strongly in favor of encouraging migration of Dutch men and women to the city. Nevertheless, he also recognized that there were limits to that endeavor. From the very beginning of the VOC's activities in the archipelago, slavery had been an "accepted" source of labor. There was an acute shortage of labor, which led to the hiring of Chinese laborers, but also to the purchase, through indigenous channels, of enslaved persons—slavery was widespread and an extensive trade in slaves existed long before the arrival of Europeans. The VOC used its considerable power to forcibly abduct residents of various islands and transfer them to places where workers were needed—for the construction of Batavia and for the cultivation of spices in the Moluccas. In an expedition to Siau island (north of Celebes [now Sulawesi]), for example, hundreds of men, women, and children were kidnapped to be employed in the harvest of nutmeg.[31] The project was only partly successful since there was, of course, little desire to work for the Dutch. Therefore, alternatives were explored. When famine struck in southern India, several VOC ships set out to recruit the suffering population as slaves. Within colonial society no critical voices are known to have been raised about this use of slave labor—even though it was at odds with the traditions and customs *in patria* (more about this later). The Dutch norm—no slavery—appears to have been easily set aside for the acceptance of slave ownership on a large scale. Indeed, within a short time more than half the population of Batavia consisted of enslaved people.

Related to this, at least in part, were changes in the norms surrounding marriage and sexuality. Enslaved women were often seen as providers of sexual services. Monogamy had been the predominant norm in Europe for centuries, but that was not the case in much of Asia, where polygamy was either permitted de facto or widely practiced through the keeping of concubines by the rich and powerful. Even in less well-off social circles, maintaining a concubine was not uncommon. Here, too, European norms tended to be abandoned quickly as people arrived in the East. The first governor-general, Both, had already argued in favor of formally allowing concubinage.[32] Coen,

however, opposed it. In 1620 he issued a decree aimed at forbidding concubinage by imposing fines on cohabitation outside marriage.[33] Adultery
was even to be punished by the death penalty.[34] This step was an extension
of his aim to make the city attractive to Dutch women, and he managed to
persuade the VOC to cooperate. Concubinage and the sexual exploitation
of female slaves could not, however, be suppressed with this single measure:
the surplus of European males and the "supply" of Asian women, voluntary
or otherwise, played a significant role in this matter—up until the end of the
colonial period, concubinage remained a common phenomenon.

Slavery and concubinage show that interpersonal relationships—
institutions linked to labor and gender—were very quickly adapted to what
was customary in Asia. There is no evidence of opposition to this trend. It
is perhaps characteristic that the pastor and the church council, prominent
participants in civil society in the Netherlands, were muzzled in Batavia and
had to swallow their criticism of Coen's aggressive policies.[35] Ultimately, the
company was in charge and its commercial interests always prevailed. Batavia had itself no city rights or other means to distance itself from the VOC
and was therefore unable to act as countervailing power. The character of the
VOC-state, moreover, changed over time. In 1684 Banten was eliminated as
a competitor and the hinterland was finally pacified, which resulted in strong
expansion into surrounding areas. Here, once again, Chinese entrepreneurs
played a major role. The sugar industry flourished under their leadership,
and for a long time sugar became crucial to the region's economy. However,
the position of Chinese operating outside Batavia was not regulated—the
"delegated authority" of the captain of the Chinese community in Batavia
was not extended to the region beyond the city walls. In this vacuum, "wild
west" situations developed that would eventually culminate in the Chinese
massacre in Batavia in 1740.

With the opening up of Batavia's hinterland and the increasing control
the VOC acquired over the northern coast of Java (the Pasisir) through trea-
ties with local rulers and various sultans of Mataram, the center of gravity in
the colony started to shift. The trade-oriented city-state of Batavia increasingly became a territorial state, generating important and ever-growing
income from taxes and "feudal rights." For example, the obligation of the
peasants of Priangan to provide labor for their local lord was used by the VOC
to establish the forced culture of coffee, for export to the Netherlands. In this
way, the main political axis, which originally ran between the Dutch and
Chinese communities, began to shift to one that ran between the Dutch and
the Javanese. Increasingly, the key problem became how the Dutch could

coexist alongside the very large Javanese population. The VOC did not actually develop any new institutions to deal with this. Around 1680, each ethnic group was allotted space outside the walls of Batavia—one or more of its own *dessa*s (urban villages). This segregation was symbolic of the fragmented society that had emerged. At the same time, the colonial elite increasingly adopted the customs of the Javanese princes of the surrounding states, even developing for themselves new forms of ostentatious display of luxury based on the examples around them.[36]

In the language of Acemoglu and Robinson: in the beginning an attempt was made in Batavia to use relatively inclusive institutions, like those developed in western Europe, for the organization of the colonial economy, in order to stimulate and attract other groups of merchants.[37] This experiment was relatively short-lived, however, and it was eventually displaced by a system of extractive institutions, often copied or directly adopted from local examples, through which the VOC and its officials used the state to appropriate any surpluses. The norms and values that were customary in the Netherlands turned out to be unable to provide the guidance that the new circumstances demanded of them: once in the East the Dutch quite easily took to keeping slaves. Norms of social conduct rapidly changed, and, generally speaking, people did not seem to have found it a problem to live in the two different "worlds" that belonged on opposite sides of Cairo. The VOC consciously kept these separated, as the example of slavery shows.

Slavery

In the autumn of 1596, a ship that had been captured from the Portuguese while carrying enslaved people from Africa (called Moren in the sources) entered the harbor of Middelburg.[38] It was the intention of the ship's new owner, Pieter van der Haegen, and its captain, Melchior van den Kerckhoven, to sell the enslaved people there, but this met with resistance from the Middelburg authorities. Mayor Adriaen Heindricxsen ten Haeff protested against this to the States of Zeeland—the highest authority in the province—which handled his protest on November 15. Ten Haeff's position can be read in the States' minutes: "that ships from Guinea arrived here carrying perhaps one hundred *Moren*, men, women and children, all of them baptized Christians, and therefore they should not be owned as someone's property or sold as slaves, but given their freedom, without anyone claiming to own them."[39]

The States of Zeeland announced the following Sunday in all churches that the Africans would be given their freedom the next day. They would then have the opportunity to choose a trade or enter employment so that they could provide for themselves. To this end, a viewing day was to be organized on the Monday, so that people could choose who to employ from the released slaves. They were expected to educate the Africans they hired according to Christian principles and teach them a trade. In the States' minutes it was recorded as "bring them up in fear of God, and with respect for all morals, as befits good Christians, and properly teach them manual skills, a trade or some other skill such that they will be capable of and willing to exercise."

Van der Haegen appealed against this decision to the States General; he was from Rotterdam, which made it a legal issue between two provinces, so the States General was the place to handle the dispute. His appeal was denied, but in its deliberations resulting from a second appeal, the States General judged that the ship's owner could do with the Africans "as he wishes." He was then allowed to recapture the scattered group of Africans, after which he set sail with most of the enslaved. A small number remained behind—it is known that a few months later a group of nine Africans was buried in the local cemetery.

This story captures a defining moment in the history of Dutch capitalism. Slavery is an important topic for a number of reasons. According to the thinking on economic development inspired by Amartya Sen (among others), in which the ability to make meaningful decisions about one's own life is key, slavery is the complete opposite of the "agency" that is central to Sen's approach.[40] People who are enslaved are deprived of their ability to make independent decisions—their agency is appropriated by the slave "owner." However, those who are enslaved will continuously struggle to reclaim their agency. The slave owner must continually use force or the threat of force to maintain the institution, otherwise the enslaved will run away or refuse to work or follow orders. This violence systematically structures slave-based societies, which are cut off from other, more cooperative institutional solutions for their institutional problems. Violence also exists at the expense of trust, one of the basic conditions for social development. And this in turn means that the development potential of this type of society is limited in the long term; slavery is one of the best "predictors" of economic stagnation and underdevelopment. This applies not only to societies that are largely based on slavery but also to the societies from which the enslaved were taken by force.[41]

Incidentally, this does not necessarily mean that a slave-based economy is inefficient or by definition associated with low income levels. On the

contrary, there are strong examples—Barbados in the seventeenth century—
of slave-based economies with high GDP per capita, although the GDP was
extremely unevenly distributed and clearly did not provide a high level of
well-being for the majority of the population.[42] Ancient Rome's economy
is another example of a relatively productive economy—by the standards of
the time, at least—based on large-scale slavery. Slave-based economies are
striking examples of how high levels of productivity can go hand in hand
with low levels of well-being and limited long-term development potential.

One aspect that receives relatively little attention in discussions about
the historical significance of slavery is that late medieval and early modern
societies in northwest Europe were unusual in that slavery had no place in
them.[43] Slavery used to be common in almost all complex societies, even in
that of highly developed China, where people could sell their child or wife
when debts were incurred that could no longer be paid off. Such debt bondage was an almost universal phenomenon. Indeed, the VOC came across it
everywhere it set foot: in India, Indonesia, Thailand, Ceylon (Sri Lanka),
China, and even in the relatively egalitarian society inhabiting the Banda
Islands. Next to debt, the other source of slavery in complex societies was
warfare, through which conquered peoples or the inhabitants of captured
cities were enslaved. In western Europe, however, these forms of slavery had
disappeared by the Middle Ages. The Church had long preached that Christians should not be enslaved and certainly not bought and sold as such. Also,
to replace debt bondage the instrument of bankruptcy had been developed,
aimed at clearing the debt and giving the person a new start. Real slavery was
first transformed (in the seventh to ninth centuries) into the more benign
serfdom, which had in turn given way to market-driven relationships: land
leasing, wage labor, and capital-market credit. The absence of slavery in
late medieval northwestern Europe is one of the strongest arguments for
the proposition that it was inhabited by relatively egalitarian societies, and
therefore most suitable for a general process of economic development in
the sense of Sen. Only in the Mediterranean region—especially in Portugal
and Spain—did slavery continue on a limited scale, mainly because of the
supply of captured Muslims, who likewise did everything they could to seize
Christians for their own slave markets.[44]

The legal status of slaves and slavery had been regulated in the Low Countries. Most famous is the ruling in the second half of the sixteenth century
by the Great Council of Mechelen, the highest legal body of the Habsburg
state, not to return a runaway slave to his "owner," a Spanish merchant who
was visiting the Low Countries, since slavery (*servitus personarum*) was not

recognized as a legal institution. According to the legal scholar Gudelinus, who recorded this ruling, slaves were immediately free once they entered an area where slavery was not recognized.[45] The ruling confirmed that the Low Countries, a relatively egalitarian society with the features of a capitalist market economy, would continue to outlaw slavery in its domestic labor markets (although serfdom continued, albeit on a small scale, in the remote rural Achterhoek region). Moreover, during the revolt against Spanish rule, a popular level of discourse arose in which the intrinsic and inviolable freedom of Holland (and later the Republic) was magnified. Defending the privileges of self-rule of the cities and provinces of the Netherlands was at the heart of this "ideology of freedom." The freedom of the young Republic was placed in direct contrast with the "slavery" that prevailed in Spain.[46] It was not so much the physical subjugation associated with slavery that people had in mind, rather the lack of political freedom that prevailed in a country ruled by a monarch. Occasionally, however, the concept was also expanded to include slavery in the modern sense, which was described in equally disapproving terms. This all goes to show that around 1600, slavery, however it was defined, was unacceptable in the Dutch Republic.

The pressing question therefore arises of why the inhabitants of this state, one in which slavery had disappeared and freedom was of paramount importance, began to make extensive use of forced labor after 1600. In the decades to follow, attitudes began to shift because Dutch merchants and ships' masters were exposed to the slave trade and to slavery itself. Up until then the Portuguese had almost complete control of the slave trade, but they had become enemies of the Dutch through Philip II of Spain's succession to the Portuguese throne in 1580. The rapid expansion of Dutch shipping to distant destinations in the 1590s—to Indonesia via the Cape and to various Atlantic destinations—suddenly broadened horizons. The events in Middelburg must be seen against this background. In fact, the debate in 1596 shaped the 250 years that followed. On the one hand, it confirmed that slavery was not to become a Dutch institution: the principled opposition by mayor Ten Haeff meant that no slaves would be sold in Middelburg and that the slave-free status of the Netherlands was to be continued. This decision was guided by an existing institutional structure in which slavery had no place, and the Dutch were able to resist the temptation of gaining access to an extensive and relatively cheap source of labor.

On the other hand, however, the States General accepted the argument that property rights over the slaves brought to Middelburg should be respected, that the slave owner had the right to regain his "property"—or, at least, to gather the enslaved again by force—and to take this property with him to places where slaves could be sold. In a way this was consistent with the judgment of the Great Council of Mechelen. After all, it had stipulated only that slaves brought to the Low Countries had to be released, and there had been no judgment on slavery in general. This double standard—sometimes summarized as "preacher in the Netherlands, merchant over the border"— would become characteristic of the Dutch attitude toward slavery. We have already seen that in Asia, from the first contacts around 1600, slave labor was used by the VOC without moral misgivings. In the Netherlands, concern was expressed about this by the *classes* (councils) of the Reformed Church in Walcheren and Amsterdam, who in 1628 and again in 1629 condemned slavery in various terms. Amsterdam's *classis* wrote that it was "not Christian to own slaves," and Walcheren was even more to the point in judging that the keeping of slaves "by the Christians in the East Indies was unedifying and impermissible."[47] However, the Reformed Church council and its pastor in Batavia defended slavery as an institution that belonged in Asia, just as the pursuit of freedom belonged in the Netherlands, and with that the discussion regarding Asia came to an end for the time being.

The VOC quickly learned to deal with the special situation arising from the two separate moral codes and institutions surrounding slavery. VOC employees were prohibited from taking enslaved individuals back with them to the Netherlands. As households of VOC employees and other free citizens often owned dozens of slaves, it was difficult for them to part with the services they provided. After 1652 it became customary for those returning to the Netherlands to take their slaves with them to Cape Town, where they could be sold at a good price. In exceptional cases, when a household really could not do without a slave (for example, a wet nurse), there were special, high "passenger" fares for bringing slaves, but special permission still had to be obtained in advance.[48] The authorities were equally disapproving about bringing a concubine from Asia. In this way, double moral standards became spatially institutionalized.

In the Netherlands there remained, nevertheless, an undercurrent that was critical of slavery in the VOC and WIC spheres of influence. In his well-known travel account, Dierik Ruiters charted in 1623, as one of the first to do so, the extent of slavery in the Portuguese trading empire in Africa and Brazil and, on the basis of his personal experiences, spoke out strongly against this institution. In 1628, the WIC (founded in 1621) asked the church councils of Walcheren and Amsterdam for advice on the issue of slavery, before deciding whether or not to enter the slave trade. The strongly worded response was perfectly clear.[49] The theological underpinnings were supplied by Pastor Festus Hommius of Leiden, who argued that slavery was a direct violation of the teachings of the scriptures that prohibit stealing. The WIC then appointed a committee to study the issue, after which nothing more was heard about it.[50] Having buried the religious objections, the WIC felt free to actively engage in the slave trade.

According to Pieter Emmer, criticism faded into the background after 1630, when the WIC really started to concentrate on expansion in Brazil, where it could not manage without a substantial and regular supply of enslaved Africans.[51] Most of these Africans were put to work on the plantations that the original Portuguese owners continued to operate—reluctantly—under Dutch rule.[52] Although the Dutch were latecomers to this trade, from the 1630s onward they increasingly succeeded in obtaining a share in the triangular trade between Europe (the Netherlands), western Africa, and Brazil, and later Surinam. But all this was taking place far away from the Netherlands and largely out of sight of most Dutch people. Occasionally the WIC was criticized for its participation in the slave trade, but there was no real resistance, and in time theologians developed other arguments—for example, the story of Ham, the cursed son of Noah—that vindicated slavery with the authority of the Bible.

The Dutch share in the slave trade can be seen in the summary of the Trans-Atlantic Slavery Project, which has gathered all available data (table 6.1) of the slave trade between Africa and the Americas. These figures will always be underestimates of the true volume of trade flows since not everything was registered, but they do give an impression of the participation and shares of the various European powers in the slave trade. The sheer size of the trade immediately catches the eye. Already in the sixteenth century—the initial phase—the Portuguese had shipped around 280,000 slaves from Africa, an average of 2,800 per year, which corresponds to the population of a rural town in Europe during this period. In the seventeenth century the numbers increased to a maximum of close to 30,000 slaves per year, owing to the English, French, Dutch, and Danish joining the trade. The Netherlands' share in the slave trade was relatively modest: only for a short while in the mid-seventeenth century—the 1640s (during the failed colonization of Brazil, with its plantation economy), around 1660, and again in 1670—was the Netherlands the largest trader of slaves, although this cannot be seen in the period averages because in the other years of the period the Dutch were far less active.

According to these data, a little over 550,000 slaves were transported by Dutch ships to the New World, but these are minimum estimates. The

TABLE 6.1. Numbers of Enslaved Persons Traded by European and American Countries (Atlantic Trade), 1501–1866, Totals per 25 Years, Numbers of Embarked Persons

	Spain	Portugal/Brazil	Great Britain	Netherlands	American Colonies	France	Denmark/Baltic	Total
1501–25	6,363	7,000						13,363
1526–50	25,375	25,387						50,762
1551–75	28,167	31,089	1,685					61,007
1576–1600	60,056	90,715	237	1,365		66		152,373
1601–25	83,496	267,519		1,829				352,844
1626–50	44,313	201,609	33,695	31,729	824	1,827	1,053	315,050
1651–75	12,601	244,793	122,367	100,526		7,125	653	488,065
1676–1700	5,860	297,272	272,200	85,847	3,327	29,484	25,685	719,675
1701–25		474,447	410,597	73,816	3,277	120,939	5,833	1,088,909
1726–50		536,696	554,042	83,095	34,004	259,095	4,793	1,471,725
1751–75	4,239	526,693	832,047	132,330	84,580	325,918	17,508	1,923,315
1776–1800	6,415	673,167	748,612	40,773	67,443	433,061	39,199	2,008,670
1801–25	168,087	1,160,601	283,959	2,669	109,545	135,815	16,316	1,876,992
1826–50	400,728	1,299,969		357	1,850	68,074		1,770,978
1851–66	215,824	9,309			476			225,609
Total	1,061,524	5,848,266	3,259,441	554,336	305,326	1,381,404	111,040	12,521,337

Source: Trans-Atlantic Slave Trade—Estimates database, SlaveVoyages, accessed March 21, 2022, https://www.slavevoyages.org/assessment/estimates.

actual numbers were much greater, perhaps as high as 850,000. The VOC's trade in slaves has been estimated by Van Rossum to be 37,854 to 53,544, but the total numbers needed to supply VOC establishments in Asia with slaves were much larger: somewhere between 660,000 and 1,135,000—much more than the WIC's Atlantic trade.[53] This trade was largely in the hands of Asian merchants and (former) VOC employees, who on their own initiative set out to supply Batavia and other markets with their "merchandise." In both East and West, slavery and the slave trade were big business; just how important their contribution was to GDP and the labor force will be discussed in chapter 8.

Conclusion

In this chapter we have analyzed four major institutional innovations or changes that were part of a transition to a new phase of capitalism in the Netherlands and abroad. Two of these were innovations of a domestic nature—the Wisselbank and the VOC's organizational model—while the other two were closely linked to overseas expansion: the creation and establishment of the new city and port of Batavia, and the use of slave labor.

With the establishment of the Wisselbank and the Bank van Lening, Amsterdam tried to steer the development of the financial sector in the right direction and, in particular, combat instability arising from speculation and manipulation of exchange rates. This was a great success, considering the Wisselbank provided a stable foundation for this sector until the 1790s. The Wisselbank and the Bank van Lening were also copied elsewhere (Sweden and England, for example), and these institutions became the forerunners of the central banks that today, just as then, seek to control and stabilize monetary and financial systems. And as already noted, the Wisselbank contributed significantly to the flourishing of the national and international financial systems, of which, in the eighteenth century, Amsterdam would become the pivot. In a sense this also created a paradox: instead of curbing speculation, the stable environment created through the Wisselbank eventually led to more speculation. We have already mentioned speculative trading in VOC shares. Despite repeated efforts by the States General to limit speculative trading, in Amsterdam a lively trade in futures developed that made it possible to speculate on a rise or fall in share prices. A well-known account of these speculative practices was recorded in 1689 by the Portuguese Jewish trader in stocks Joseph Penso de la Vega. He described an extremely complex market in which it was possible to speculate on movements in share prices in a variety of ways. Not only Dutch stocks and bonds but increasingly those of other countries and states were traded on the Amsterdam Stock Exchange. As we will see in chapter 8, toward the end of the seventeenth century there was a growing surplus of savings in Holland, and this surplus found its way into government paper from all surrounding countries. Large trading houses increasingly concentrated on organizing this market for international capital, enabling these houses to expand and become banks of substantial size; cashiers, who had been banned in 1609 (as competitors of the Wisselbank), also made a comeback. Financial capitalism was not banned from Amsterdam owing to the setting up of the Wisselbank, but its tendency to at times destabilize the economy was curtailed.

The transformation of the one-off trading company into a corporation with a long-term strategy and financial model was one of the factors behind the success of the VOC. The enormous investments in trading posts ("factories"), harbors, fortresses, and urban infrastructure that were made created a relatively stable and, compared with the competition, well-funded global commercial enterprise that for nearly two hundred years controlled large volumes of trade between Asia and Europe, and, at least as important, between Asian ports themselves. The formula introduced by Coen, by which profits from transactions within the Asian network were used to finance trade with Europe, remained successful until about 1680. The VOC also proved its flexibility by developing new trade flows: after the dominance of spices in the early years, textiles (silk and cotton) from India became increasingly important, followed by coffee and sugar (from Java) and tea (from China).

Two developments nevertheless undermined the VOC's long-term success. In the last quarter of the seventeenth century its inter-Asian trade network began to unravel, partly because Japan became increasingly isolationist and was no longer prepared to export its silver, which the company had been using as a means of payment in its trading transactions. More and more silver had to be shipped from Europe to Asia to make up for the shortfall. At the same time, the company changed its dividend policy. In its early years, the strength of the VOC had been to invest profits rather than distributing them to shareholders. In the eighteenth century, payment of high dividends became standard, even if little or no profit was made (see chapter 8).

The story of Batavia, where at first an attempt was made to establish a port matching the Dutch model, but also where this aim was abandoned at an early stage, is also more or less representative of other ports and settlements that were established in the process of overseas expansion. Cape Town experienced similar development, albeit its Dutch character was somewhat more resilient—yet there, too, slaves were used extensively to meet the high demand for labor. Competition with the indigenous San and Khoikhoi for land—people who, from a European perspective, did not hold clear property rights (they, of course, held a different view)—complicated things in no small way. Paramaribo was from its very beginnings the port of a slave-based colony. Only in New Amsterdam—later New York—did a tradition and a range of institutions emerge that continued to build on its Dutch heritage. The absence of slavery in the latter colony seems to be explained by an absence of large-scale production facilities. In Surinam and the Cape Colony, crops were grown for export to Europe and the supply of passing European ships. In New Amsterdam, the Europeans produced food for their own consumption and traded imported goods against whatever they wanted from the Native American population.

Our comparison of institutional changes prompted by the rapidly developing form of capitalism in which the Republic participated around 1600 shows, above all, that the "excesses" of capitalism experienced in the Republic were curbed, that the pursuit of short-term profit was restrained by institutional buffers, meant to ensure long-term thinking—generally with positive effects for the economy and society. Such corrections and buffers figured less prominently in its overseas expansion: nobody prevented the use of slaves, nor was the creation of "extractive institutions" impeded. There was, in a sense, a moral and institutional bifurcation within the Dutch economy and society. Dutch freedom was, at home, preserved and remained by and large intact. In Indonesia, South Africa, and Surinam freedom was severely constrained, even denied.

7

The Republican State and "Varieties of Capitalism"

Perhaps nothing was a more sensitive issue in the urbanized and commercialized Netherlands during the seventeenth and eighteenth centuries than the price of bread. Bread was by far the most important staple in people's diet—the potato did not become a serious competitor until after 1770. Increasingly, the middle classes ate wheat bread, while artisans and wage laborers sometimes ate rye bread and sometimes wheat bread. The really poor turned to gruel from barley or buckwheat as their staple, thereby avoiding the high milling taxes on wheat and rye.[1] For the majority of the population, the price of bread was therefore the most significant barometer of well-being: when grain was scarce—owing to wars that hindered supply or to poor harvests—the price of grain shot up and dearth threatened. If enough grain circulated on the market, the price of bread could remain low and the purchasing power of wages was relatively high. Indeed, then there was perhaps even room for some luxuries.

High grain and bread prices could also lead to civil disorder and rioting, even higher mortality, undermining political stability. For the urban authorities of the Republic it was therefore important to regulate the price of bread and to intervene if things threatened to get out of hand. In the Middle Ages, most cities of western Europe had developed forms of intervention in the grain and bread markets in times of scarcity. One key instrument was bread-price regulation: urban authorities determined what the price of the bread should be or, using a slightly different approach, determined what, for a fixed price, the weight of a loaf of bread should be. The development of bread-price regulation in the Netherlands after the Revolt built on practices established earlier. Jan de Vries has written a splendid book about how that developed further in the Netherlands when important innovations were implemented after 1590.[2] The new system of bread-price regulation, introduced by Amsterdam in 1596 and subsequently adopted by almost all cities in the country, was based on a detailed reconstruction of the cost of bread from a mix of fixed and variable costs, the latter fluctuating with changes in the price of grain. In the rest of Europe, the regulation of bread prices compensated bakers not only for rising grain prices but at the same time for their unchanging fixed costs too, to the detriment of consumers. The Dutch system worked better because of its fine mesh, ensuring that the bread price benefited both bakers and consumers and that there were no incentives to deviate strongly from the official price. Furthermore, in times of shortage the market remained transparent, and increases in bread prices could be "managed"—by selling subsidized grain, for example, local authorities could keep bread prices reasonably well under control.[3] In part, this system also compensated for the fact that because of high excise duties and fixed costs, especially in Holland and Zeeland, bread was expensive. For municipal authorities there was a lot at stake, because food riots were a common phenomenon in premodern Europe. The remarkably low number of such riots in the two centuries following 1596 suggests the success of their approach, and this impression is reinforced by the observation that high food prices did not lead to additional mortality. Food scarcity, in other words, was very unpleasant but no longer lethal, as it still was in the Southern Netherlands and in France.[4] Regulation of the bread price also safeguarded a significant source of government income; excise duties on milling and duties on beer were the most important cash cows of the early Republic.

The bread market in the Republic was, therefore, even more regulated and coordinated than it had been during the Middle Ages, with a decisive role for urban governments. The grain market, on the other hand, was almost entirely unregulated (apart from a few taxes, and regulations on weights and measures). This illustrates how in the capitalism of the seventeenth and eighteenth centuries quite different forms of regulation existed side by side. A theoretical framework has been developed for the present-day economy that analyzes these "varieties of capitalism." The varieties-of-capitalism literature shows that there are decidedly different ways of organizing capitalist economies, which in practice may coexist and compete with each other. In their classic book on the topic, Hall and Soskice distinguish two basic models:

"coordinated market economies" and "liberal market economies."[5] Both are market economies, but in the coordinated variant government and various forms of cooperation among private companies—and trade unions and government institutions—play an important role. Germany is often cited as an example of the coordinated model, but generally speaking this also applies to the Scandinavian countries and the Netherlands and Belgium. In liberal market economies—of which the United States and the United Kingdom are seen as classic examples—the role of the market is much greater. Both models have their advantages and disadvantages. The coordinated market economy focuses more on the long term and is more stable, but for rapid innovation liberal market economies have the advantage.

These two models can be considered Weberian ideal types. Since 1980, for example, the Netherlands has developed from a "pure" coordinated market economy into a mixture of both types.[6] It has also been suggested that more than two models exist: a southern European, more family-network-based capitalism is considered to be a third type. Applying these concepts to early modern capitalism is not without risk, particularly as the context differs significantly. On the one hand, in the premodern economy the influence of the market was overwhelming—the cushion of the welfare state that has absorbed many hard knocks in the twentieth century was still largely absent (although not completely so, as we will see). The highly commercialized Netherlands seems almost like a paradise for entrepreneurs striving for unlimited profit. If we dig a little deeper, however, the role of government stands out across a broad stretch of economic activity—often even to the point of being directive, as the example of bread-price regulation demonstrates. In the previous chapter we also encountered strong government measures in the form of regulation of money flows (with the establishment of the Wisselbank) and the expansion of trade and shipping with the East and the West. The WIC and VOC were creations typical of a coordinated market economy. (In this context, for the WIC's and VOC's competitors the role of the states in their overseas expansion was often even greater.) Such interventions were, moreover, not those of a rent-seeking feudal state but those of a "modern," "capitalist" state that made innovative contributions to the commercial success of its merchant traders.

In order to interpret this mix of free market forces and government intervention and control, we must delve deeper into the character of the state in this period. The Republic, on the one hand, was perhaps the purest example of Karl Marx's dictum, boldly articulated in chapter 1 of the *Communist Manifesto*: "the executive of the modern state is but a committee for managing the common affairs of the whole bourgeoisie." The Revolt enabled the social group of merchants and entrepreneurs to consolidate their grip on power, which they did indeed use to defend the interests of "the whole bourgeoisie." On the other hand, the Dutch state was deeply rooted in society, through its manifold connections with civic institutions. In a monarchy, the court was in many ways a world unto itself.[7] In the Dutch Republic, on the other hand, the regions were more or less autonomous, as were the cities within them, and within these cities a substantial part of the population had citizenship rights and access to civil organizations.

Access to power was also relatively simple. We will show how that worked in practice in this chapter, where we examine three aspects of the political economy of the Republic: the constitution and social composition of the administrative elite, the involvement of the middle class in the governance of the economy through the guilds, and the manner in which the institutions of the Republic maintained a social safety net for the labor market. Our purpose is to demonstrate that for a state so connected to its civil society, a pure liberal market economy was not an option. In other words, the "new capitalism" that arose after 1600 had features that we now associate with coordinated market economies.

The State and the New Capitalism

The new capitalism of the seventeenth century, just like capitalism today, did not have a clear, unambiguous structure but was more like a barrel filled to the brim with conflicting interests. It was such a conflict of interests that came to a head during negotiations prior to the Peace of Munster (1648). For almost two decades, conflicting interests among the towns of Holland had held the province in political deadlock: those cities dedicated to European trade expected to benefit from a peace treaty with Spain, while its industrial cities feared competition, especially from the Southern Netherlands.[8] What was striking then—and still is today—was that the hierarchy of importance in political arenas was first local, second regional, and then—and only then— national. William Temple, in one of the best contemporary books about the Republic, *Observations upon the United Provinces*, from 1673, sums it up succinctly:

> To discover the first spring and motions [of their government], it must be taken yet into smaller pieces, by which it will appear that each of these provinces is likewise composed of many little states or cities, which have

several marks of sovereign power within themselves and are not subject to the sovereignty of their province.[9]

The state structure that evolved during the Revolt was meant, taking into account the international situation the Republic found itself in, to facilitate cooperation, especially military efforts, while at the same time allowing room for the pursuit of a variety of interests, including economic interests. This was accomplished through the division of administrative roles. Constitutionally it looked messy, but it worked.

As explained in the previous chapter, the army and navy were not only essential for the defense of the Republic's territorial integrity, they also played a major role in the creation, protection, and expansion of its trading empire. These tasks were entrusted to the central institutions of the state, the States General and the Council of State (Raad van State): the States General made policy and maintained contacts with foreign powers, while the Council of State was responsible mostly for implementing policy. Both institutions comprised representatives of the seven provinces that together composed the Dutch Republic. In the States General, each province had one vote, irrespective of the size of its financial contribution to the Republic's endeavors. The composition of the Council of State, on the other hand, took some account of the differences in size and prosperity. The central institutions of the Republic were, therefore, representative bodies of the provinces. Unanimity was required on important issues. Holland, as the largest and richest province, often determined the course to be taken, but if the other provinces worked together they could block Holland's plans. It was informally accepted that Holland could pursue its own foreign policy when that suited it. Indeed, the advocate of Holland (named "grand pensionary," a kind of prime minister) maintained his own contacts with the Republic's diplomats, and at the signing of the Treaty of Westminster in 1654 a separate and extremely controversial clause was secretly added that was signed only by Holland.

In addition to the States General and the Council of State, the stadtholders from the House of Orange also embodied the central power of the Republic, but in a manner that clearly indicates the limitations of the Republic's central institutions. Formally, the provinces appointed stadtholders. Usually the stadtholders appointed by Friesland and Groningen were different than those of the other provinces. Sometimes provinces even refused to appoint a stadtholder: Holland did without a stadtholder from 1650 to 1672 and again between 1702 and 1747. The powers of stadtholders were unclear and differed by province. However, the stadtholders from the House of Orange were also commanders in chief of the army and navy, and in that capacity they took part in the Republic's military campaigns, so they had a vested interest in strengthening the political core of the Republic.

A significant part of the state's activities were incorporated in public-private partnerships. Although the VOC and WIC are the best known examples of this, the army and navy also made extensive use of privately owned enterprises for recruitment, payments, and provisioning. A high level of discipline was a notable feature of the Republic's army, which can be largely attributed to regular payment of its soldiers. While in other countries soldiers sometimes waited years for their pay, Dutch troops were usually paid on time. This was due to the efforts of *solliciteurs-militair*, in fact bankers who supplied commanders of army units with the money needed to pay their troops. That money was to come from the provinces' payment offices, but those offices had to contend with their own cash-flow problems. When cash was in short supply the *solliciteur-militair* came to the rescue and provided the unit commander, with whom he had a contract, with the necessary funds—at a price, of course.[10]

The provincial States provided the link between the local level, where much power to decide and act lay, and the institutions that had to guard the common interests of the Republic. Everywhere, meetings of the provincial States were attended by representatives from city and countryside. With the exception of the States of Friesland and Holland, these two elements, city and countryside, were in balance. In Friesland, each of its three rural districts had one vote, while the eleven Frisian cities (towns, actually) together had only one vote. In Holland, on the other hand, the predominance of the cities was enormous: eighteen towns against one rural representative. The cities and the nobles representing the countryside sat alternately on behalf of their provinces in the Republic's institutions; in some cases the rotation of sittings was scheduled well into the twentieth century. The intention was, of course, to prevent these positions from becoming a permanent bone of contention. On the board of the Admiralty of the Meuse, located in Rotterdam, sat seven representatives for the southern part of Holland (one each on behalf of the nobility and the cities of Dordrecht, Delft, Gorinchem, Schiedam, Den Briel (Brill), and, of course, Rotterdam) and a member representing each of the other provinces, with the exception of Groningen.[11] On the board of the VOC's chamber in Zeeland, situated in Middelburg, there were nine representatives from Middelburg, two from Vlissingen, and one from Veere. From 1647 a representative for the region of Groningen was included.[12] In this way strong personal ties were forged among local government, national institutions, and companies.

The preponderance of local and regional interests over national interests was also visible in public finances. The States General had hardly any income of its own.[13] The main central source of income was duty on imports and exports levied by the Republic's five Admiralties, but these were once again composed of regional representatives—see the example of the Admiralty of the Meuse, above—who were known to often give priority to the commercial interests of their own ports, and expected the States General to make up any subsequent shortfalls in revenue. The central institutions depended mainly on contributions from the regions, where most of the taxes were levied, which in turn depended on collection at the local level. But extensive local powers to tax almost automatically could have led to free-riding, with some localities understating their ability to contribute. For many taxes, however, such free-riding was circumvented by setting quotas or amounts in advance: each town or village had to contribute a fixed percentage or a fixed amount to the total sum required. After Friesland had claimed for many years in succession that it could not afford to pay its quota of the "general means," as the Republic's common taxes were called, Holland garrisoned a few army units in Friesland, to avoid—as a lender of last resort—having to make up the deficit.[14] They made the Frieslanders pay in one way or another.

In Holland, which contributed nearly 60% of the general means, it was essential that a balance was found between local and national interests. This was achieved by leaving much to the initiative of the regents of the eighteen cities with the right to vote in the States meetings, while at the same time keeping them under close scrutiny. As in all of Europe, the Dutch tax system was fundamentally regressive, relying as it did primarily on excises that taxed daily necessities and thus affected the poor just as much as the rich. From the later seventeenth century, some efforts were made to mitigate the worst effects. We know from the eighteenth century that when a new poll tax was introduced, use was made of the social networks of the urban middle class to ensure a fair distribution of the tax burden. At the same time, for these types of taxes progressive rates were applied.[15] With the distribution of the most important excise duties in the Republic, measures were taken to ensure these had less impact on the price of (the cheaper) rye bread and more impact on the price of (the more expensive) wheat bread.[16] In 1679–80, reforms were implemented that shifted fiscal pressures from the broad masses to items that affected mainly the higher social classes.[17] This suggests that local authorities were trying to create broader support among taxpayers. But they, too, were subject to close scrutiny by the province. Holland's Finance Office demanded monthly statements of receipts, and from 1650 onward these were even published, to achieve maximum transparency and to demonstrate to the citizens of any one city that they were not being disadvantaged by another.[18]

A great deal of regulation and implementation in the Republic was left to local authorities, both in the cities and in the countryside. As long as neighboring cities, towns, and villages were not obstructed in any way, local elites could go about their business as they pleased. The way in which political elites were recruited also differed from place to place, between and even within provinces. In the east of the Netherlands, citizens had some say in appointments, while in the west they had only very limited input. From a social point of view, local governments, which sent delegates to the provincial States, who in turn delegated members to the States General and other central bodies, were drawn from relatively small groups of local elites. The revealing term used by contemporaries was "family government." In the modern literature, the term "patrimonial state" is used to describe it, or "familial state."[19] These terms cover two situations. One refers to the fact that political and administrative functions were not acquired through elections or bestowed according to transparent criteria, but through familial connections. The other refers to the situation in which companies, especially those engaged in colonial trade, were run by institutions that were half political and half commercial, connected through family links. The tendency to arrange matters in this way can be found throughout seventeenth-century Europe, including the Dutch Republic. What is peculiar to the Netherlands in such matters was the involvement of urban politics in this complex mix of interests.

In this environment entrepreneurs and elites, in particular, benefited from the economic boom. In Gouda, while the numbers of "capitalists" declined in the course of the seventeenth century, the size of individual fortunes increased.[20] Among the 250 richest inhabitants of the Republic in the seventeenth century, the proportion who lived in Amsterdam was strikingly large. Among them were quite a few who owed their wealth to expansion overseas. Some had made their fortune in high-ranking positions in the VOC: Cornelis Speelman (the 12th richest), Joan van Hoorn (13th), Cornelis van der Lijn (77th) and Willem van Outshoorn (132nd) had all been governors-general in Batavia, while Wouter Valckenier (25th), Rijklof van

Goens (50th), Constantijn Ranst (81st), Andreas Cleyer (137th), Leonard Winnincx (162nd), and Gerard Demmer (218th) owed their prosperity to other positions they held in the company. It is striking that expansion across the Atlantic in the seventeenth century did not produce the same degree of riches, perhaps because there was greater international competition in the market for slaves, as well as those for sugar and other tropical goods.[21] As we shall see, the average worker did not get poorer. Growing inequality was mainly the result of the increasing wealth of the upper class.

During the seventeenth century the spheres of business and government became more distinct.[22] This was mainly because the combination of private and public roles that had previously been common had become so time-consuming that it was no longer workable. A similar division of roles—for the same reasons—also took place within influential families: one son would be prepared for a role as public administrator, while the other found his place "in the business." An increase in the number of councilors with a law degree can be seen everywhere throughout the seventeenth century. In Leiden, the increase in numbers of lawyers began in the mid-seventeenth century. In Amsterdam this increase had begun even earlier. Of the thirty-two *regenten* (members of the ruling elite) appointed in Amsterdam between 1600 and 1619, only six had an academic degree, but of the thirty-nine appointed between 1620 and 1639, sixteen held a university degree. Toward the end of the century it was exceptional for a regent, in Leiden or Amsterdam, not to have completed university studies before being called to higher office. Such professionalization also meant that urban regents moved in increasingly small social circles. Ultimately, regent families had invested in public careers and they wanted to reap the benefits. Over the course of the century, fewer and fewer new families appeared on the scene.[23] The personal separation between state and capital can be seen in a list of the fifty richest Dutch citizens of the seventeenth century. Senior state officials and merchants are well represented in the list: sixteen senior officials and twenty-one merchants. The merchant-regent combination, however, was exceptional in this group of the superrich; only four persons in this select group were active in both politics and commerce.[24]

None of this alters the fact that the constitution of the Republic offered a great deal of scope for local and regional economic interests. The province of Holland, which had by far the greatest international interests, more or less pursued its own foreign policy. In the national arena, decision-making required lengthy negotiations in order to reconcile divergent local interests.

In 1638 François van Aerssen, the right-hand man of Stadtholder Frederik Hendrik, tried to explain to the French ambassador how this worked:

> The Prince of Orange is in a different position from the King [of France], who only has to express his wishes. Here one needs money to put ideas into effect and this goes slowly; it can be obtained only from the provinces . . . by a demonstration of some major advantage. . . . They can be led only by persuasion. . . . This cannot be done without much controversy and loss of time.[25]

It is easy to recognize in this complaint a shortcoming—a loss of time—but the policies that resulted from such consultations could count on broad support.

Entrepreneurship and the Guilds

Although the international reputation of the Dutch Golden Age draws primarily on the role that the Dutch played in world trade, the Republic was at the same time an industrial powerhouse in the period immediately preceding the Industrial Revolution. This was in part due to the fact that the Republic, and especially Holland, developed during this period into the most important region in Europe for industrial technological innovation. Two examples can illustrate this. In the sixteenth century there was no silk industry whatsoever in the northern Netherlands. It was set up in Holland by migrants from the south, who arrived there in the years following 1585; Amsterdam and Haarlem, in particular, became the focal points of the industry. A quantitative impression of the size of the industry is hard to come by, but according to the entrepreneurs themselves in Amsterdam in 1642 more than 20,000 people were dependent in one way or another on silk manufacturing. In a city of about 150,000 souls this was a surprisingly, perhaps even improbably, high proportion. By way of comparison, in Lyon in 1660 more than 3,000 people worked in the local silk industry; an equal percentage would have amounted to 7,000 silk workers in Amsterdam, significantly less than the 1642 claim. Whatever the case, that silk was an important product in Amsterdam is certain: in the period 1667–68 some 31,500 items made from silk fabric were exported from the city. Manufacturers in Holland introduced many new fabrics, such as *floers* (velvet), *lamfers* (crêpe), and *fulp* (deep-pile velvet), as well as new manufacturing techniques, of which the ribbon frame, or silk engine loom, was the most important. This loom, developed in Leiden in 1604 for woolen fabrics, was subsequently made suitable for silk in Haarlem, spreading from there throughout Holland to all of Europe.[26] By 1622, sugar had become another significant industry, even though thirty years earlier sugar refining was all but unknown in the Netherlands. By then, the number of refineries in Amsterdam had increased from three or four in the late sixteenth century to twenty-five. Several other towns in the Republic also had sugar refineries.[27]

Other new industries also emerged in the Dutch Republic during the decades around 1600. Papermaking developed rapidly in the rural Veluwe district in the middle of the country, where lots of clean water was available, with twenty-five active mills in 1625, rising to sixty in 1660, while in the Zaan area, north of Amsterdam, twelve paper mills were active in 1660. In the course of the seventeenth century, Dutch paper would come to dominate European markets.[28] The decaying textile centers of Holland were transformed, and by 1622, Leiden, with its forty-five thousand inhabitants—three times as many as in the mid-sixteenth century—had become Europe's second-largest textile center after Lyon, producing a wide variety of novel woolen fabrics.

These industries displayed a lot of innovation, technical as well as institutional. Patents granted by the States General rose to around ten per annum during the 1620s and 1630s, before stagnating at a much lower level of three to four annually during the rest of the seventeenth century, although some of the decline was compensated by an increase in patents granted by the States of Holland.[29] For many new developments, however, it made little sense to apply for a patent. Moreover, many innovations were incremental and also collective—that is to say, they emerged gradually within a certain industry, without one particular inventor being able to stake individual ownership of the new idea. Tellingly, we do not know which shipbuilder created the first *fluyt*, although it was possibly the single most important industrial breakthrough of the Dutch Golden Age. We do know who invented—and patented—the sawmill, but other industrial mills were developed anonymously. The rural Zaanstreek to the north of Amsterdam in 1630 was home to no fewer than 191 industrial windmills; in all of Holland there were, moreover, 86 sawmills and 73 oil mills. In 1595 a group of entrepreneurs patented a fulling mill with the States of Holland. After their patent expired in 1612 the innovation rapidly spread to other textile centers. The ribbon frame was patented in 1604, allowing the mechanization of the ribbon-making industry. Improved equipment was also introduced in soap boiling (1618) and leather printing (1628), to name just a couple of examples.[30]

Industry benefited from the high quality of human capital in the Republic. In Amsterdam at the end of the seventeenth century, three-quarters of men were literate and more than half the women were able to write their own name when registering their marriage banns.[31] Even before 1600, the inhabitants of the Low Countries—north and south—were considerably more numerate than the average European.[32] In addition, in the seventeenth century the number of higher education programs in the Republic increased spectacularly.[33] And training opportunities for practical trades also multiplied, both within and outside the guilds.[34] The abundant supply of skilled labor in the Republic was reflected in premiums paid to skilled workers being considerably lower in Holland during the seventeenth and eighteenth centuries than in the rest of Europe.[35]

Industry could also benefit from numerous and active entrepreneurs. Obviously, this was the era of small enterprise, and not every baker or butcher could be labelled an entrepreneur. But if we try to limit the class of entrepreneurs to those who were in a position to take "judgmental decisions about the buying and selling of goods and services," it has been estimated that around 12.5% of the workforce in the province of Holland might qualify. This percentage applied in the countryside as well as in Amsterdam around 1620 (somewhat arbitrarily, this excludes guild trades). Entrepreneurs presumably acted strategically and used external funding to finance their businesses. Data from Leiden in 1620 and 1660 and from Gouda in 1650, both industrial towns, show many builders and craftsmen among those who contracted loans through notaries (Gouda) or by registered annuities with the local aldermen (Leiden).[36]

Start-ups were often supported by local governments—although some of this might have been merely tempting businesses to move from one place to another. This tradition had already started in the late Middle Ages and was by no means unique to the province of Holland or the Dutch Republic, but can be found in many places. Still, the towns of Holland were remarkably active in this area, especially during the seventeenth century. During the 1610s, eight towns in Holland offered support to eighty-eight newly established enterprises. This support ranged from rent-free premises to subsidies or licenses protecting their markets. Perhaps most interestingly, entrepreneurs might be supplied with cheap or even free labor from the orphans cared for by municipal institutions.[37] In the 1680s, Huguenot refugees from France were offered support by various towns interested in their know-how in the silk and publishing industries.[38]

All this brings us, almost inevitably, to the issue of the role of the guilds in this capitalist economy.[39] The strong growth of the Dutch economy and population after 1590 was accompanied by an increase in the number of guilds, especially in the rapidly growing cities of the west of the country. Between 1560 and 1670, the number of guilds in Holland and Zeeland doubled from around 550 to 1,100. In the same period, the number of guilds in Groningen, Friesland, and Drenthe remained virtually the same, and even decreased in the remaining provinces, in a pattern resembling more or less the distribution of economic growth across the country.[40]

A lot has been written recently about the role of guilds and comparable organizations. Did guilds act as a brake on the development of the capitalist economy, or were they in fact a stimulus? Sheilagh Ogilvie, in many publications, argues that guilds blocked innovation and redistributed income for the benefit of a relatively small group of insiders—the established master craftsmen.[41] S. R. Epstein, on the other hand, has argued that, primarily owing to their role in the training of new generations of craftsmen, the guilds and their members were a link in the chain of technological advancement of European industry during the centuries leading up to the Industrial Revolution.[42] Both authors postulate a general thesis, but can we actually generalize in this way? The historical record of this period, including that in the Dutch Republic, is full of contradictory indications.

As associations of entrepreneurs, guilds could potentially contribute to the economy in a number of ways. They organized the training of craftsmen, they set standards for the quality of products, and they lobbied the authorities for measures that would benefit business. In addition, they had an important social function. In the seventeenth century a considerable number of guilds set up their own insurance funds. For a small weekly contribution, members were assured of benefits in the event of illness or death. Hundreds of guilds had such funds; in Amsterdam there were only two that did not. Amsterdam's council also actively supported guilds in this policy. For example, peat carriers were allowed to add a small amount to their bills to cover contributions to their insurance fund. As the peat carriers had a monopoly on the transport of peat within the city, their clients were forced to pay. In other cities this support was less extensive and insurance funds were also less common.[43]

Although in collective memory guilds have a reputation for being strange "clubs" that try to keep membership numbers as low as possible, this was hardly the case in seventeenth-century Holland: entry fees were low there compared with other countries. In Germany, guilds set requirements related to family, religion, and lifestyle—not the case in Holland's cities. Those who could produce a certificate of professional competence and were a citizen of the city could join a guild with little hinderance.[44] In Amsterdam, for example, membership of the bakers' guild was wide open for newcomers.[45] It can be deduced from records of Amsterdam's marriage banns and citizenship registers that about half the master bakers in Amsterdam came from Germany. These people would have paid 10 guilders for guild membership and—unless they were marrying the daughter of one of Amsterdam's citizens—on top of that another 30, and later even 50, guilders for citizenship rights. At the time these were substantial sums of money, which the city council used to finance its orphanage and other social services. Newcomers would, furthermore, have to demonstrate that they were competent craftsmen—for example, by serving for two years under a master baker, who also had to issue a certificate attesting to the candidate's good conduct. The main obstacle for an aspiring baker was not these formal requirements, however. Anyone who wanted to become an independent baker had to acquire a bakery. That required a substantial investment, and even those who had the necessary money could not just buy a bakery as these often remained in the same families for many generations. In spite of all these hurdles, it is significant that so many of Amsterdam's bakers were nonetheless of foreign descent.

It is equally significant that an even greater share of bakers' apprentices came from Germany.[46] Marriage banns show that in Amsterdam Germans made up 90% of bakers' apprentices. Not all of these apprentices will have settled permanently in Amsterdam. After all, in Germany it was a requirement in many places that a master craftsman had first to complete some years of travelling employment before his admission to the guild, a period in which the young craftsman learned the skills of the trade during a series of paid apprenticeships in various cities. In this way he became familiar with a variety of products and the techniques by which they were made. The rules of the bakers' guild of Aurich, which lies in Germany to the northeast of Groningen, stated in so many words that an aspiring master baker must first have worked in Holland for two years, followed then by another six months under a master baker in Aurich. This provision makes it immediately clear how closely the German and Dutch labor markets were intertwined. Some of these baker's apprentices would later also become masters in Amsterdam's bakers' guild, although the majority were destined for a life of wage labor.

The openness of Amsterdam's guilds was largely due to the attitude of the city council, which refused to facilitate discrimination. There was, for example, no guild in the diamond sector because many Jews were employed in it—they could not formally join a guild and would therefore have been seriously disadvantaged if such a guild were established. How different the situation was in cities in the east of the Netherlands. In the mid-seventeenth century, at the insistence of guilds and church councils, in which guild members often had a prominent place, ecclesiastical demands were linked to citizenship rights: new citizens had to be confessing members of the Calvinist Church. In Utrecht, such measures were explicitly aimed at disqualifying Catholics from citizenship. In the eastern regions, entrance fees of guilds for outsiders were also significantly higher than in Holland.[47] This may be one of the reasons why cities in the east hardly grew during the seventeenth century.[48] In Holland, on the other hand, guilds were asked for their opinions, they could also petition the local government on their own initiative, but they had no formal role in making the ultimate decisions.

That guilds, innovation, and economic growth went hand in hand is evident among the artisan painters.[49] Visual art is one of the economic activities of the Dutch Golden Age that still enjoys worldwide renown. The works of Rembrandt, Vermeer, and Hals belong to the canon of Western art. Nevertheless, just a few decades before these artists produced their masterpieces, painters and their works of art were of little significance in Holland. In 1570, cities such as Amsterdam, Haarlem, Leiden, and Utrecht each had a mere handful of artists, on average 3.3–3.4 per 1,000 inhabitants. In other cities (e.g., Delft and The Hague) this average was lower, even significantly lower, less than 2 per 1,000 inhabitants. In cities without a guild (e.g., Leiden and Dordrecht) the number of painters per 1,000 inhabitants grew slowly between 1570 and 1640, whereas the sector grew strongly in the decades following the establishment of guilds in Amsterdam (1579), Rotterdam (1609), Delft (1611), Utrecht (1611), and The Hague (1620, when its guild was reformed). Naturally, the creation of a guild was not the only stimulus: growth spurts took place in Delft in 1580, in The Hague after 1590, and in Rotterdam after 1600 without any institutional changes being made at the time.[50] Still, in this sector in which process and, especially, product innovations occurred frequently and where a high level of quality was achieved—to which the "Dutch masters" displayed in countless art museums around the world still attest—almost all those masters were members of a guild.[51]

In Holland, art was produced on an industrial scale, but it remained a craft-based industry. What happened in industries where the scale of production was somewhat larger? Leiden grew into one of the most important textile centers of Europe in the seventeenth century, with the focus on woolen fabrics. Thanks to immigrants from the Southern Netherlands,

"New Drapery" was introduced around 1600.[52] Woolen fabrics from Leiden were exported all over Europe. Guilds played a minor role in Leiden's textile industry.[53] But the city's administration helped small producers to benefit from international markets by setting up "halls," or markets, where cloth was provided with a mark attesting to its quality and passed on for international trade. In addition, these textile halls also functioned as banks for cloth producers, enabling small manufacturers to raise capital. Incidentally, "halls" were also introduced by other cities and for other industries—for example, the famous pipe manufactories in Gouda.[54]

The picture is equally mixed for shipbuilding. Major innovations had taken place in the fifteenth and sixteenth centuries in cities where the industry was organized in guilds.[55] This culminated in the development of the *fluyt*, a ship design that would remain dominant throughout the seventeenth century.[56] During the seventeenth century, some of the yards for building new ships moved to the Zaanstreek, a rural district north of Amsterdam where no guilds existed.[57] There, many innovations in woodworking techniques were developed. Nevertheless, the largest shipyards remained in the cities, with their guilds. In Amsterdam, both the local Admiralty and the VOC established shipyards in the mid-seventeenth century where hundreds and eventually more than a thousand people found work. These were the largest industrial workshops in the Republic. The most important workers in these yards were the ship's carpenters, who were organized in Amsterdam in their own guild.[58] Because guild members inevitably lived close to one another, on islands where their slipways were, they formed tightly organized communities. It is no wonder that their conditions of employment included long-term contracts and high wages.[59] Moreover, because ship's carpenters were all contracted employees, their guild functioned almost like a modern-day union.

When it comes to the economic role of the guilds, this period in Dutch history displays a mixed picture. Judging from experiences in cities in the east of the country, the guilds were indeed an institutional obstacle to economic development. In Holland, on the other hand, the increase in the number of guilds and their active participation in economic governance turned out to be compatible with growth, and there are indications that they also supported such economic growth. In the relatively exceptional industries where significant increases in scale were taking place, guilds as well as other models of organization could be found. There was clearly progress in levels and quantity of human capital, although this cannot be attributed solely to the guilds.

The guilds were, however, more than just straightforward economic institutions. In some ways, they were also miniature versions of republican society as a whole, and membership was an education in republican citizenship.[60] The guilds shared many features with other corporative bodies and in some sense with the Dutch Republic as a whole. These institutions of republicanism all had regulations (known as "privileges") that gave them a degree of autonomy.[61] They had their own sources of income and, thus, financial independence. The regulations stipulated that each institution be governed by its own board, which was elected from, and often by, the members, who were called "brothers" or "sisters" in the case of guilds and militias, and "citizens" in the case of cities.

In many corporative institutions, members or their representatives met intermittently and made decisions on matters affecting the entire corporative community. Republicanism, therefore, was more than just a type of constitution: it provided a complete model for society. For example, republicanism embodied an imprecise but nevertheless very powerful ideology, the basic tenets of which were captured in the word "freedom."[62] That word meant, then, almost the opposite of what we understand it to mean today. To be "free" in the republican sense meant "bound to the organization." The criticism of Philip II during the Dutch Revolt was that he curtailed that freedom. Since the medieval Italian city-states, no European state, with the exception of the Swiss Confederation, allowed so much agency to its corporative, or republican, institutions as the Dutch Republic.[63]

The fact that the Republic was able to develop into a technological hotbed was due to a combination of factors.[64] Of course, fast-growing domestic markets and exports abroad were helpful. As for silk manufacturing, everywhere new activities and techniques were being introduced by migrants and subsequently adopted and further developed by local entrepreneurs. This usually involved refinements rather than breakthroughs. There were relatively few obstacles to new technologies, and attempts to resist them were rare. The Republic was a literate society in which reading and numeracy were present in a large proportion of the population. Publishing enterprises thrived, making books and knowledge readily available. In other words, this was a society whose level of human capital was high. In addition, the authorities and civil society played an important role in the technological progress of the Republic: they regulated industries, certified products, promoted the training of skilled workers, and provided opportunities for sharing risk. In the Dutch Republic, capitalism and producers' organizations went hand in hand. In many respects guilds were part of the fabric of society, in its economic performance and otherwise.

Poor Relief and the Labor Market

One of the big questions is, of course, what consequences the economic developments we have described had for "labor." Karl Marx was convinced that in the mid-seventeenth century "the Dutch were more overworked, poorer and more oppressed than all other Europeans put together."[65] That sounds powerfully conclusive, but the evidence suggests that the situation was actually much more complex.

During the boom of the seventeenth century there was a huge demand for labor in industry and the services sector. Furthermore, there was the inevitable problem of poverty—inevitable because the demand was mainly for proletarian labor, while at the same time the labor market was quite unstable. Long-term employment contracts were the exception rather than the rule; many people were hired on a weekly or even daily basis. And seasonal fluctuations in labor demand resulted in significant unemployment during the winter months, while insurance against unemployment, sickness, and old age barely existed. Those who were confronted with such difficulties had to appeal for poor relief. In addition to responding to an economic challenge, the authorities saw poor relief as an instrument for promoting a sense of community, about which there were also concerns. The influx of immigrants and the new religious balance resulting from the Reformation undermined, contemporaries believed, traditional loyalties to local society. Poor relief counterbalanced such forces of disintegration.

Nowhere were such problems more visible than in the center of merchant capitalism, Amsterdam, a city that around 1585 was a magnet for migrants from all over Europe. The rapid growth of the city's population, from about thirty thousand in 1560 to more than a hundred thousand in 1622, and climbing further to two hundred thousand in the second half of the century, was entirely due to immigration. In the first quarter of the seventeenth century, perhaps as many as half the inhabitants of Amsterdam had been born outside the Dutch Republic. Many had arrived with the flow of refugees from the Southern Netherlands following the fall of Antwerp in 1585, which also led to enormous population growth and a transformation of the economy in cities such as Leiden and Haarlem. Overall during the seventeenth century, most immigrants came from Germany and to a lesser extent from Scandinavia. In 1685, the revocation of the Edict of Nantes led to a new stream of refugees to the Republic, this time French Huguenots.[66] Dutch cities attracted highly productive immigrants, which created a cumulative process of urban growth characteristic of the Golden Age—and a feature of dynamic urban economies in general, as, for example, analyzed by Krugman and others for contemporary urban systems.[67] Contemporaries were, at the same time, acutely aware of the potential downsides of migration, including the risk of impoverishment, which many Huguenots experienced.

An important source of information on labor markets is the registers of marriage banns of the city of Amsterdam. In addition to recording the place of origin of applicants, these registers often noted the occupations of the couple to be married. This also immediately points to a limitation of figures based on this source: for some occupations, marriage was difficult. Seafarers are a clear example of this, which means that their numbers are probably underestimated. Nevertheless, in spite of the "ifs" and "buts" we can still say a lot about the labor market in Amsterdam, which was dominated by first-generation immigrants, either from elsewhere within the Republic or from outside its borders. In certain occupations—for example, bakers—hardly any were born in Amsterdam: as we have seen, the labor market for bakers was entirely in the hands of German migrants. Sailors also often came from Germany, as well as southern parts of Scandinavia.[68] Of the latter, it has been shown that most grew up on farms. Their agricultural skills were useless in Amsterdam, but their muscle could be put to good use on board a naval or VOC ship.[69]

Many migrant men found work requiring little or no training. According to registers of marriage banns, this accounted for one-third of the jobs in Amsterdam in the second quarter of the seventeenth century. Because unskilled workers were generally less likely to marry than men in skilled occupations, the proportion of these jobs could have actually been as much as half. The Dutch also found work in the merchant navy and even signed up on VOC ships, although the VOC was not a popular employer because of the high mortality rate among its crews: during the seventeenth and eighteenth centuries probably only one-third of its one million European employees survived to return from Asia.[70] Migrant women mostly worked in domestic service, which provided work for an estimated twenty thousand people, predominantly women. In addition, many women probably worked in the informal economy; they sold fruit, drink, and other cheap products on the streets.[71] Some were active as prostitutes, as Lotte van de Pol demonstrates, "a necessary evil because of the large numbers of dissolute seamen in the city."[72]

Of course, how much individual workers could earn was highly dependent on the type of work and how often they actually had work. The modern-day labor market, with its large numbers of nominally "self-employed" workers, who in fact work under dubious contracts that make them essentially wage earners without stable employment relationships, is once again beginning to display characteristics of the premodern labor market. Pay data from that period suggest a continuity in employment that was often lacking in reality. Nevertheless, since wage data were collected in Holland and the Republic in the same way as in other countries at the time, it is still possible to make some meaningful observations about the situation in the seventeenth century.

The first thing to note is that nominal wages increased slowly during most of the sixteenth century but soared after around 1580. By 1600 they had already more than doubled compared with the situation in 1500 and by 1650 had even quadrupled. Then, around the mid-seventeenth century, growth petered out. In the western Netherlands this stagnation lasted until the mid-nineteenth century, when wages once again showed a clear rise.[73] Both skilled and unskilled workers benefited from this increase, as well as the master craftsmen who often employed these workers. But these advances were largely offset by increases in the cost of living. If we look at real wages, corrected for inflation, we see a sharp increase between around 1580 and 1620, followed by a sharp decline during the first decade after the Twelve Years Truce, when the economy was clearly faltering, and a second period of increase in subsequent decades—an increase that continued even until about 1700—mainly because prices began to fall in the second half of the seventeenth century.[74] Initially, workers particularly in the western Netherlands benefited from the increase in wages, but in the course of the seventeenth century the gap in purchasing power between the western and eastern parts of the country continued to shrink.[75]

These discussions about the development of real wages have for a large part been based on what men—often employed in the construction sector—earned. Nevertheless, women were also highly active in the labor market. Foreign visitors were often amazed at the economic independence of Dutch women who, as recent research has shown, were active across a broad front in the labor market. Even more extraordinarily, if they did the same work as men, they were also paid the same wage, as Elise van Nederveen Meerkerk has shown for textile spinners. The wages of women in this market were determined largely by the scarcity of labor—they benefited from the high demand for labor in the first half of the seventeenth century and were, thus, all the more affected by the slump in the labor market of the eighteenth century.[76] The structural disadvantage of women lay, however, in their access—or, more to the point, lack thereof—to other segments of the labor market. Most guilds were closed to women, and their education was not as advanced as men's, meaning that for the most part they had access only to low-skilled jobs, which paid relatively poorly. There were exceptions, however. A widow who continued a business that had previously been run by her husband was sometimes able to actively participate in some of the better-paid occupations.[77]

It remains a matter of contention whether wages really were higher in the seventeenth century than in the late Middle Ages. If daily and weekly wages are anything to go by, the differences cannot have been very great. It is even possible that *daily* wages were lower in the seventeenth century, but that *annual* incomes were higher. There are many indications that after the Reformation much more work was done each year, owing to the disappearance of dozens of religious holidays. It could just be that between 1530 and 1630 the number of days worked increased by fifty, perhaps as many as one hundred, per year.[78] However, the increase in the length of the working year can be interpreted in two ways: as welfare gain through higher incomes being earned, or as welfare loss because apparently more hours and days of work were necessary to earn a decent income. Throughout the seventeenth century, builders in Amsterdam were the highest paid laborers in Europe; in 1600 their colleagues in Antwerp were earning just as much, but by mid-century those wages had fallen behind.[79] An important explanation for these high wages was the high level of labor productivity. In the shipping industry, for example, improvements were realized between 1550 and the 1620s—coinciding precisely with the period of major wage increases—in the ratio of tonnage to distance traveled, on the one hand, and the size of the crews on board, on the other. This was the period when the Dutch developed their unmistakably successful ship design, the *fluyt*. This design stood out because of its favorable balance between large cargo space and small crew numbers, which was reflected in freight costs that decreased steadily. After 1630, the development of new ship designs stagnated and decreases in freight costs were much smaller.[80]

Despite the high level of wages, most workers were unable to earn a steady income, owing to the precarious nature of employment relationships. Short-term fluctuations—for example, due to weather or a personal setback—would result in an abrupt interruption of income. In a number of sectors, such as merchant shipping, the military, and—especially for women—textiles, pay was structurally so low that it was difficult at any time to keep one's head above water. Sooner or later many people found themselves in need of social support. Unfortunately, the organization of poor relief was just as precarious as the labor markets themselves.[81] There was, of course, nothing organized at the level of the national government: all poor relief was local. Only in Friesland were some provincial regulations in place, but these had no other purpose than to provide a framework for a system that was local in design and implementation. Villages generally had few amenities and usually exported their poor to the cities, which traditionally had a large number of institutions that dealt with poor relief in various ways. Some of these focused on the sick; for others it was the elderly; while still others were there for all the poor. In northern parts of the Netherlands most of the care was extramural—that is, the poor lived on their own and received support in cash and kind. The latter included bread, clothing, and footwear, and, in winter, fuel. Such support was never enough to make ends meet, as the example of Hendrikje Slackebaarts, a widow in Zwolle, shows. She lived with three children and her mother in upstairs rooms at the Broere church, which were made available to her for free by the poor board. Each week she received 8 stuivers (a stuiver was one-twentieth of a guilder) in poor relief from the city and another 4 stuivers from the Reformed parish because she was a member of that Church. In addition, her children each received a shirt from the city's poor-relief organization. Nevertheless, three-quarters of the family income was earned by Hendrikje through taking in sewing work.[82]

Hendrikje Slackebaarts's situation was typical for many widowed or abandoned women of that time. Everywhere they were overrepresented among those who had to depend on poor relief. In Zwolle, two and a half times as many women than men were beggars. More than 80% of those women worked in the textile industry, while for men the proportion was a little more than 25%.[83] In Delft, more than 50% of the female poor worked in the textile sector; for men the proportion was a bit less than 25%. The services sector was the source of income of another 25% of the female poor in Delft (the recourse for a comparable number of the male poor was enlistment in the army).[84] Delft and Zwolle were not ports, otherwise maritime shipping would have undoubtedly also featured prominently in these figures.

Almost everywhere, poor relief was funded from voluntary contributions. In Sneek, more than half the income of the poor-relief board came from church collection bowls. This transparent form of collection, where fellow citizens could see how much each was donating, amounted to an effective form of social coercion; the amounts collected remained remarkably stable throughout the seventeenth century.[85] In Amsterdam, voluntary contributions were also the main source of income for institutions providing for the poor. In 1638, an official of the Roman Catholic office for elderly poor relief received "the sum of five hundred guilders, which was brought to his house in the evening by someone who wished to remain unknown; on the bag was written the word 'charity.'" Two years later another official of the same institution received "a donation of fifteen hundred guilders, which money . . . in a bag thrown over the door to his house by someone unknown."[86] At that time you could buy a modest, middle-class house in Amsterdam for 1500 guilders.

Such events, but even more so the weekly donations raised for the poor all over the country in small amounts, tell us much about the value the bourgeoisie placed on providing a social safety net for their less-fortunate fellow citizens.[87] While religious inspiration was undoubtedly an important consideration, naturally such charity was also motivated by self-interest. Not in the sense that employers had the supply of labor in mind, but rather, it seems, that generous donors hoped that poor relief would help keep the poor pacified. This generally worked very well. In November 1630, however, food riots took place in Gouda and Leiden. Something similar happened in Haarlem on October 5, 1693, and again in the autumn of 1698 in Gouda, Rotterdam, Delft, and Haarlem. Otherwise it remained remarkably quiet in this respect in Holland throughout the seventeenth century.[88] Furthermore, the authorities and the urban elites were well aware that most of the poor were not idlers or spongers, and that for most of the year they contributed to prosperity by functioning as a source of labor. When in Amsterdam in 1681 it was proposed to impose stricter conditions on access to poor relief, the regents of the Nieuwezijds Huiszittenhuis, the municipal institution for poor relief, objected, saying that "this would lead to the exclusion of all sorts of laborers and seafarers." And yes, it was true that among migrants from elsewhere there were also some freeloaders: "The wheat is contaminated with chaff, but we leave it to the Lord to sift that out."[89] In other words, it was better to accept that sometimes money would also go to people who actually did not need it. Elsewhere, however, people were becoming less generous, as we will see in the next chapter.

In the seventeenth century penal workhouses were set up in several places, including Holland, to experiment with demanding compulsory labor from inmates in exchange for providing poor relief. The idea originated in England, where it spread widely. Subsequently, a prison-workhouse was opened in Amsterdam in 1596, and several other cities in the Republic followed suit in the twenty-five years that followed. Rasphuis and Spinhuis, penal workhouses in Amsterdam where, respectively, men rasped Brazilian wood for the paint industry and women spun yarn for the local textile industry may have been daunting institutions, but in quantitative terms their contribution to local poor relief was quite limited.[90] The vast majority of the poor had their own accommodation and were for the largest part of their income dependent on their own labors.

For the authorities, poor relief was a balancing act. On the one hand, the incentive to work had to be maintained, while, on the other, the Dutch economy was dependent on immigrants, especially in Holland, and it was the quality of social services that was part of Holland's appeal. Sailors were known to have purchased the citizen's rights of Amsterdam so that their children could have access to the city council's orphanage. There, they were better fed and received more training than they would in the almoner's orphanage, where children from poor families without citizen status ended up.[91] International comparison has shown that during the seventeenth and eighteenth centuries the western provinces of the Republic spent the highest proportion of their GDP—about 3%—on poor relief of all European regions. Although this percentage was lower in the eastern provinces, even there it was higher than the European average.[92]

Conclusion

It is often assumed that public authorities in early modern Europe were either uninterested in, or else incapable of, creating effective economic policies, other than imposing tariffs on foreign competitors. S. R. Epstein has argued that their most important contribution was to overcome the political fragmentation that inhibited economies of scale and made economic transactions more insecure.[93] This could, almost by definition, be achieved only by national governments. Local government was, in this take on the issue, a major part of the problem, if not the problem itself. Ogilvie has argued that most early modern authorities were likely to strike deals with republican institutions like guilds.[94] Both authors cast doubt on the possibilities of economic growth under such institutional regimes. Our analysis does not confirm their pessimism.

The new capitalism that had emerged in the Dutch Republic during the decades around 1600 emerged and flourished precisely under the circumstances that Epstein and Ogilvie have identified as the main handicaps of medieval and early modern economies: political fragmentation and a large role for local middle-class organizations such as guilds. Although we have not been able to find consistent evidence for the guilds' contribution to growth of all industrial sectors, we did find it in some. Moreover, and probably more significantly, we have not found consistent evidence that the guilds inhibited the Dutch economy's growth potential during its Golden Age. The country's economic performance improved while it was under the influence of strong civic organizations.

As Peter Lindert found for modern capitalist societies, this economic development coincided with the population having access to a range of welfare institutions.[95] Although these institutions offered a paltry level of support by the standards of the twenty-first century, they were probably better than what could be found in most contemporary societies. Welfare benefited workers in general, but females in particular.

Charles Tilly has observed that much state activity affecting economic development was related, in one way or another, to warfare. In his theory of state formation he distinguishes capital- and coercion-intensive paths of institutional development. While large agrarian states like Prussia and Russia were clear examples of the latter model, the Dutch Republic is presented by Tilly as the prime example of the capital-intensive route of early modern state making.[96] As we have demonstrated in this chapter, capitalism and state formation were indeed in many ways two sides of the same coin during the seventeenth century. The Dutch Republic supported overseas trade with money, arms, and privileges. Conversely, capitalists sorted out funding and other problems for the state's armed forces.

So, can we say that the Dutch Republic was an early modern example of a coordinated market economy as defined by the varieties-of-capitalism literature? Perhaps it is stretching the two models back in time a little too far, to make a meaningful distinction between liberal and coordinated market economies. In many regions markets were insufficiently developed to call them "liberal." And governments did not have the instruments then that they do nowadays, to claim a coordinating role in economic life. The distinction nonetheless serves a purpose, even for the seventeenth century. Long before the arrival of the "modern" state, capitalism was benefiting from institutional contexts that did much more than clear away obstacles and make room for private enterprise. Authorities in the Dutch Republic made policies that they hoped would benefit their citizens. Capitalists benefited more from those policies than workers or the middle classes, but workers and the "middling sort" were still benefiting from the economic boom. The institutional makeup of the Dutch Republic, moreover, gave much agency to the local communities where ordinary people had most to expect from policies that would benefit them too. How they would fare under less favorable circumstances is the topic of the final chapter of this book.

8

Capitalism and Inequality in the Eighteenth Century

No dimension of inequality is more compelling than inequality in mortality rates. One occasion when this became apparent was during the Christmas flood of 1717, which struck mainly in Groningen and neighboring Germany, claiming more than ten thousand lives. It was the deadliest storm surge in recorded history in the North Sea area. Most victims came from the poorest strata in the Groningen countryside. Groningen's agriculture was already a capital-intensive business that used a significant amount of wage labor. In the self-image of the Dutch, the solidarity that grows from the struggle with water is a popular theme, but when that struggle became a matter of life or death, as in Groningen in 1717, the fate of the poor was often different from that of the rich. What made the difference was the construction of the house in which people took shelter—was it solid and, if so, was it made of stone or was it a hut of wood and grass sods—and where it stood, whether on safe, high ground or low and close to a dike. Storm surges created many more victims among the poor than among the rich.[1]

In essence, a major criticism levelled at capitalism is that as an economic and sociopolitical system it leads to ever-increasing inequality. It produces inequality between the social groups involved in the production process—the small class of capitalists and the large group of workers, or, in our example, the gentry and capitalist farmers of Groningen and the agricultural laborers without significant assets. This issue came to a head in the eighteenth century, by which time the Republic had experienced centuries of economic growth. In chapter 1 we saw that this polarization in the distribution of wealth played a key role in Marxist thinking on the emergence of capitalism. Today, when we talk about social inequality, we are often talking about another, albeit closely related, dimension of inequality—the unequal distribution of income. Both forms of economic inequality tend to increase during the process of economic growth, as Piketty, for example, has shown for later periods.[2] Similarly, Scheidel claims in his world history of inequality that growing disparities are "normal," and that only external shocks—warfare, pandemics, the collapse of the state, and revolutions—act as "great levellers."[3] This is the first layer in the criticism of capitalism: its undeniable benefits will always be very unequally distributed. For this reason, we begin this chapter with the question: By how much did inequality of income and wealth increase in the early modern period? Did economic growth lead to polarization, to the disappearance of the middle class, as Marx's *Verelendung* hypothesis maintains? Was the increase mainly an urban phenomenon, the result of the unequal distribution of profits earned from international trade, or did this process also have agricultural roots and were similar developments to be found in the rural countryside?

The second layer of criticism concerns the sociopolitical consequences: growing inequality undermines citizenship and civil society and stimulates corruption and rent seeking. After all, in highly unequal societies the checks and balances needed to combat corruption and other forms of rent seeking may be absent. To use the concepts developed by Acemoglu and Robinson, were the inclusive institutions that had once facilitated growth now replaced by extractive institutions that suppressed growth?[4] Is there systematic evidence that morality was undermined by the opportunities for greed created by the market economy?

The third layer of criticism argues that inequality undermines the basis of capitalism itself. Van Bavel argues that the egalitarian socioeconomic relations from which capitalism emerged, as highlighted by the new institutional economics (North, Acemoglu, and Robinson), are undermined by the inequality resulting from capitalist development. Capitalism, like a Moloch, devoured the "children" it produced, something that in the long run would even lead to economic and sociopolitical stagnation, drying up the capitalist impulse. Van Bavel's wavelike view of capitalist development is based on this mechanism: economic polarization leads to bad governance and rent seeking, which results in economic stagnation, if not decline.[5] Do we find evidence for this in the Netherlands during the seventeenth and eighteenth centuries?

These issues gained in urgency because the winds of fortune that had been propelling the Dutch Republic forward during most of the seventeenth century were changing direction in the eighteenth. For a variety of reasons, the Dutch found it increasingly difficult to maintain their economic leadership in the world economy, while at the same time economic growth was slowing down. These changes forced various economic sectors to change course, but they also added a new edge to the distribution of wealth and income.

We have structured the argument of this chapter as follows: First we focus on the development of inequality of wealth and income, asking how strong the increase was in the seventeenth and eighteenth centuries, and whether this points to the disappearance of the middle classes and the rise of extractive institutions. Next we review the pattern of economic development in the eighteenth century, paying special attention to the growing importance of the plantation economies based on slavery, as this plays such a large role in the current debate about capitalism. Other sectors that became more important during the eighteenth century were agriculture and finance. Whereas growth in the sixteenth and seventeenth centuries had been broadly based on, and had resulted in, a rapidly growing demand for labor, in the eighteenth century it became skewed, dependent on a few major activities and without the same employment-generating impact, leading, in the long run, to a crisis in the urban system of Holland and Zeeland. Finally, we discuss the governance of the country, the opportunities for increased rent seeking, and the evolution of civil society.

Income and Wealth Inequality

We start with the bare facts about the evolution of income and wealth inequality. Did the Golden Age breed greater inequality? How unequally was economic growth distributed? There are good reasons to be pessimistic about this, as has been demonstrated by a great deal of research. The merchants of Holland, and in particular those of Amsterdam, became extremely wealthy during the period in which the country's role in international trade expanded dramatically. At the same time, real wages were at best stagnant, as the overview of real wage developments in Europe produced by Robert Allen has shown.[6] There is no doubt, therefore, that income disparities also increased, as has been confirmed by a reconstruction of the evolution of income inequality in Holland.[7]

In Europe during this period inequality was usually much greater in the cities than in the countryside. Urbanization—often the best indicator of economic growth—has a "natural tendency" to result in increased inequality at both regional and national levels. In 1561, a year for which we have excellent data on the estimated inequality of income distribution in the cities, towns, and villages of Holland, the Gini coefficient of the cities was 0.52 (for the richest city, Amsterdam, it was 0.55), whereas for the countryside it was 0.35, and for Holland as a whole 0.56.[8] By international standards this was not excessively high. On the basis of similar data, it has been estimated that the Gini coefficient for Holland was 0.50 in 1500 and 0.63 in 1732, indicating a substantial increase in inequality during the sixteenth and seventeenth centuries. The share of the richest 1% of the population increased from 10% of income in 1500 to 15% in 1732 (and 14% in 1808). Over the same years, the share of the poorest 50% of the population declined from 19% in 1500 to 12% in 1732 (and later to 11% in 1808).[9]

Data on the distribution of wealth are patchier, but display a similar trend. The share of households in Leiden possessing no taxable wealth increased from 76% in 1498 to 92% in 1722, while in the same period the top 1% of wealthy households saw their share of total wealth rise from 21% to 59%, clearly underlining the capitalistic nature of this industrial town, where people who are literally classified as "capitalist" in the tax registers were a small minority. Leiden, as the largest industrial city in the country, may have been exceptionally unequal; in Amsterdam the share of the people possessing no taxable wealth was slightly lower: 84% in 1631 and 79% in 1674.[10]

Two "capitalistic" developments explain the increase in income inequality. The first is the change in the functional distribution of income, leading to a divergence between wage income and total income. The share of wages in total GDP declined considerably, from an estimated 56% in 1500 to 41% in 1650.[11] Income from wages tends to be much more equally distributed than income from capital or land, and this decline in the share of wages had large consequences for total income inequality. The second development was the increase in wealth inequality, which also strongly affects income inequality. To sum up, income and wealth inequality in the Dutch Republic match the pattern predicted by critics of capitalism. There is no doubt that inequality of wealth and income increased substantially, and that the proceeds of the economic growth that occurred were distributed in a highly skewed way. Whereas in the fifteenth and sixteenth centuries the Netherlands was, by international standards, a relatively equal society, in the eighteenth century it began to match and perhaps even overtake its neighbors in its level of inequality.

International comparisons put these numbers into perspective, however. Near stability in real wages between 1500 and 1800 was already quite an achievement; in large parts of Europe real wages declined over the course of these three centuries. In other urbanized regions—Flanders and Italy—the upward trend in inequality was also present, but without a parallel process of economic growth, thus undermining the idea that growing inequality was caused solely by growth. There, wealth inequality also went up sharply, polarizing the social economic structure.[12]

An alternative and interesting method for comparing estimates of inequality for premodern societies has been developed by Milanovic, Lindert, and Williamson. They measure what they call the inequality possibility frontier, which indicates the maximum level of inequality possible in a country for a particular level of income (see figure 8.1, taken from their article).[13] The idea is that the higher the GDP per capita, the more "surplus" is available to be distributed unevenly. In very poor countries whose GDP per capita is almost equal to the "subsistence minimum," the maximum possible inequality will be much lower than in rich countries, which would have a larger surplus to distribute. Translated into the concepts developed by Acemoglu and Robinson: in societies characterized by extractive institutions, income inequality will be close to the maximum level, whereas in countries with inclusive institutions, the Gini coefficient of the income distribution will be well below the maximum level, thanks to the existence of a large middle class that benefits from the inclusiveness of the institutional framework.[14]

If the data on the income inequality of Holland and England before 1800—two pioneers of capitalism—are set against their inequality possibility frontier, it turns out that both countries were actually quite far removed from this frontier. The long-term trend displays, moreover, a widening gap between actual inequality and maximum possible inequality, while, in contrast, all types of noncapitalist societies, from the Roman Empire in 14 CE to Java in 1880, are much closer to the maximum (see figure 8.1). Income inequality far below the maximum level indicates the persistence of inclusive institutions and the vitality of the middle class, positioned between the poor and the elite. Inequality did increase, but by much less than would be expected on the basis of an "extractive" development path. Clearly, the middle class maintained its position within the income distribution and may even have increased in size.

There is a third angle from which to approach the issue of income inequality. The story of inequality in distribution of income and wealth is dominated by cities, where the greatest wealth (amassed by merchants active in international trade) and the greatest poverty normally existed side by

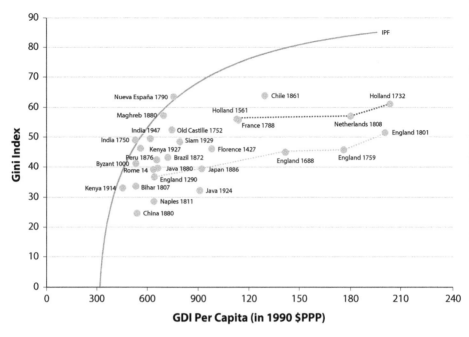

FIGURE 8.1. The relationship between gross domestic income (GDI) per capita (in 1990 dollars) and the Gini index of income distribution, showing the inequality possibility frontier (IPF). *Source*: Reproduced from Milanovic, Lindert, and Williamson 2011, 265.

side. This, however, overlooks the role of agriculture and the countryside in the development of capitalism. As we have explained in previous chapters, the Dutch countryside was by no means uniform, and there were considerable regional differences between coastal regions and the inland provinces, divisions still visible around 1800. Peaks in labor demand were solved in the coastal regions by hiring migrant workers from Germany, while the inland provinces, except for peat cutting, made hardly any use of such workers. Markets were well developed there, too—the inland provinces had wage labor, and interest rates on the mortgage and capital markets were almost as low as those in Holland—but there was less dependence on the market. In general terms, there was a direct relationship between the inequality of rural structures in different parts of the country and the extent to which the market economy had been able to penetrate them and agricultural productivity had increased.[15]

Data on the inequality of property distribution in the countryside around 1800 illustrate the differences between the "capitalist" agriculture in the coastal provinces and the "peasant" agriculture of the inland provinces. In

TABLE 8.1. Inequality in the Countryside around 1810

	Agricultural Labor Productivity (Netherlands=100)	Households without Cattle (%)	Gini Coefficient of Cattle Distribution
EASTERN REGIONS			
Drenthe	77	9	0.49
Overijssel	60	29	0.55
Gelderland	74	32	0.66
WESTERN REGIONS			
Holland	125	73	0.86
Zeeland	155	71	0.84

Source: Soltow and Van Zanden 1998, 63.

Drenthe, a province with a favorable land/person ratio, over 90% of the rural population owned some cattle, and the inequality of cattle ownership—a measure of rural inequality—was low (table 8.1). Zeeland and Zuid-Holland were at the other extreme, with less than 30% of rural households owning cattle, and a much higher Gini coefficient of cattle ownership. The regional differences in labor productivity ran largely parallel with this: labor productivity in the coastal provinces was at least double that of inland provinces (table 8.1). This neatly fits the Marxist prediction: where there had been a breakthrough favoring agriculture based on wage labor productivity increased sharply, while in regions where peasant farming was most common productivity rates lagged behind.

The coastal provinces were thus much more productive, but at the same time inequality was larger there than in the inland provinces. If we take into account not only income and assets but also a broader selection of indicators of prosperity, it is not evident that the higher levels of productivity in the capitalist provinces also led to higher living standards. In this respect, the northern provinces especially did well, at least judging by data from the first half of the nineteenth century (we have no comparable data for the years before 1800). In the north, inequality was relatively low (after all, the really rich lived in the western regions of the country) and life expectancy relatively high; by contrast life expectancy in the large cities of the Randstad (the agglomeration of major cities in the west of the country) was relatively low owing to the endemic prevalence of all types of diseases (table 8.2). Literacy was also high in the north, partly because of Protestant predominance, and extreme

TABLE 8.2. Ranking of Indicators of Standard of Living in the Provinces of the Netherlands, 1800–1850, Ordinal Scale, Ranking from Best (1) to Worst (11)

	Height of Military Conscripts 1821–28	Meat Consumption 1807–8	Infant Mortality 1840–51	Poverty 1850–51	Inequality 1808	Literacy 1813–19	Average
NORTH							
Groningen	6.5	7.0	4.0	3.5	2.0	2.0	4.2
Friesland	8.0	2.5	2.0	9.5	5.0	3.0	4.9
EAST							
Drenthe	1.0	4.0	3.0	1.0	1.0	1.0	2.3
Overijssel	11.0	7.0	6.0	2.0	3.0	6.0	5.5
Gelderland	3.0	5.0	5.0	3.5	9.0	6.0	5.6
Limburg	4.0	10.0	1.0	7.0		11.0	5.8
North Brabant	5.0	10.0	7.0	5.5	6.0	10.0	7.5
Utrecht	2.0	1.0	9.0	8.0	7.0	7.5	6.3
WEST							
Zeeland	10.0	2.5	11.0	5.5	4.0	5.0	7.1
South Holland	9.0	7.0	10.0	9.5	8.0	7.5	8.0
North Holland	6.5	9.0	8.0	11.0	10.0	4.0	8.1

Source: Noordegraaf and Van Zanden 1995, 419 (table 13.1).

poverty was relatively rare. Income levels were indeed highest in the western regions of the country, but owing to the much higher levels of inequality in the cities, as well as their unhealthy living environment, "broad prosperity" was lower than, for example, in Drenthe or Friesland. Incidentally, the data used for this comparison predominantly date from a time—the first half of the nineteenth century—when the cities of Holland were experiencing a crisis, and thus perhaps exaggerate this impression of the situation.

The figures from the beginning of the nineteenth century in table 8.2 suggest that the connection between economic growth and well-being is not straightforward. Did Holland fare relatively poorly here because of its polarized structure of wealth or that it was the most urbanized province and cities were in crisis at the time? As we will demonstrate below, the urban crisis was linked to the specific growth path of Holland in the eighteenth century, which did not lead to a strong growth of employment. Other provinces were in the long run better off, benefiting from the dynamic growth in the economy of Holland, without paying the price of high urbanization.

The Economy in the Eighteenth Century: A New Pattern of Growth

The patterns of inequality that we observe in the eighteenth century were not simply a result of the economic growth of the seventeenth century. In the eighteenth century, the Dutch economy underwent a number of important structural changes that affected social outcomes. It was almost inevitable that the Dutch leading role in global trade would not last forever. In the words of Immanuel Wallerstein: "To be at the summit is to be certain that the future will not be yours."[16] Wallerstein believed that this inevitability was the result of the increasing competitiveness of other states. Paul Kennedy saw it as an international relations problem. International hegemony comes at a high cost. The hegemon comes under pressure from all sides by countries that can benefit from the technological and institutional innovations of the hegemon's leading economy. Those countries are at the same time building their military potential. Opponents are becoming stronger and are many; the pressure they jointly exert will eventually become too much.[17] This problem did indeed affect the Dutch Republic in the eighteenth century, manifesting itself significantly in 1715, when the States General was forced to discontinue interest payments on the national debt for nine months and subsequently unilaterally lowered the interest rate on that debt. The Republic's bankruptcy made it clear that the financial limits of the state had been reached. In the opinion of Jonathan Israel, this marked the end of Holland's dominance in world trade.[18]

Scale was a major factor here. Despite its greater prosperity and capital strength, the Netherlands, with a population of roughly 2 million, was a small player on the world stage: the United Kingdom had about 6.5 million inhabitants, France no less than 19 million. In the past, the Dutch Republic had compensated for its relatively small size by taxing its population and resources more intensively; by the effectiveness of its state, army, and navy; and occasionally by sheer luck (escaping the fate of being fully occupied by foreign—mainly French—armies). European competitors had learned from these experiences, and caught up in all respects, increasing the pressure on the Dutch Republic. The English, in particular, looked to the Dutch Republic for inspiration in fiscal policy.[19]

Catching up by the neighbors goes a long way to explain the end of the Dutch miracle. Nevertheless, seen from close up, the Republic's economy did not perform so badly during the eighteenth century. Even the economy of Holland—long the driving force behind the Dutch economy, now hit extra hard by setbacks—continued to grow throughout the eighteenth century, thanks especially to the strong performance of its agricultural sector. Although industry did indeed stagnate, the services sector also showed a positive performance.[20] So the problem was not so much a shift from growth in the seventeenth century to decline in the eighteenth century but rather a structural change in the economy, an adaptation to new circumstances.[21] While traditional drivers of economic growth—from the Baltic trade to textiles and brewing—became less competitive for a variety of reasons, other parts of the Republic's economy grew in the eighteenth century: agriculture, trade with Asia, the plantation economy in South America, and the financial sector.

In the fifteenth and sixteenth centuries, agriculture seemed to be the weakest link in the Dutch economy: the country produced insufficient food to feed itself and had to import large quantities of cereals from the Baltic region to meet the demand for bread. The capitalist transition that the countryside and agriculture experienced did not herald the end of Dutch agriculture, quite the contrary. Stimulated by rapidly growing demand from the cities for agricultural products, which enabled processes of specialization and intensification, agricultural productivity in the coastal provinces displayed a gradual, but nevertheless strong, increase.[22] The stagnation in the growth of cities in the late seventeenth and eighteenth centuries allowed the supply of agricultural products to gradually outstrip domestic demand. Dairy farming had always produced in part for export, a pattern that was further reinforced in the eighteenth century when the growing English market became increasingly attractive. Specialized crops such as madder—a red dye for textiles, increasingly grown on the clay soils of Zeeland and South Holland—also made a significant contribution to export growth. These trends continued to the point that, in monetary terms, by 1800 agricultural exports completely offset imports. In the nineteenth century, a large export surplus would even arise (which continues to this day), and the agricultural sector developed into one of the strengths of the Dutch economy.[23] In the second half of the eighteenth century, when agricultural prices were rising again (after a dip in the 1730s and 1740s), the countryside also became increasingly prosperous.

In international trade and shipping—the mainstay of the Randstad economy—competition increased, mainly because of English expansion in this sector, but the Republic's position remained relatively strong until around 1780.

In the seventeenth century, the Republic had been leading the trade between Europe and Asia: more Dutch ships passed the Cape of Good Hope than those of all other European countries combined. In the eighteenth century, competition from English and, to a lesser extent, French ships increased noticeably, and by the end of the century English and Dutch ships were sailing this route in equal numbers. In spite of this, because Dutch ships were considerably larger they still carried more cargo to Europe.[24] The Dutch East India Company (VOC) continued to grow during this period, also in terms of turnover. In Asia, however, the balance sheet slid into the red, mainly owing to rising costs. For quite some time these losses were compensated for by income earned in Europe from goods brought back from Asia, but profitability was under increasing pressure.[25]

The VOC's strategy began to change, however—one of the most concrete examples of changing entrepreneurial behavior during this period. The success of the VOC in its early years, as we saw in chapter 6, was made possible by large-scale investment in a network of trading posts, a vast shipping fleet, sailors and soldiers, and fortifications to protect its activities. In the seventeenth century, dividend payments fluctuated from year to year, in step with results, but after around 1710 dividends were always paid out, even in years of poor performance. It looked as though the shareholders were taking more than their fair share. In years when losses occurred, dividends could be paid only by taking on additional debt. The burden of the debt, which had been minimal in the seventeenth century, continued to increase during the course of the eighteenth century.[26] As a result, funds available for investment in forts, ships, and crew steadily declined, and the position of the once so powerful company deteriorated. Maintaining control over production monopolies in the Moluccas and Ceylon (Sri Lanka) became increasingly difficult, and VOC employees became—illegally—more active in establishing their own trading interests, while the profitability of the company as a whole was declining. There was little or no knowledge of this outside the company: although it kept complex accounts from which these financial data could be reconstructed, it was "economical" with providing information about the actual state of affairs. During the tumultuous 1780s these problems became acute. Even so, the company continued to pay out dividends, presumably to give the impression that nothing was amiss. Ultimately, in 1799, all this led to the VOC being declared bankrupt, after being cut off from its Asian supplies for several years. External circumstances clearly played a role in its demise, but policies concerning debt and dividends, which could be seen as rent seeking, focused on short-term interests, also played a role.[27]

But in the eighteenth century the VOC remained extremely important for the Dutch economy, and it was by far the country's largest private employer. The VOC had always been dependent on foreign employees, but their representation increased further, rising from about 20% of its sailors in 1700 to approximately 50% by the end of the century. A similar increase took place among its soldiers, rising from 35% in 1700 to about 80%.[28] Low pay and high mortality made the VOC less attractive for Dutch employees. However, for German migrant workers, who had few alternatives and for whom the meager wages nevertheless provided purchasing power, the VOC remained an acceptable option.[29]

An even more important source of growth was the Atlantic plantation economy, based on slave labor on the so-called Wild Coast (Wilde Kust), the stretch of coastline between the Orinoco delta and the Amazon River, in particular Surinam.[30] In the 1660s this area had changed hands a number of times between the English and the Dutch, but in 1667, when it happened to be in Dutch hands, it was definitively allocated to the Republic under the Peace of Breda. Exploitation of Surinam was specifically undertaken with the foundation in 1683 of the Society of Surinam, a joint venture between the City of Amsterdam, the Dutch West India Company (WIC), and the wealthy Aerssen van Sommelsdijck family, which had noble pretensions and saw this as an opportunity to establish its own overseas fiefdom.[31]

The Society of Surinam created the infrastructure for the establishment of plantations that were to be operated under private ownership. The relationship between private and public actors was extremely complicated here, but the involvement of private investors, the semi-public WIC, and the City of Amsterdam was a clear signal that all parties expected to profit from the colony in some way. However, European migrants were very reluctant to take up work there. The only interest from inhabitants of the Republic was for managerial positions, and even to fill those posts it was necessary to regularly encourage people from other European countries to apply: only Portuguese Jews, French Huguenots, and Swiss came forward. The work on the plantations themselves was done by enslaved Africans.

At the turn of the eighteenth century, about 1,000 slaves were being transported from Africa each year to one of the Dutch plantation colonies in the Americas. That number increased to 1,500–3,500 by the mid-eighteenth century, and in the 1770s was sometimes as high as 5,000.[32] The increase was caused partly by the high rate of mortality among the enslaved, but also because they frequently escaped into the forests to join Maroon (escaped slave) communities hiding there. Maroons regularly carried out raids on individual plantations, and in 1757 they took part in a major uprising that took six months to bring to an end. A similar uprising occurred in 1763. Even then, this meant no end to the protests and attacks from the forests, where the Maroons regularly formed alliances with the indigenous peoples, for example the Arawaks and the Caribs.

As the plantation economy in Surinam grew, the impact of colonial, slavery-based activities began to be felt in the Republic too. Recent research indicates that—under certain assumptions—the Atlantic slave economy at its peak, around 1770, contributed about 5% to the income of the Republic and about 10% to that of the province of Holland.[33] For slavery in Asia, these figures are more difficult to calculate, in part because slaves in Batavia and other VOC establishments mainly served in households, and it is not immediately clear how such services would have contributed to GDP in the Netherlands. Slaves on the Banda Islands who harvested nutmeg are an exception, since they, like slaves in Surinam, did produce a commodity for direct sale on the Dutch market.

A different approach to get an understanding of the importance of the slavery-based sector is to calculate the proportion of the total labor force that was enslaved in the "greater Netherlands," which we can consider (somewhat arbitrarily) to comprise the Netherlands plus the VOC's establishments (including the Cape Colony) and the plantation economy of Surinam. Van Rossum has estimated the size of the slave population in the VOC's domains and the Atlantic region, on the basis of which it can be estimated how many slaves were economically active (assumed to be about 70% of the total).[34] The population sizes of Holland and the Netherlands are also known, and in normal circumstances the working population is about 35%–40% of the total population (the assumption being that women, children, and the elderly are not employed in the wage economy). Further, the large contingent of VOC employees (about twenty-eight thousand at its peak) also needs to be taken into account. Calculations based on these data indicate that in 1650 slavery accounted for about 6.8% of the labor force of the "greater Holland" (which would comprise all workers in the province of Holland and in Surinam, the Cape Colony, and the remaining VOC domains) and about 3.8% of the working population of the greater Netherlands. In 1770, at the height of Dutch use of slaves, these proportions are as high as 24% and 14%, respectively.

With calculations like this, the question is always: What is a lot and what is not? The proportion of 14% means that one in seven workers in the greater Netherlands economy were slaves—and six in seven workers were free. In the Dutch Republic itself the proportion of enslaved was zero, while in VOC settlements such as the Cape Colony 50% or more were slaves, and in Surinam the proportion was almost 100%. Whatever the case, one in seven workers suggests a higher contribution to national income than the recent estimates of 10% and 5% for the province of Holland and the Republic, respectively. The difference is partially explained by the fact that, curiously, the VOC was not included in the estimates of the share of slavery in GDP.[35]

In the seventeenth and eighteenth centuries, those parts of the economy based on forced labor were relatively dynamic—there are reasons why its share increased over time. In the seventeenth century the VOC was one of the drivers of economic growth in the Netherlands, while in the eighteenth century the Atlantic economy became one of the sectors to maintain a rising trend more or less right up to the 1780s. Indeed, Surinam and the slave trade there became increasingly important for the Dutch economy as a whole, and with that the issue of the presence of slaves on Dutch territory returned.

To grow, Surinam's plantation economy required not only labor but also capital. From the mid-eighteenth century, capital flooded into its economy, at the same time enabling financiers to gain control of the plantations. In 1753, Willem Gideon Deutz, a descendant of a banking family that had been active in the international financial markets for almost a century, launched an investment fund that focused exclusively on Surinam. Its initial activities were a failure, but soon the fund attracted millions of guilders, which were made available to consortia of plantation owners. In doing so, the profitability of those enterprises was not assessed too critically, and, in any case, was often difficult to predict. One of the reasons why plantations needed extensive credit was that it took years before the cultivation of tropical crops actually started to pay off. In the meantime, the owner had to go into debt to acquire his land and to buy slaves to work it. Deutz, and soon other bankers too, collected the money needed from Dutch private investors and savers and had to ensure the safety of those investments. They took receipt of the coffee and other crops produced to sell in Europe and, conversely, were also allowed to supply the plantations with provisions they needed.

Soon the bankers had a large say in the entire business, but because they were not familiar with the situation in Surinam this was not necessarily a good thing. The planters probably received far more credit than they could use, let alone repay. The Society of Surinam, which itself did not exploit plantations, made most of its earnings from import and export duties and other levies and did nothing to restrain investment. This was a classic bubble in the making—and it would soon burst. In 1773 it did just that. A new uprising of Maroons in Surinam and a financial crisis in Amsterdam together created a "perfect storm." From then on it proved difficult to run the plantations profitably.[36]

The plantation economies on the Wild Coast were thus heavily dependent on another element of growth in the eighteenth-century economy: financial services, and especially those dealing with governments.[37] The Deutz family firm was again a prominent pioneer in this. In the seventeenth century, Weduwe Deutz & Co had started to provide credit to the Austrian government in exchange for supplies of mercury, which it sold in Amsterdam. Investors in the advances provided by Deutz to the Austrian government were promised an annual interest rate of 5%. Those investors also bore the risk, although it is not clear whether they fully realized that Deutz took no responsibility for the security of the loans. Apparently, investors founded their confidence in the venture on the company's reputation.

At the beginning of the eighteenth century, the British government also began to draw on the large supply of savings available on the Dutch market. The surplus of savings was available partly because the States of Holland between 1715 and 1780 consolidated its debt position. English bankers based in London, often of Dutch descent, sold British government bonds in the Netherlands through a network of Dutch contacts. By 1770, of an estimated 250 million guilders of foreign debt held by Dutch investors, more than 200 million was invested in British government securities. Despite the low interest rates of British paper, they were popular because they were issued by Parliament and, thus, investors were not at the mercy of the unpredictable whims of a monarch. The Leiden textile entrepreneur and millionaire Pieter de la Court van der Voort, who in 1738 had invested more than one-third of his capital in English bonds, put it this way: "Whoever puts their trust in the promises of supreme powers [princes, the Bible, etc.] is often deceived." He had already sent his son Allard to London in 1710, where he had him make contact with Theodore and Jacob Jacobsen, "people known for their enormous wealth, as well as being very good people" according to the account of his travels. From then on, the Jacobsen firm looked after the investments of the De la Court family and various other Leiden capitalists.[38]

However, the supply of British government bonds fluctuated, and, owing to a lack of domestic opportunities, Dutch investors lent to other countries that were less creditworthy than the British. In particular, the French government, and later also American rebels, both of whom were at war with the British, began borrowing money in the Republic. This was just one of the bones of contention leading to the Fourth Anglo-Dutch War (1780–84). In the 1780s, income from interest on investments in foreign government bonds increased to such an extent that it was greater than income from investments in Holland itself.[39] This played out on the eve of the French Revolution, a crisis that would shake the entire continent and have far-reaching consequences for financial markets.

This overview, in combination with the GDP estimates discussed in chapter 2, shows that on the one hand the economy continued to grow—GDP per capita increased in the long run—but on the other hand the character of growth changed significantly during the eighteenth century. This is, of course, the fate of all market economies: their continued vitality depends on their ability to deal with growth and structural change, the rise and decline of new and old industries. The flowering of agriculture was bringing prosperity to the countryside and weakening incentives for structural change, and in the long run this had negative consequences for the kind of economic growth based on industrialization, the dominant paradigm of the nineteenth century.[40] Even more problematic is the other growth industry, international financial services, and in particular the exports of domestic savings abroad. It created a new income stream of the yield of those investments to the Netherlands, which might have crowded out competing industrial exports—an early version of the Dutch disease from the 1970s, which was based on export income from natural gas. Moreover, it was an activity that generated hardly any employment, while at the same time the demand for labor was shrinking in the textile and beer industries. It is no coincidence that among the middle class concerns about employment of the urban poor mounted. Until the early 1800s, the welfare system of Holland's cities was able to absorb the blows, but in the nineteenth century it was severely cut as part of the liberal reforms of the period.

The third dynamic sector, slave-based plantation economies and the slave trade, was in retrospect even more problematic than agriculture and international services. We have in chapter 6 already sketched the negative long-term effects for the societies involved of a system based on harsh, violent coercion; it is the ultimate negation of "development as freedom" in Sen's approach, the extreme "extractive institution" from the perspective of Acemoglu and Robinson. Growth occurred in the eighteenth century in the Netherlands, but slave labor made it clear that the costs of these structural changes were being passed on to "external" parties.[41]

Too Small, Too Rigid?

Investments abroad, in particular in the public debts of other European states, were problematic for another reason: they were seen by contemporaries as an indication that the elites had put their own interests above those of the country. Critics sensed very clearly that something had changed. An anonymous pamphlet published in Leiden in 1748, a period of political protest, described it like this:

> Until a century ago, people had their hands on the plow, and they did not seek to enrich themselves with the property of others. They did not need much, because then Leiden did not boast any of the gilded carriages now to be found in its streets. Then, everyone was commercially active and was prepared to work in the factories to keep them running . . . [while now] they indulge their uninhibited desires in regal homes and aristocratic feasts. I could tell you much more! Reformation! Reformation! If not, we will perish.[42]

This point of view was subsequently echoed by historians well into the twentieth century. They observed a reduction of numbers of elites in public office, a shift from entrepreneurial to rentier elites, and how these rentiers were increasingly investing abroad—starving Dutch firms of the capital to expand, it was argued.

There are indeed indications that from around 1700 senior positions in the cities and, therefore, also many high positions of state were no longer open to newcomers. In Zwolle, the number of new family names found among the city's regents began to decrease from the mid-seventeenth century, reaching its lowest point in the last quarter of the century; three-quarters of the councilors came from families that had previously held office in the city's administration.[43] A "new oligarchy" also emerged in Leiden during this period,[44] and in Amsterdam the number of newcomers in the city council had never been so low as it was between 1702 and 1748.[45] In Rotterdam, furthermore, no fewer than 83% of the city councilors appointed in the same period were either the son, son-in-law, brother-in-law, uncle, or brother of another councilor; in Hoorn the proportion was 79% and in Zutphen 67%. This was often the result of deliberate policy, which, in a number of cases, was even specified in writing, in a "contract of correspondence." In such a contract, local regents promised one another to give preference to relatives when filling vacancies. Nepotism seemed rampant. However, in the second half of the eighteenth century, the number of new families participating in city councils increased significantly when Orange stadtholders were reinstated all over the country—after being excluded from office for almost half a century—bringing the numbers of newcomers back to the levels of the first half of the seventeenth century. This change must cast serious doubt on the contrast between the two centuries.[46]

TABLE 8.3. Number of Merchants and Entrepreneurs among the 250 Richest Inhabitants of the Republic, 17th and 18th Centuries

	Position in Ranking				
	1–24	25–49	50–99	100–250	Total
17th century	11	14	20	59	104
18th century	12	12	24	58	106

Source: Data from Zandvliet 2018, 129–404.
Note: Widows of merchants, bankers, etc., are counted as entrepreneurs, but not their heirs.

The number of merchants and entrepreneurs among the 250 richest inhabitants of the Republic did not decrease noticeably, neither in total nor in their representation in various categories of wealth. Table 8.3 shows that among the top 24 richest inhabitants of the Republic in the seventeenth century, 11 were active merchants or entrepreneurs; in the eighteenth century this number was 12. Among the rich ranked just below the absolute top, the number of merchants and entrepreneurs remained likewise virtually unchanged. We should not attach too much significance to the exact numbers—there is no systematic source available to inform us about the capital of individuals—but the similarities in numbers for the two centuries are nevertheless remarkable and a refutation of the idea that the elite abandoned trade and industry.

In the past, elite families were also reproached for investing an increasing proportion of their assets passively, in public debt, at home and abroad, and no longer in companies that would have sustained the country's prosperity. Data for the seventeenth century are scarce, but a consistent pattern emerges from those that are available. During that period, urban ruling families in Holland invested their money mainly in real estate—houses and land; at most only one-fifth was of their money was invested in active businesses.[47] Trade and transport did not have an important place in the portfolios of these families in the seventeenth century, as it had done in the sixteenth century when many councilors were active businessmen. Starting in the second half of the seventeenth century, the share of government bonds in investment portfolios increased rapidly, often to more than half, replacing real estate as the most important source of investment revenues. This was directly related to the strong growth of government debt in Holland during this period. In the eighteenth century, foreign bonds also became popular with these investors. Although Dutch and British bonds offered a low interest rate, they provided a great deal of security.[48] In other words, whatever problems the Dutch economy experienced after 1700, it is difficult to see how they might have resulted directly from elite investment decisions. Moreover, the boom in plantation loans during the 1770s demonstrates that investors were happy to embrace opportunities when they emerged—even if those came at a considerable risk.

Would another economic policy have made a difference for the economic fate of the Republic? In the second half of the seventeenth century, several European governments had embarked on policies—generally referred to as "mercantilism"—to improve their country's prosperity. Opinions differ about exactly what "mercantilism" means, but whatever the case, the Republic noticed the consequences. Several wars in this period clearly had an economic dimension, in addition to dynastic and military-strategic objectives. Some had the clear objective of undermining Dutch commercial hegemony. The consequences for the Republic as an exporting and trading nation were quite negative. As a result, in the mid-eighteenth century there was discussion about whether to end the Republic's own free-trade policy, although ultimately it was left intact.[49] Undoubtedly, shifting the burden of taxation from heavy excise duties toward more reliance on customs duties might have relieved pressure on the cost of living and on nominal wages. Adam Smith had already identified this in his *Wealth of Nations* (1771) as the essence of the problem experienced by the most advanced economy of his time.[50]

It was not that contemporaries in the Republic became aware of the nature of their problems only through reading *The Wealth of Nations*. Those problems were the subject of constant discussion throughout the eighteenth century. That discussion had become urgent because of the towering debts the Republic had incurred during its wars against Louis XIV of France between 1672 and 1713. The burden was particularly heavy on Holland, which was the only province that had been creditworthy enough to run up debts on that scale.

By the beginning of the eighteenth century, the States of Holland was in serious financial trouble. The military expenses of the Forty Years' War between the Dutch Republic and France from 1672 to 1713 led to more than half the regular revenue being spent on interest payments on the national debt. As well as interest payments, in 1711, 1712, and 1713 prize money had to be promised to induce people to purchase securities: their bond also functioned as a coupon in these first state-run lotteries—a move born of dire necessity. In 1715 the States General could no longer meet its obligations, and for eight months nothing at all was paid out, followed by a unilateral interest-rate cut. In effect, this amounted to a temporary state bankruptcy.[51] Nobody could miss the signs that something had to be done.

In the seventeenth century, the Republic had set up an effective public-finance system based on the confidence of taxpayers and investors in the national debt. Above all, this trust was the product of the decentralized state structure of the Republic. Elsewhere, monarchs tried to strengthen the structure of their states through centralization, but for a variety of reasons this often backfired. The fact that the political elites in the Republic's state's assemblies themselves invested in its public debt was interpreted by investors as a sign of confidence: those regents would see to it that the system remained solid.[52] Even wider circles of the population, however, were directly interested in the national debt. In the absence of savings banks, broad groups in society invested their money in public debt paper. And they used those debt securities as collateral for other financial transactions, so the national debt also functioned as a lubricant for the entire economy.[53]

The authorities were aware of the need to maintain this public trust. In various provinces, among them Friesland, Overijssel, and Gelderland, representatives of the middle classes were explicitly involved in decision-making around fiscal measures. In Holland and Gelderland, entries in the tax registers were made the responsibility of the neighborhood representatives rather than the city council. In the eighteenth century, when the system was under great pressure, local officials decided to tax themselves and increase the tax burden for those with higher incomes (above 600 guilders). In this way everyone could see that the ruling class was also contributing to revenues.[54]

During the seventeenth century, there had been one other factor that played a significant role in the viability of the fiscal system: Holland took responsibility for the lion's share—58%—of public spending and carried nearly all of the Republic's public debt. By the eighteenth century, however, Holland became ever less effective in fulfilling the role of "linchpin" in the economy. Conflicts over public finances within Holland not only affected the province itself but also weakened the entire Republic because no other province was in a position to take over Holland's coordinating role.[55] In the second half of the eighteenth century, the Orange stadtholders attempted to do so, but that led mainly to cronyism, not to real reform.[56]

The overall quality of governance does not seem to have been undermined by the economic changes of the eighteenth century. Levels of cooperation between provinces on matters of taxation were fairly to very stable until the 1780s, when they were challenged by a revolutionary movement. Although the tax burden in the Netherlands was exceptionally high—especially in the province of Holland—only rarely did this lead to tax riots or other signs of reduced legitimacy. The elites made efforts to demonstrate their own contributions. A spectacular example of just this was the *liberale gift* of 1748: a levy of 1% on assets up to 1,000 guilders and 2% on assets above that amount. This tax was a response to a French invasion in 1747 and extensive riots against the system of tax farming in the wake of the invasion. The authorities responded by forcing the rich to pay twice as much as the middling- and lower-income groups.

More generally, after around 1680 the ruling elite was forced to recognize that the possibilities for collecting tax revenue through higher indirect taxation had reached a limit. Subsequently, taxation of income and assets increased, and the tax system in Holland became more progressive as a result. Obviously, the system of taxation in the Republic remained far from ideal. The fact that each province levied its own taxes, and within each province each city maintained its own privileges and customs in this matter, meant that the overall setup was inefficient from a bureaucratic point of view, allowed substantial variation in tax burden between provinces, and, as would become apparent in the nineteenth century, was one of the obstacles preventing further economic growth and unity. The breakthrough needed to create a national tax system would not come until after 1795, and even then progressed only in fits and starts. Local and regional privileges were some of the basic principles on which the Republic was founded.

Capitalism and Civil Society

In earlier chapters we argued that Dutch capitalism benefited from a strong civil society—from organizations such as guilds and civic militias—and from responsive local governments. Did structural economic change and increasing inequality undermine these civic institutions and by implication the quality of the society built around them? To start to answer this, we first look at a specific type of institution—the drainage board—which is considered particularly characteristic of the Netherlands and about which a relatively large amount is known.

We have already seen that in the late Middle Ages these bottom-up institutions arose for the management of water in low-lying parts of the country. Drainage boards are sometimes thought to be the place where the special version of Dutch democracy called the *poldermodel* took root. That, however, gives them too much credit, since they had no role in the parliamentary structure of the Republic. Nevertheless, drainage boards certainly facilitated the participation of broad groups in political decision-making in rural areas, and that in itself would have created societal resilience. The connection between drainage boards and democracy in the Netherlands is also happily made in the international literature. After presenting many examples of societies that collapsed because they were unable to find a solution to ecological challenges, Jared Diamond, in his *Collapse: How Societies Choose to Fail or Succeed*, ends by highlighting the Dutch "success story." According to Diamond, this can ultimately be traced back to the solidarity resulting from collective life below sea level, in a polder, where everyone had to contribute to keeping the water out.[57] But could this idyllic medieval cooperative withstand the rise of capitalism and the growing inequality that capitalism entailed? What did the rise of agrarian capitalism mean for the organization of water management?

Tim Soens, who studied water management in late-medieval Flanders, observed there a process of increasing concentration in land ownership and use that eventually led to a small minority of large landowners having decisive influence on the administration of the polders.[58] At the same time, the distance between the executives of the polders and the daily practice of water management increased. The newly wealthy in late-medieval Flanders saw land ownership as a commercial investment, so when the benefits no longer outweighed the costs they reduced their investments in dikes to a minimum, leading to neglected maintenance and numerous victims from the floods that resulted from this neglect. In the northern Netherlands, too— for example, in Groningen—the "communal" dike organization of farmers disappeared and a rural elite emerged that saw positions in the organization of water management as a family asset, at the expense of the quality of the water management. The seriousness of the 1717 floods in Groningen, the event with which we opened this chapter, was possibly a consequence of these changes in the administration of its water management.[59]

This pessimistic view of developments in the management of water can be countered with the fact that after 1580 the number of storm surges with serious consequences for the population and for agriculture decreased, and extensive land reclamation by draining land and impoldering began. Whatever the case, the Netherlands did not suffer from extensive flooding due to failing water management; 1717 was an exception, not the rule. However, Milja van Tielhof, after systematically describing the institutional development of water management in the Netherlands, has combined these two contradictory observations into a nuanced assessment.[60] There are indeed indications that an oligarchic administrative culture emerged in the drainage boards. In the sixteenth century, their meetings were public, and all stakeholders were invited to attend through announcements in church or by other means. Often those meetings took place in the open air, where every-one who wanted to attend could—and perhaps did, given the importance of the findings. After inspection of the dikes, a "verdict" was delivered on the spot: a decision was made as to whether each landowner had properly maintained her or his section of the dike or watercourse. Gradually, how-ever, these meetings had become more private in nature; according to Van Tielhof, the reason for this change was sometimes stated to be "that people with little land often had the loudest voice." Indeed, voting had often been on the basis of "one (wo)man, one vote,"[61] which meant that those with small holdings could collectively outvote the large landowners. Large drainage boards moved their meetings to the cities, in part prompted by the growing ownership of rural land by city dwellers and in part because city councils obtained seats on such boards. In the process, they may have made it more difficult for ordinary farmers to attend.

In the background, the commercialization of water management also played its part. Traditionally, each landowner with land alongside a dike was responsible for that part of the dike and was expected to maintain it with his or her own labor. From the sixteenth century onward, however, this traditional system was increasingly converted into an obligation to pay a tax—in proportion to the total amount of land owned—to meet the cost of maintaining the dike. Under this arrangement, not only the parcels located directly alongside the dike contributed to its maintenance but all land that it protected, even if that land was sometimes dozens of miles away. This "communalization," a logical consequence of the vigorous commercializa-tion of the countryside, provided greater flexibility and, ultimately, broader support. The broadening of support came, however, at the expense of direct involvement. Landowners now paid their taxes, and dike maintenance was outsourced to specialists—dike workers and contractors—who worked throughout the region on behalf of the water-management organizations—the polder administrations and drainage boards. This professionalization of water-management responsibilities helped to reduce the number of floods. Whereas, for example, in the sixteenth century a modest number of drainage board administrators had been illiterate, this had become unthinkable by the eighteenth century, and professional advisors and contractors were also hired to help maintain the infrastructure of waterworks. Executives of the polder boards came from increasingly smaller circles, and sometimes a par-ticular family would hold control over a polder for many years. The "broad participation" (the term is Van Tielhof's) that had been characteristic of the late Middle Ages deteriorated as a result of these developments, although the drainage board, certainly by the standards of the early modern period, remained an example of an institution with strong links to civil society.[62]

Guilds are another example of an institution with such links. The number of guilds grew considerably between 1670 and 1784, and as collectives they were successful in protecting the working conditions of their members.[63] Indeed, pleas from the guilds to protect "established" craftsmen were acted upon by the city authorities. Their employees, if they had any, were often also organized in servants' guilds (organizations of wage laborers, trade unions of a sort).[64] The effectiveness of these organizations is evident from the fact that from the mid-seventeenth century until well into the nineteenth century wages for skilled labor remained largely unchanged. However, behind this so-called wage stability all sorts of hidden changes were taking place: employers would adjust working hours to suit themselves, or would manipulate to their advantage a worker's secondary benefits. In times of economic hardship, for example, lower winter wages would be applied for longer periods and the higher summer wages for shorter periods.[65] In general, though, workers in this sector were able to defend themselves relatively well against the problems occurring in the industrial sector.

Craftsmen had the social capital to combat increased economic uncertainty through self-organization. This is evident from the increase in the number of voluntary social insurance schemes. Traditionally, this was a role that guilds fulfilled, but independent insurance funds for sickness and funeral expenses had already emerged in the seventeenth century. Their members were, certainly initially, often united on the same basis as guild members— that is, having a shared occupation. In a social sense these organizations were quite similar to the guilds, but formally they were independent. Their number doubled in the eighteenth century to just under five hundred.[66]

All this reeks of rent seeking. That impression is, however, contradicted by other data. In Amsterdam, access to the local guilds had been made a lot easier when, in 1668, a formal denizen status was introduced as an alternative to proper citizenship. This very cheap denizen status led to a substantial increase in the numbers of Amsterdammers with potential guild membership. The local tailors' guild between 1730 and 1811 recruited a third of its membership among German immigrants, and more Amsterdam tailors had been born elsewhere in the Dutch Republic than in Amsterdam itself. In the local surgeons' guild, not quite half of the members came from Amsterdam in the second half of the eighteenth century, less than in the population as a whole.[67]

Together these developments indicate, once again, that capitalism in tandem with republicanism had brought about numerous changes, but that those changes did not necessarily lead to an erosion of civil society, nor to a deterioration in the living conditions of ordinary people. In cities, for example, craftsmen could, through the guilds, prevent the burden of economic problems being placed unilaterally onto their shoulders. And although in rural areas the direct involvement of the average farmer in water management declined, the quality of its organization improved, to the benefit of all farmers. The distribution of the burden required to maintain it also improved. Local institutions proved, even after a century of flourishing capitalism, still to be socially resilient.

The strength of these kinds of local institutions was again evident in the 1780s, when the Netherlands, like other parts of the Atlantic region, was swept along by a wave of revolutionary movements that began with the American War of Independence in 1776. In the case of the Netherlands, its revolution is often portrayed as being fundamentally conservative.[68] Statements by both its supporters and the revolutionaries themselves tell a different story.

Over the course of the eighteenth century, many people in the Republic became convinced that the country was in decline. Criticism of those who were held responsible for this—once again, "the elites"—swelled to hurricane strength. Pamphlets and commentaries appeared, and in the 1770s and 1780s competitions were even held to establish what had gone wrong and offer solutions.[69] For a long time, all of this agitation did not trigger a political response. That changed as a result of the dramatic impact the Fourth Anglo-Dutch War (which broke out in 1780) had on the Republic. Suddenly, proposals for reform acquired a great degree of urgency and practical significance. A typical example of this was the appearance in 1781 of an anonymous pamphlet, entitled *To the People of the Netherlands*, that linked fundamental considerations about the causes of the decline with practical proposals for institutional reform.[70] It was written by someone who understood the art of sedition (much later it was revealed that the author was a dissatisfied nobleman called Joan Derk van der Capellen tot den Poll): the analyses were simple and recognizable to all. The work was distributed for free and "went viral." According to this pamphlet, the problems the Republic had to contend with were entirely due to one person, stadtholder William V. Fortunately for the pamphlet's author, there was no television in the eighteenth century, otherwise it would have been immediately obvious that the man who in "the media" was portrayed as a semi-tyrant was, in fact, a waverer who considered himself unfit for his high office, dominated by his wife, Wilhelmina of Prussia, and by his chief counselor, the Duke of Brunswick—both from Germany.[71]

One of the striking elements in the pamphlet is the emphasis it placed on the interests of trade, especially when we consider that the author was a nobleman from one of the inland provinces. The pamphlet included the following remarkable passage:

> The people who live in a country, its residents, citizens and farmers, the poor and the rich, big and small, together are the true owners, lords and masters, of the land and can say how they want to be governed. A people is a large society. The governors, the authorities, the magistrates, the prince . . . are only the directors, the administrators, the stewards of this company or society.[72]

In his following sentences, the author even compared the society of the Republic to the VOC, arguing that just as the Heren XVII ran the VOC, so should the country be run as a whole, with the directors acting on behalf of shareholders, as politicians should do on behalf of their citizens. And, so stated the pamphlet's author, when it came down to the citizens' economic interests, to which the directors had to pay attention, trade had to come first. In the mid-seventeenth century there had been no stadtholder and the country was run by urban elites such as Johan de Witt. At that time, according to the author, "commerce flourished more than ever, and everyone, big and small, prospered, both in the maritime and inland provinces."[73] The freedom then enjoyed by the inhabitants of the Republic brought out the best in them. Now, said the pamphlet, that freedom is threatened by the Prince of Orange and his military accomplices.

The second striking element is the emphasis placed in the pamphlet on corporative bodies as the institutional backbone of the republican state system of the Dutch Republic. According to the author of *To the People of the Netherlands*, ever since the ancient Germanic period the Dutch had been used to participating in decision-making through meetings. Guilds, militias, and sworn councils had for centuries undertaken the task, on behalf of citizens, of keeping a close watch on the conduct of the political elite. Together these organizations formed a dense network that shaped society, especially in the cities.

The pamphlet's impact was enormous. Not long after its distribution, mobilization of male citizens began on a large scale. In October 1782 some 1,500 inhabitants of Deventer signed a petition in which various demands were made regarding feudal service in the countryside (to be abolished) and the distribution of votes in the States of Overijssel (to be revised in favor of cities). The signatories totaled an estimated two-thirds of all adult males in

Deventer. At the beginning of December, the citizens of Deventer elected eight civilian commissioners who, together with four initiators of the petition, formed the first Patriot action committee of the Republic. Two new petitions were organized by the committee, this time calling for free city council elections to be held and for the recommendations usually made by the stadtholder for the composition of the council to be ignored. In short, these petitions were aimed at restoring the political autonomy of Deventer. Half the signatures under both petitions were collected through the guilds. The movement was, thus, firmly rooted in the city's republican structure.[74] In March 1783 a so-called *burgervrijkorps* (free corps militia) was established in Deventer, exactly according to the recommendations of *To the People of the Netherlands*. In no time the *vrijkorps* had about three hundred members, who practiced their military skills every week—as well as, in between their drilling, discussing the latest political developments.

The example of Deventer was soon followed in many other cities, towns, and villages, and not just in Overijssel. The Patriots, as they now called themselves, did not want to overturn the entire social order; they continued to operate within the framework of republicanism.[75] In 1785 they produced their own analysis of the problems facing the country: *Design to Make the Republic, through a Wholesome Association of City Regents and Citizens, Internally Happy and Strong on the Outside*.[76] In this pamphlet, which came to be known as the *Leids Ontwerp* ("Leiden draft," named after its place of publication), the form of government of the Republic was praised for having a "certain degree of virtue, of perfection, of even simplicity." According to the authors, the power of William V's court had increased to the extent that the Republic was suffering from excessive central coordination, with the result that civic institutions could no longer function properly.[77]

The Patriot Revolution progressed remarkably well, and in 1787 large parts of the country were actually under the control of people who, if not sympathetic to the Patriots, at least did nothing to prevent them from having their way. In May 1787 joint units of the *vrijkorps* even achieved a minor military victory, near Vreeswijk in the province of Utrecht, by chasing off a unit of the regular army. Total victory seemed within reach. That this did not come about was due to the intervention of the Prussian army. William V was married to Wilhelmina of Prussia, sister of the Prussian king, and since she refused to watch passively as her husband was gradually ejected from office, she persuaded her brother to send his army to the Republic at a time when the French threatened to intervene in favor of the Patriots. In September and October 1787, the Patriot Revolution was quashed without significant opposition.

Fearful of reprisals, thousands of Patriots fled abroad. Most of those who did not return home ended up in France. Given the leading role played by the guilds and civil militia, it is not surprising that among those refugees were many craftsmen and middle-class citizens—that is, members of corporative bodies.[78] Their flight could easily lead us to conclude—mistakenly—that there was little support among capitalists for society's corporative structures. In the 1780s Amsterdam was a Patriot stronghold, and even after the French invasion in 1794–95 its city council would for many years strive to preserve its guilds against French attempts to abolish them.[79] Their main motive for doing so was the preservation of local autonomy, which threatened to become subordinated in French efforts to create a unified state. Ultimately, this resistance by Amsterdam and many other cities in Holland would be in vain, but Amsterdam's attitude underlines once more that capitalism and corporatist republicanism could go hand in hand, even at the end of the eighteenth century.

Conclusion

There can be no doubt that the new capitalism that took shape in the Dutch Republic around 1600 not only propelled the country to center stage in the league of nations, but also radically changed Dutch society. The course capitalism in the Republic followed in this was, however, not always one that the literature would lead us to expect. Inequality did increase, but not linearly, nor to the extent predicted by critics, and the development of income distribution indicates the continued importance of a sizeable middle class. Moreover, it is not always clear which causes were behind the increase in income inequality. Urbanization was probably a factor; elsewhere in Europe, inequality increased with urbanization but without economic growth or capitalism.[80] The domestic working class benefited much less from the prosperity brought by capitalism than did the richest families; the real incomes of the employed did not decline much if at all, and in that respect the Netherlands contrasted favorably with the rest of Europe. In the globalizing world of the eighteenth century, the negative effects were mostly passed on to people outside Europe. Within Europe, migrant workers suffered from poor conditions of employment, such as those with the VOC, but the fact that those migrants continued to seek employment in the Netherlands suggests that things were no better at home.

Nor had capitalism dug its own grave. In the eighteenth century, the Dutch economy changed, but the sectors that provided growth—such as

the financial sector and the Caribbean plantations, as well as agriculture—
were and remained strongly market oriented. The Dutch also thought about
their own society in capitalist terms: they saw it as a "company," and politicians as "administrators" who had to perform their tasks on behalf of the
"shareholders"—that is, the country's citizens.

The institutions of civil society, which had such an important role in the
emergence of this new capitalism, turned out to be remarkably resilient.
Guilds continued to be a significant force in the cities, and in the countryside
institutions for water management generally functioned as they were meant
to. The latter was achieved in part through professionalization, a development
that took place at the expense of the participation of ordinary farmers. The
elites played a great, perhaps even an increasingly important, role in society,
and at times they tended to close their ranks to newcomers. But that, too, was
part of a general trend in Europe, with the emergence of absolutism as the
most extreme variant, under which the structures of participation that had
emerged in the Middle Ages, via communes and parliaments, came under
severe pressure. In regions that did not undergo capitalist development, in
southern and central Europe, opposition to absolutism was less successful
than it was in the core countries of capitalism, those around the North Sea.[81]

The top tier of the wealthy in the eighteenth century comprised as many
entrepreneurs as it had in the seventeenth; the idea that society had been
taken captive by rentiers turns out to be incorrect. The wealthy elites were,
moreover, quite aware of the social responsibilities they bore, something
they were vigorously reminded of on several occasions by rebellious movements rooted in society's corporative bodies. The Patriot movement of the
1780s was a strong example of this. Without the intervention of the Prussian
army, that movement might well have brought about a republican revolution
based on the corporative institutions that remained so dominant in Dutch
society, a revolution that would have had the active support of many elite
families, who still viewed local autonomy as the institutional cornerstone
of their capitalist system.

Slavery became much more important for the Dutch economy than it
had been in the seventeenth century. In Asia, slave numbers crept up slowly,
but in the Atlantic parts of the Dutch colonial empire the number of slaves
in 1775 was four times higher than it had been in 1700.[82] The dualistic way in
which the Dutch handled the institution of slavery did not change during the
eighteenth century. When in 1736 the Hoge Raad (Supreme Court) heard
the case of the runaway slave Claes, who had escaped from his captivity in
Curaçao by hiding on board a ship, the court judged that he was not to be

released, even though Claes himself argued that slavery was not accepted in the Netherlands and that he was therefore a free man. In putting his case, Claes's lawyer referred to the well-known judgment of the Great Council of Mechelen.[83] The Hoge Raad, however, ruled that theft was involved: the runaway slave, being property, had stolen himself. The court also argued that slaves were necessary for the colonies. The situation of a runaway slave was considered different from that of a slave accompanying a master who was returning to the Netherlands. In the latter situation—certainly if the slave had also converted to Christianity—the States General judged in favor of the ex-slave residing in the Netherlands.[84]

Another version of this decision was published by the States General in 1776. On the one hand, it emphasized that everyone should in principle be recognized as a free person, while, on the other hand, it also ruled that slaves who came to the Netherlands were to be freed only after they had spent six months in the country; with special court permission this period could be extended to twelve months.[85] This statement by the States General was probably inspired by the famous Somersett case (of 1772), which banned "chattel slavery" on English soil and led to the release of large numbers of slaves—in England, at least. The situation in the British colonies was left up in the air.[86] The case was the starting point of the movement to abolish slavery, even though the practice was to flourish in the years that followed. In England there had been an estimated fourteen to fifteen thousand slaves, which indicates that the issue for English society was much more significant than in the Netherlands, where it concerned at most a few dozen slaves.

The British abolition movement was motivated by the fear that slavery would irrevocably erode the right of personal freedom in Britain itself, as well as horror at the violence that accompanied it, in particular among religious minorities like the Quakers.[87] The Republic was more effective in protecting itself from such impacts: the VOC discouraged bringing slaves to the Netherlands, and jurisprudence gave a relatively large degree of room for the emancipation of slaves who set foot in the Netherlands, thus alleviating fears like the British ones of a deterioration of the traditional freedom of citizens.

9
Conclusion

Capitalism has increasingly been called into question in recent years, in particular since the global financial crisis of 2008—after such criticism had been pushed into the background during the 1980s and 1990s by a triumphant neoliberal ideology. By examining one of the first examples of a capitalist market economy, the Netherlands prior to 1800, we hope to contribute to the debate. The region followed its own development path within western Europe: it was relatively marginal in the High Middle Ages, being an "under-developed" marshy delta around 1000, and outside the foci of feudal growth in Flanders, northern France, and western Germany. But it participated fully in the wave of institution building and economic development (albeit from an initially lower level), and was, in its struggle against Habsburg Spain, probably better able than those core regions of medieval development to defend the medieval institutional legacy. Whereas in the rest of Europe the "republican" sociopolitical structures and institutions were increasingly suppressed by the rise of absolutism, the economic success story was this "latecomer," with its institutions rooted in the High Middle Ages but adapted to the new exigencies of the Golden Age. This continuation of republican constitutionalism was the real Dutch divergence during the seventeenth and eighteenth centuries.

The Netherlands was one of the pioneers of capitalism, with its economy, certainly in the west of the country, being predominantly market oriented as early as the fifteenth century. That orientation has never changed since, although, of course, as in any market economy, there have been fluctuations in the relative importance of the allocation of resources through the market and through other mechanisms, such as the state and the household.

We began our research with two major questions in mind: Where did capitalism come from, and how did it change society? To investigate these questions we have drawn on the case of the Netherlands, which is an instructive example for three reasons. First, the Dutch economy has shown a long upward trend ever since the Middle Ages. There were certainly periods when growth was slow, but over the longer term the economy has been growing ever since records began, starting in the mid-fourteenth century. Second, the Netherlands was an early adopter of the principles of the market economy. This is evident from the early development of capital, land, and labor markets, as well as from the massive levels of participation in those markets. Indeed, capitalism was not a phenomenon found only in cities, with their concentrations of trade and industry. It also extended to the countryside, where as early as the late Middle Ages farmers produced products for urban markets with the help of wage labor. Third, especially during the seventeenth century, the Netherlands was the leading economy in the world. During that period, Dutch ships dominated the world's seas and Dutch merchants spun an intercontinental commercial network in which grain, wine, spices, sugar, tobacco, porcelain, and humans were bought and sold. They developed new ways of doing business, the best known of which is the financing of commercial enterprises through the issuing of shares. There can be no doubt that the activities of the Dutch during this period were part of a budding capitalist economy. We have also shown in this book that in the Dutch context the Golden Age did not constitute a break with the past, nor with the period that followed. Rather, it was an intensification, an acceleration, of a process of economic growth that had begun centuries before and would continue for centuries thereafter. That observation enables us to understand both the roots and the consequences of that seventeenth-century boom as part of the emergence and ripening of capitalism as an economic system.

Following in the footsteps of Douglass North and the new institutional economics (NIE), we have examined this process of economic development in the institutional context in which it took place. In other words, our approach is that of political economy. Deviating from North and his colleagues, however, we understand politics to be broader than the narrative of property rights and representative institutions that many NIE authors tend to emphasize. After all, in a capitalist society, it is not only the capitalists who must be motivated to allow their economic transactions to be settled through the market: everyone must be encouraged to participate in commercial transactions. Distributing the returns from growth among a broad selection of groups provides them with an incentive to make an effort, to be creative, and to contribute in all kinds of other ways to a prosperity that can benefit them both as individuals and collectively as a society. As Putnam and others have shown, civil society in a more distant past had already created opportunities for large groups to participate in decision-making on social issues. And it is precisely in this respect that, next to continuous economic growth, we recognize a second constant. From the meeting of merchants in Tiel in 1015—reported by Alpert of Metz—until the French occupation in 1795, this corner of the European mainland was administratively divided into a large number of more or less autonomous units. That administrative autonomy turned out to provide an ideal environment for capitalist experimentation. Our analysis to a large extent concerns, therefore, the successes, but also the problems, of the interaction between these autonomous administrative units and the markets that functioned in them.

This brings us to the discussion of the origins of capitalism and its relationship to the social system that preceded it: feudalism. Historical "reality" is always more obdurate than the theories and models developed by social scientists would suggest. To begin with, the idea that feudalism was characterized by stagnation and hierarchical relations, by "extractive institutions," and thus by a lack of economic growth, has become questionable. Both Duby (for France, in particular) and British economic historians such as Campbell have emphasized how dynamic the "early growth" of the European economy was when, as from around 950, the feudal system was developing.[1] In England, this transition, which came about suddenly after the Norman Conquest in 1066, is most clearly marked in time; it led there to a sudden wave of surplus extraction and production, of which the boom in the construction of large churches observed by Buringh and colleagues is a striking example.[2] In the Southern Netherlands a similar, but more gradual—and over time also more far reaching—flourishing of the economy, particularly in the cities, was experienced during the expansion phase of the feudal system. The new forms of surplus extraction introduced at the time, such as tithes for the Church and banal rights for local lords, allowed the emergence of a relatively wealthy elite—concentrated in monasteries and castles—which provided a major impetus for the growth of international trade and the emergence, as yet on the margins of the feudal system, of cities. Just as England is a good example of this process within the dimension of time (with 1066 as the tipping point), the region that is known today as the Netherlands provides an excellent example of these changes within the dimension of space. After all, feudalism was not consolidated in the area north of the Rivers IJ and Ane, where "Frisian-Drenth freedom" predominated, with the result, unsettling for those who view feudalism as an impediment to growth, that the north of the country lagged behind the rest during the great wave of economic and urban growth between 950 and 1300. Although the Frisians dominated the region's international trade until around the year 1000, in the centuries to follow the "free" part of the Netherlands clearly lagged behind the development of the "feudal" region to the south of the major rivers, Meuse and Rhine.

There is another reason for reevaluating feudalism: the power of rulers and monarchs was limited. The feudal system arose from the disintegration of Charlemagne's Carolingian Empire, and the fragmentation of power that followed could be counteracted only when local lords could gain support from other parties, such as the Church, the nobility, and, especially, the gradually developing cities. Central to feudalism was the pledge of reciprocal allegiance between lord and vassal—the lord needed vassals to be able to go to war, the vassal needed the lord to consolidate and legitimize his local power. Such reciprocal relations also developed between monarchs and cities, through which the urban, mercantile bourgeoisie managed to establish a strong position in the sociopolitical balance of power, thus laying the foundations for a civil society that would become characteristic of the new sociopolitical terrain. More generally, the feudal balance of power was flexible and open—even bodies that regulated water management could establish for themselves a more or less independent position within it, to name a typically Dutch example. The consultation economy—so characteristic of Europe in the present as well as the past—was thus a feudal invention, which is also illustrated by the emergence of "states," or parliaments, in which the different social classes were represented and through which they negotiated with their rulers on matters of taxation and warfare.

We do not want to present feudalism as an institutional paradise. It was an effective system of surplus extraction, with the ruler, for example, claiming that he alone owned all the land. In economic history, feudalism has the image of being a strict hierarchical system. This is mainly based on the English model, where feudalism did not emerge gradually but was introduced by the Normans after they had conquered England in 1066, imposing their own version on a subject population (this trajectory would also lead to the emergence of a booming market economy).

Dutch feudalism, however, was positioned at the other end of the spectrum, owing to its geographic proximity to "Frisian freedom." For example, although the Count of Holland did claim "wastelands" (especially the dunes) to be his, he did not claim ownership of all land. This less rigid approach helped Holland to become the center for the transition to a market economy. In much of the available literature, as discussed in the previous chapters, specific environmental factors—the exploitation of the central cushion-peat bogs and the subsidence of the peat country that followed—are identified as important causes of the transition to a market economy that started in Holland. As a result of that transition, peasants came to own their land and managed to shed feudal rights and obligations, allowing them to respond as rational, market-oriented producers to the ecological crisis that slowly arose after 1370. This transition to a market economy was not accompanied by violence and took place in a society that, for a preindustrial society, was characterized by relatively small inequalities in income and wealth and, again by the standards of the time, a relatively high and rising level of human capital, as well as favorable relationships between men and women. From the flourishing of capital markets experienced in the fifteenth and sixteenth centuries, to which large numbers of the population had access, we conclude that there was a relatively high level of confidence in markets and institutions. The economic miracle of the sixteenth and seventeenth centuries must ultimately be attributed to this—that almost everyone, including women, could safely borrow and save money at low interest rates, which they did on a large scale.

The transition to a rural market economy occurred against the background of a European-wide "late medieval crisis," which had a variety of outcomes.[3] In the Netherlands this outcome was shaped by the simultaneous but unrelated ecological crisis that severely restricted the capacity of the regional agricultural sector to feed its own population. This had far-reaching consequences for agriculture, but also stimulated overseas trade, especially with northern Europe, and the building of a substantial fleet to fetch grain for Dutch markets. It also gave a boost to the levels of urbanization in Holland and Zeeland, because of the shift in the economy's center of gravity from agriculture to industry and services. Cities, as a result, also became increasingly important in political decision-making. Indeed, by the mid-sixteenth century the County of Holland had become something of a coalition of cities, whereby it was important that the urban landscape was evenly composed of numerous small towns and cities, and a limited number of larger cities, each with its own profile and dynamics (Leiden specialized in textiles, Delft and Gouda in brewing, Amsterdam in shipping and trade, and so on). The big difference between urban evolution in the Netherlands and northern Italy, Europe's other leading region at the time, was that in each region of northern Italy one city—Florence in Tuscany, for example—managed to acquire a dominant position at the cost of the independence and civil society of the other cities (in Tuscany, Pisa or Pistoia, for example). After 1400, this process of concentration of power in Italian city-states was accompanied by the gradual disappearance of the countervailing power of the communes. By contrast, in the Netherlands the cities remained in competition with one another, as well as with their ruler. This latter struggle forced them to cooperate, in spite of their diverging interests.

The cooperation between the cities of Holland and Zeeland provided the foundations upon which the Dutch Revolt of 1566 was built: without this bond they would not have been able to successfully wage war against domination by Spain, a country whose empire then spanned the world. The Revolt certainly displayed features of a "capitalist revolution" in the sense that the bourgeois elite of the country (mostly in the west) led and financed the resistance, in an at times uneasy coalition with the "proletariat" of seafarers, fishermen, and craftsmen, who provided the manpower and the revolutionary spirit. The bourgeoisie came to power, but—and here the comparison with a classic bourgeois revolution ends—it was in fact already in power prior to 1566, although it was at that time hampered and even undermined by the absolutist claims and interventions of the Spanish crown. The issue of religious freedom was symptomatic of the conflict, and as we have seen a solution for this was chosen—the model of the Calvinist Church, combined with religious tolerance—that satisfied the desires of the (urban) middle classes.

The Revolt was one of two developments shaping the "new capitalism" that emerged in the decades around 1600. The other important development was the establishment of a "world economy," initially under the leadership of Portugal and Spain. We have described this economic acceleration in terms borrowed from Braudel's thinking on capitalism. For him, capitalism is mainly associated with the great flows of capital that arose along with the emergence of the market economy, and with the nodes in the networks of those flows, occupied by bankers and merchants. Spatially, these networks show a high degree of inequality: there is a center upon which the flows converge, where capital and entrepreneurship are concentrated, and that center tends to move when more favorable conditions arise elsewhere. The economic boom in the Netherlands after 1585 was particularly intense because two shifts reinforced each other: there was a relocation of the economic center of the Low Countries from Brabant to Holland and, parallel to that, the economic center of gravity within the European economy was also on the move, from northern Italy to the North Sea region. This coincidental shift of the centers of both regional and European capitalism was further amplified by massive flows of high-quality human capital sparked by religious conflict (Protestant merchants from the southern Netherlands and Jewish merchants from the Iberian Peninsula).

The changes in the geography of capitalism, which, incidentally, were followed in the second half of the seventeenth century by a further shift of capitalism's center of gravity toward England, also help to answer the question of the relationship between cycle and trend in the growth of the Dutch economy. On the one hand, we see a trend of consistent growth in GDP per capita from about 1350 to 1800, the hallmark of a market economy in which new productivity gains are constantly being realized, albeit relatively slowly before the nineteenth century. Not even the environmental crisis after the 1370s, nor severe economic headwinds in the eighteenth century, managed to break this trend in growth. This is what one may expect from a market economy—and the process of consistent growth is one of the strongest indications that Holland functioned as a market economy. Growth happened across all sectors: in agriculture and trade, but also in industry. During the seventeenth century, the Dutch Republic, and Holland in particular, set the pace for technological progress in Europe. Growth in GDP per capita was also accompanied by improvements in well-being across a broad spectrum of social dimensions: education levels gradually increased, violence became increasingly the monopoly of the state, gender inequality was relatively limited (by preindustrial standards), civil society developed strongly, and, in cities as well as the countryside, various forms of political participation existed and continued to operate. Only life expectancy and health status did not develop favorably, probably because of the growth in the populations of cities, with their higher mortality.

On the other hand, the cyclical element in the growth curve—in particular the boom between 1585 and 1620—was mainly the result of the geographic shifts described by "Braudelian" capitalism, as a result of which the Republic suddenly became the center of the economy of western Europe and, in some ways, of global trade. This was, in particular, accompanied by demographic change—an acceleration of population growth due to mass immigration during the boom, followed by a slowdown in demographic expansion after 1670, when the economic center of gravity shifted to London. The first wave of "modern economic growth," as characterized by De Vries and Van der Woude, consisted of a combination of these two movements: the growth trend of GDP per capita and the rise and relative decline of the Republic as the nucleus of the capitalist world economy.[4]

These economic developments were underpinned by state formation. The downside of local autonomy was a lack of coordination. Before the Revolt, all autonomous units were ultimately dependent on a ruler, who had the symbolic authority and the real financial and military means to both provide protection and impose his will. That changed in the Netherlands as a result of the Revolt, which led to the creation of a state in which all those autonomous villages, towns, cities, and regions worked together, while clinging tenaciously to their freedoms. This was an important step. In the Southern Netherlands, capitalists were compelled to participate again and again in the dynastic "projects" of their Burgundian and, later, Habsburg monarchs, projects against which they repeatedly rebelled. In the Republic of the Seven United Provinces, a new scale and alignment of interests occurred simultaneously. The new state put all its might behind the capitalist expansion that took shape at this exact time. The stadtholders, who functioned as military commanders, were restrained and subordinate to the representative institutions.

This cooperation also enabled the Republic to assert itself militarily. The Republic's activities abroad would not have been possible without the systematic application of organized, large-scale violence. That, too, was organized in a capitalist manner—the VOC and the WIC were both trading companies and war machines at the same time. In Europe, economic motives were an important factor during the almost continuous wars. Although the stadtholders, as military leaders, used their troops on a few occasions to settle domestic conflicts, there was no support for permanent leadership based on military repression, and the stadtholders themselves rarely sought such conflict. There was no permanent government that could function as the "executive committee of the bourgeoisie." Indeed, in the Republic negotiation was constantly necessary to achieve political results.

At the same time, military might was an integral part of the capitalist expansion of this period, and despite its relatively small population the Netherlands grew into a military superpower in the seventeenth century. Within Europe, but much more so in Asia, Africa, and America, its army and naval fleet were used to open up new markets for Dutch capitalists. Violence was an instrument available for use in the capitalist expansion, and nowhere was this more apparent than in the slave trade and the extensive use of forced labor in Asia and the Americas. It is an exaggeration to say that "primitive accumulation" was a direct result of this particular form of exploitation, but it is evident that the slave trade and slavery were part of the capitalist repertoire.

In part because of the great military efforts required of it, the Republic was a perfect example of a society that combined considerable prosperity with high levels of taxation, with taxes carefully calibrated to give them legitimacy. It was for the latter reason that citizens were involved in establishing tax assessments. In the eighteenth century, taxes even began to show a modest degree of progression, forcing the richer inhabitants to pay a larger percentage of their income than did the poor.

The growth spurt from 1585 to 1620 also saw fundamental economic changes. In chapter 6, we analyzed the two most important ones: the advent of financial capitalism and overseas expansion. Before 1600 capitalism made use of well-organized financial markets, but had no banks, no bankers, and virtually no specific financial sector. With the arrival of this sector—initially from Antwerp—institutional innovations were introduced to curb its negative effects and to exploit for the common good the new opportunities that arose. We have outlined the Wisselbank and the VOC, as a share-based company, as examples of such institutional transformation. In other words, the new institutions were adapted to fit the circumstances of the Republic. These innovations were in all sorts of ways very successful. The Wisselbank contributed significantly to the stability of the country's financial markets, and the VOC was able to develop a long-term strategy that was the basis for its sustained success. In the process of expansion abroad, however, capitalism was not "contained" but allowed to develop without restriction; the trading of slaves on a large scale and the use of slaves in both the Eastern and Western Hemispheres are the best examples of this. We have argued that the insights from NIE help to explain the growth of well-being in a society with inclusive institutions such as the Netherlands. They also make clear, not only why slavery was a morally unjust institution (also from the perspective of the Dutch, who had lived in a slavery-free society since the late Middle Ages), but also why it created a society based on high levels of direct, personal violence that was doomed to stagnate in the long run. It is clear that many in the Netherlands understood at least to some extent these links, as they tried with considerable success to keep the home country free from this institution. One of the consequences of this was that slavery was not seen as a threat to the quality of Dutch society, helping to explain the lack of support for the movement to abolish it.

The Republic was a bourgeois society with a market-oriented, capitalist economy. To understand its development—and to answer the second set of questions raised in chapter 1, about the consequences of this capitalist breakthrough—we introduce here the concept of "the Low Countries' Paradox," recently outlined by a group of Flemish historians.[5] The "paradox" is that two developments that appear to be in conflict with each other nevertheless occurred simultaneously in the Low Countries. On the one hand, these authors observe a significant increase in social inequality between 1300 and 1800, but, on the other hand, during the same period the middle class seems to have continued to grow in numbers, and the related bourgeois values and norms to have remained firmly anchored in society. In other words, on the one hand the pessimistic prediction of Marxists that economic development in a capitalist market economy leads to growing wealth disparities between the rich and the rest of society is confirmed; on the other hand, growing city populations and an increasing degree of urbanization strengthened the position of the middle class and the civil society they supported.

Analysis of the development of income inequality in Holland in relation to the inequality possibility frontier indicates how the paradox can be explained. While inequality in Holland increased significantly between 1500 and 1800, at the same time the distance from the inequality frontier grew larger, an indicator of strong middle-class growth. The cities of Holland were, on the one hand, the drivers of higher incomes and greater inequality, but, on the other, the locus of citizenship and its institutions—and this continued more or less unabated, as the example of the Patriot movement discussed in chapter 8 shows. The transformation of the capitalist dynamic discussed in chapter 5 also played a part in resolving the paradox—the stability of the system was improved precisely by restraining the capitalist impulse with the help of institutional innovations such as the Wisselbank and the fixing of bread prices, and by the further expansion of the guild system. The specific variant of capitalism that emerged after 1600 had, as we have shown, characteristics that are similar to those of the "coordinated market economy" of the twentieth century.

Abroad, however, such institutional constraints were rarely, if ever, in force. There, Dutch capitalism showed its "ugly face." An institutional and, thus, normative duality was characteristic of the "greater Netherlands"—which we have demonstrated mainly through the case of slavery, something that was considered normal in the East Indies, South Africa, and Surinam (in fact, everywhere outside the home territory of the Dutch Republic) but was not accepted as a permanent institution in Dutch law, and this law was enforced within the Dutch Republic itself. The institutions within the Republic were and remained (on the whole) inclusive, while the institutions in the colonies were (on the whole) extractive. The freedoms of the Dutch were preserved; the freedom of the peoples of the East Indies, South Africa, and Surinam declined or disappeared altogether. One part of the "greater Netherlands" was on a path toward the Industrial Revolution of the nineteenth century and the modern economic growth associated with it. The other parts were destined to face difficult histories dominated by inequality, colonization and decolonization, and underdevelopment.

Dutch capitalism was rooted in circumstances that were also available to peoples in other parts of Europe: regional markets, urbanization, local institutions of self-governance, technologies that were increasingly easy to access. Two, however, stand out as specific to the western areas of the Netherlands. The first was the ecological bottleneck that was overcome during the late Middle Ages by a commercialization of the countryside and the expansion of overseas trade. This forced the Netherlands onto a path of early and intense market orientation. The second was the establishment of a federal state during the Dutch Revolt that left local autonomy intact. This gave the Dutch "punch" on the international stage, while maintaining the advantages of "agency" for (local) civil society and the economic activities that emerged from those local contexts.

NOTES

Chapter 1

1. The authoritative J. de Vries and Van der Woude (1997) looks at its subject from the perspective of "modern economic growth," a topic we will tackle in chapter 2 of this book. For earlier analyses of the Dutch economy from the perspective of "capitalism," see Wallerstein (1980, ch. 2), Gelderblom and Jonker (2014), and Bavel (2016, ch. 4).

2. Beckert 2014; Beckert and Rockman 2016.

3. Contributions to the *Cambridge History of Capitalism* do not systematically make this distinction either, so that it would appear that every premodern economy with market exchange (i.e., pretty much every premodern economy—only in the Inca civilization were markets absent) was a capitalist economy, thereby stripping the term of its distinguishing power (Neal and Williamson 2014; see also Prak 2015 and Temin 2015, 1003).

4. See the discussion on peasant economies, initiated by the research of Chayanov (1966; for Java: Zanden 2004).

5. Karl Marx, *Das Kapital* (1867), vol. 1, ch. 31; see also Lourens and Lucassen 1992, M. van der Linden 1997.

6. North 1981.

7. North and Weingast 1989.

8. Acemoglu and Robinson 2012.

9. Weber (1905) 2002.

10. Putnam 1994.

11. Zanden and Prak 2006.

12. J. de Vries 2014.

13. In connection with this, there is an equally complex discussion about how feudalism should be defined. Does feudalism, in essence, concern the exploitation of serfs/peasants working the land, in particular their labor on large-scale agricultural entities (manors), or does it concern relations in social-political structures for which reciprocity between lords and their vassals is central? For this debate, see Sweezy et al. (1978); also Epstein (2007) and Duplessis (2019, ch. 1).

14. Wickham 2021, 14.

15. Bloch 1961.

16. Reynolds 1994.

17. J. de Vries 2001b.

18. Wickham 2021; Duby 1974.

19. Duby 1974. See the discussion on the feudal economy in Epstein (2000, ch. 3).

20. Howell (2010) discusses all of these dimensions for the southern Low Countries.

21. Kelly 1997.

22. Smith (1776) 1986, 197–99 (quote at 197); Zanden and Van Riel 2000, ch. 1.

23. Brenner 1976.

24. Brenner 1976. See also the contributions in Aston and Philpin (1987).
25. Broadberry et al. 2015.
26. Mokyr 2018.
27. Lis and Soly 1979.
28. Piketty 2014.
29. For a critical review, see Burnard and Riello (2020).
30. Zanden 1993.
31. Bavel 2016.
32. Fisman and Miguel 2007.
33. Bowles 2016, 115.
34. Hall and Soskice 2001.
35. Zanden and Van Riel 2000; Zanden 2005.
36. Milanovic 2019.

Chapter 2

1. Paping 2014, 15–17.
2. Bavel and Van Zanden 2004.
3. Paping 2014.
4. Bolt and Van Zanden 2020; Maddison 2004. The underlying series presented in figure 2.1 are from Broadberry et al. (2015) and Malanima (2011).
5. Zanden and Felice 2019. For 1427 a set of new estimates based on the Catasto (Florentine tax register and population survey) of that year suggest that it was smaller than the estimates presented in figure 2.2 show, but that northern Italy was more wealthy than Holland or England is beyond reasonable doubt.
6. Zanden and Van Leeuwen 2012.
7. Prados de la Escosura and Rodriguez-Caballero 2020.
8. Zanden and Van Leeuwen 2012.
9. Bavel 2016; also Bavel et al. 2012.
10. Smith (1776) 1986, 197–99 (quote at 197); Zanden and Van Riel 2000, ch. 1.
11. J. de Vries and Van der Woude 1997.
12. Prados de la Escosura and Rodriguez-Caballero 2020.
13. Mokyr 2018.
14. Goldstone 2021.
15. Bavel 2016.
16. J. de Vries and Van der Woude 1997, 713, 715, 716, 720.
17. Zanden 2002a.
18. Pleijt and Van Zanden 2019.
19. The recent debate started with the *Report of the Commission on the Measurement of Economic Performance and Social Progress*, also known as the Stiglitz, Sen, Fitoussi report, published in 2009.
20. Sen 2001. Sen's work is followed up in the economic historical contribution of Zanden et al. (2014).
21. Buringh 2011.
22. Woude 1991.
23. Buringh et al. 2020.
24. Bloch 1961.
25. Buringh and Van Zanden 2009.
26. Pettegree and Der Weduwen 2019.

27. See the discussion of regional patterns of well-being, including literacy, in Noordegraaf and Van Zanden (1995).

28. Stanton 2007, 85.

29. Woude 1982.

30. Rommes 2015.

31. Cummins 2017.

32. De la Croix and Licandro 2015.

33. Kuiper and Olde Meierink 2015.

34. Maat 2005.

35. Meinzer, Steckel, and Baten 2018. A more detailed analysis of the Dutch data from this study can perhaps answer the question of to what extent trends in Dutch stature differed from those in the rest of Europe; see also the discussion of regional trends in table 8.1.

36. See Baten et al. 2014.

37. Van Dijck 2020.

38. Pinker 2012.

39. Trends in income inequality are discussed in chapter 8.

40. See Zanden, De Moor, and Carmichael 2019.

Chapter 3

1. For more information about this episode and, specifically, the merchants' guild of Tiel, see Akkerman (1962). For information on conflicts concerning (imperial) toll collection, see Verkerk (1998, 434–35); about Alpert of Metz and his writings, Rij (1999).

2. Greif 2006b, ch. 4; 2006a.

3. Following Head and Landes (1992).

4. The following impression of the Netherlands around 1000 is based on Mostert (2009) and Bavel (2010a).

5. Lewis 1982, 186; for the mission, 94–95.

6. Bavel 2010a, 63–75.

7. Steensel 2014.

8. The term comes from German sociologist Robert Michels and is discussed in Diefenbach (2019).

9. The classic text on this is still Slicher van Bath (1948); see also Langen and Noomen (1996) and Mol (2004).

10. Mol 2001.

11. Schaïk 2008, 207.

12. Schaïk 2008, 207.

13. Blok 1985, 144.

14. Tromp 1991, 179.

15. Tromp 1991, 180; Blok 1985, 154–55.

16. Tromp 1991, 180.

17. Bavel 2010a, 75–83.

18. Wickham 2021; Duby 1974.

19. For the most extensive treatment of this feudalism-driven growth spurt of the European economy, see Duby (1974).

20. Henstra 2000; Bavel 2010a, 193–95.

21. Following Bavel 2010a, 387.

22. Koene 2009.

23. H. van der Linden 1956.

24. Following the classic study of H. van der Linden (1956).

25. H. van der Linden 1956, 17–30.

26. Ven 2004, ch. 2.

27. Tielhof and Van Dam 2006, 42–43.

28. Zuijderduijn 2008; Tielhof and Van Dam 2006, 37.

29. Tielhof and Van Dam 2006, 39–40.

30. Schilstra 1974.

31. Spek 2004.

32. Spek 2004, 590, 994.

33. Spek 2004, 590–91.

34. Slicher van Bath 1945, 717–19. On the "deviating" developments in Drenthe, see Heringa (1982). See also Ostrom (1990) and De Moor (2015, ch. 1).

35. Zanden 1999, 130.

36. Wickham 2015.

37. Buringh et al. 2020.

38. The following is based on H. de Groot (2000).

39. Vliet 2000.

40. Smithuis 2019.

41. Frijhoff, Groothedde, and Te Strake 2011, ch. 8.

42. Westrate 2008; Schaïk 1989, 59–60.

43. Schaïk 1989, 62–66.

44. Dijkhof 2004, 68.

45. Baart 1984, 26.

46. Melker 2004, 260.

47. Kaptein 2004.

48. See Kan 1988, 22–26.

49. Kan 1988, 51 and ch. 3.

50. Camps 1995.

51. Fynn-Paul 2009, 22.

52. Fynn-Paul 2009, 19.

53. Berman 1983, 225–53.

54. De Moor and Van Zanden 2012.

55. Goody 1985.

56. Berman 1983, 282.

57. Zanden, Buringh, and Bosker 2012.

58. Zanden 2009a, ch. 5; 2009b.

59. Schulz et al. 2019.

60. Richardson and McBride 2009, 172–86.

Chapter 4

1. Based entirely on *Informacie up den staet faculteyt* 1866. The complete version of this publication (and the survey of 1494) can be found at http://www.iisg.nl/nationalaccounts/enqueste/.

2. J. de Vries 1974, 84–91; Woude 1972.

3. Zanden 2002b, 133–38; Bavel 2003.

4. Jean Carondelet (1469–1545) was probably the best known of these: a Burgundian, priest, advisor to, among others, Charles V, and patron of Erasmus, he can be seen in a painting of Jan Gossaert's, now hanging in the Louvre.

5. For details on this crisis, see Epstein (2000, ch. 3).

6. Tielhof and Van Dam 2006, 40–50.

7. Campbell 2016.

8. Rommes 2015, 50–51.

9. Bavel and Van Zanden 2004, 505. The data on urbanization origins are from Lourens and Lucassen (1997).

10. Bavel 2002; Roosen and Curtis 2019.

11. Bennett 2010.

12. See the discussion in Herlihy (1997) of the patterns of social and economic change resulting from the Black Death pandemic; see also Voigtländer and Voth (2013).

13. Pleijt and Van Zanden 2019.

14. Zanden 2009b.

15. Prados de la Escosura and Rodriguez-Caballero 2020.

16. Álvarez-Nogal and Prados de la Escosura 2013; Epstein 1991.

17. Bavel 2003.

18. Zanden, Zuijderduijn, and De Moor 2012.

19. D. de Boer 1978; Bavel and Van Zanden 2004, 517–19.

20. For the migration from the countryside to the cities in this period, see D. de Boer (1978, 135–65).

21. For a detailed analysis of market traffic, see Dijkman (2011).

22. Zanden 1988; Bavel 2003.

23. Bavel 2006, 62; 2007, 294–99.

24. North 1990, 69: "the level of interest rates in capital markets is perhaps the most evident quantitative dimension of the efficiency of the institutional framework."

25. Zuijderduijn 2008, 283–85. See also the discussion in Stasavage (2011, 38–46).

26. Tracy 1990, ch.1; see also Epstein 2000, 71.

27. Tracy 1990, 83–86.

28. Zanden 2002b, 138, 148.

29. Tielhof 1995.

30. Bavel and Van Zanden 2004, 511–15.

31. Roosen and Curtis 2019; see also Rommes 2015.

32. Blondé, Boone, and Van Bruaene 2018.

33. The difference between Holland and the south (e.g., 's-Hertogenbosch) was much less at the beginning of the sixteenth century, but increased strongly over the course of that century (actually, by 1560). See Hanus 2010, 106.

34. Weststrate 2010, 270–71.

35. Wubs-Mrozewicz 2008, 46.

36. Wubs-Mrozewicz 2008, 49.

37. Zijl 1963; Bruin, Persoons, and Weiler 1984; Semih Akçomak, Webbink, and Ter Weel 2016.

38. Based on data from incunabula discussed and analyzed in Zanden (2009b). See also Dittmar (2011).

39. Schaïk 1993, 257–58.

40. Boone 2010, 80, 84, 86.

41. Prevenier and Blockmans 2000, 152.

42. Arnade 2008, 13–15.

43. G. Parker 1988; Gunn, Grummitt, and Cools 2007.

44. Tracy 1985, 1990.

45. Kokken 1991, 13–20, 30.

46. Kokken 1991, 19.

47. Stasavage 2011.

48. Among the demands yielded to Holland was the concession that correspondence would in the future be in the language of the territory concerned rather than French, and that central administrators would appoint Hollanders and not "aliens" (officials from Brabant and Flanders, for example) to important positions. See also Boone and Brand (1992).

49. Blockmans 2020.

50. Van der Wee 1963.

51. Tielhof 1995.

52. J. de Vries and Van der Woude 1997, 234–44.

53. Zanden 2001.

54. Bavel and Van Zanden 2004, 520–22.

55. Zuijderduijn 2008, 80–94.

56. Munro 2003.

57. Zanden, Zuijderduijn, and De Moor 2012.

58. De Moor and Van Zanden 2010.

59. Zijlstra 2000, 51–52 (quote at 52), 133.

60. Bavel 2010b; 2016, ch.4.

61. Allen 2001.

62. De Moor and Van Zanden 2012.

63. See Zanden, Rijpma, and Kok 2017, 196.

64. De Munck, Lourens, and Lucassen 2006.

Chapter 5

1. For a picture of Hooft, his family, and his ideas, see Dudok van Heel (1981), H. van Gelder ([1918] 1982), and Tielhof (2002, ch. 1).

2. The text of this speech is available in H. van Gelder (1925, vol. 2, document #10; quotes at 7–8).

3. Tielhof 2002, ch. 1.

4. Pirenne 1927.

5. Prak 2018, 15–16, 298–99.

6. Epstein 1991.

7. Boone and Prak 1995; see also Parker 1977.

8. Lantschner 2015.

9. De Munck 2018, chs. 1–2.

10. Meij 1980; Rooze-Stouthamer 2009, 103.

11. Grayson 1980; Nierop 2000, 11–12.

12. Tracy 2008, 101, 105.

13. Pollmann 2019.

14. Koopmans 1990, 27.

15. Rowen 1972, 70. For the original wording in Dutch, see Groenveld and Leeuwenberg (1979, 30).

16. Tracy 2008, 176; see also Fritschy 2003, 66.

17. Tracy 2008, 177n46.

18. Tracy 2008, ch. 10.

19. Israel 1989, ch. 2; J. de Vries and Van der Woude 1997, 665–68; Gelderblom 2000, 15–22; Lesger 2006, ch. 4; see also Foldvari, Van Leeuwen, and Van Zanden 2013.

20. L. Lucassen and De Vries 1996, 148–49.

21. Diederiks and Spierenburg 1995, 169–70.

22. Kuijpers 2005, ch. 2 and 376.

23. J. Lucassen 2002, 200.

24. Kaptein 1998, 187–99.

25. Lesger 2006, 69–70 (tables 2.2 and 2.3).

26. Gelderblom 2000, 116–17 and ch. 4.

27. Fuks-Mansfeld 1989, 39 (1st quote), 45–46 (2nd quote).

28. On this synergy, see Gelderblom (2000, ch. 4).

29. Unger 1978; see also Wegener Sleeswyk 2003.

30. Davids 2008, 184–85.

31. Davids 2008, 225.

32. Poelwijk 2003, 49, 54.

33. Davids 2008, 219–23.

34. Rasterhoff 2017, ch. 6; see also De Clippel, Sluijter, and Vermeylen 2015.

35. De Clippel 2006.

36. Gelderblom, Hup, and Jonker 2018.

37. Gelderblom 2013, 39.

38. Gaastra 2003, 17, 19.

39. Gaastra 2003, 19–20.

40. Gelderblom 2003, 266 (table 7).

41. Wallerstein 1980, ch. 2; Arrighi 1994, 127–44.

42. See also chapter 8.

43. Price 1994, pt. 3.

44. Elias 1903–5, vol. 1, items 75–115.

45. Gelderblom 1999, 240–41.

46. Noordam 1994, 28–29.

47. Calculated from Engelbrecht (1973, items 15–78).

48. Gelderblom 1999, 240–41.

49. Gelderblom 2013, 39.

50. Davids 1995a.

51. Zwitzer 1991, ch. 4.

52. Fritschy 2003, 66; Gelderblom and Jonker 2011.

53. J. de Vries 2019, ch. 5.

54. Hart 2014, ch. 7.

55. Fritschy 2003, 64; Gelderblom and Jonker 2011, 5–7, 26; see also Stasavage 2011.

56. Hart 2014, ch. 4.

57. Gelderen 2002; see also Haitsma Mulier 1980, 64–76; Tracy 2008, epilogue.

58. Epstein 2000, ch. 2. He modified his views in Epstein (2006, esp. 257).

59. Zanden, Buringh, and Bosker 2012.

60. Tracy 1990.

61. Nipperdey 1993; Benedict 1993.

62. J. de Vries 2008, 87–88.

63. Gorski 2003, ch. 1.

64. Stayer 1995; MacCulloch 2003, 204–12.

65. Gorski 2003, ch. 2; see also Kaplan 1995.

66. Frijhoff 2008.

67. Schilling 1992, ch. 8; Te Brake 2017, ch. 7.

68. Territories along the southern border that were won back from the Spaniards in the second half of the Eighty Years War, especially the northern rim of the Duchy of Brabant, were

ruled by the States General and had to accept a Protestant regime. Nonetheless, the majority of the population remained Catholic.

69. Prak 2022, ch. 15.

70. Fuks-Mansfeld 1989, 117–18; also Israel 1983.

71. Hsia and Van Nierop 2002; see also Kaplan 2007.

72. For the moral struggle of Holland's Calvinists with their newfound wealth, see Schama (1987, ch. 5).

73. To compare this with the situation in Germany, see Cantoni, Dittmar, and Yuchtman (2018).

74. Bos 2006, 179.

75. C. Parker 1998.

76. Schilling 1980.

77. Israel 1995, 686–88; Kuijpers and Prak 2004, 212–15; see also Dittmar and Meisenzahl 2020.

78. Israel 1995, 689–91.

79. J. de Vries 1978.

80. Spaans 1989.

81. Te Brake 1998, ch. 3.

Chapter 6

1. Nieuwkerk 2009, 12–27, quote at 27.

2. Braudel 1979.

3. J. de Vries and Van der Woude 1997, 130–31.

4. For the role of cash in the Dutch economy, see J. Lucassen (2014) and Gelderblom and Jonker (2018).

5. Mooij 2009, 32–33.

6. See also Quinn and Roberds 2014.

7. Quinn and Roberds 2014, 12–27.

8. Gillard 2004, 420; Dehing 2012, 488.

9. Gelderblom, De Jong, and Jonker 2013.

10. Gaastra 2016, 19–20.

11. See Gaastra 1989; Steur 1984; also Gelderblom, De Jong, and Jonker 2013.

12. Jongh 2011; Gelderblom, De Jong, and Jonker 2013.

13. Gelderblom, De Jong, and Jonker 2013.

14. Frentrop 2002; Gelderblom, De Jong, and Jonker 2013.

15. Gelderblom, De Jong, and Jonker 2013.

16. Sicking 2004, chs. 1–2.

17. Berman 1983, chs. 5, 6, 11, and 12; Harris 2020, ch. 9; for the Admiralty, see Bruijn (1993).

18. Dari-Mattiacci et al. 2017, 216, 219, 221.

19. Emmer and Gommans 2021; Koekkoek, Richard, and Weststeijn 2019.

20. Bodian 1997.

21. The name "Batavia" was not Coen's choice, which was "Nieu-Hoorn," after his place of birth in Hoorn (in Holland). Although Coen is seen as the founder of the Dutch settlement, the name "Batavia" had already become established through common use.

22. Goor 2015, 302.

23. Goor 2015, 137.

24. Goor 2015, 150.

25. Goor 2015, 311.

26. Goor 2015, 291.

27. Niemeijer 1996, 67.

28. Haan 1922, 75.

29. Blussé 1986.

30. Goor 1998.

31. Goor 2015, 352–53.

32. Baay 2015, 76.

33. Goor 2015, 379–80.

34. Baay 2015, 78.

35. Details about relations between the VOC and the Reformed Church in Batavia can be found in Niemeijer (2005, chs. 17–20).

36. Baay 2015, 63–68.

37. Acemoglu and Robinson 2012.

38. There are numerous descriptions of this event in the literature on the history of the Dutch slave trade. The version most based on primary sources is that of Hondius (2005).

39. All quotes from the minutes are from Hondius (2005, 20).

40. Sen 2001.

41. Nunn 2008a, b.

42. Eltis 1995.

43. Fynn-Paul 2009.

44. Fynn-Paul 2009.

45. Kralingen 2014.

46. Gelderen 1999, 31, 35, 51.

47. Niemeijer 1996, 176; see also Heijer 2021, ch. 1.

48. Baay 2015, 71–73.

49. Emmer 2019, 40; Joosse 2011.

50. Emmer 2019, 40.

51. Emmer 2019, 40.

52. Heijer 2021, 63.

53. Rossum 2015, 26.

Chapter 7

1. Jobse-Van Putten 1995, ch. 6.

2. J. de Vries 2019.

3. See also Dijkman 2021.

4. Curtis and Dijkman 2019; Noordegraaf and Van Zanden 1995.

5. Hall and Soskice 2001.

6. Sluyterman 2015.

7. Duindam 2003, 2016.

8. Israel 1982, 230–34, 282–83, 301, 304; also Hart 1994.

9. Temple 1972, 52.

10. Feld 1977, ch. 7; Nimwegen 2010; Brandon 2015, 66–70.

11. Brandon 2015, 64 (table 1.1).

12. Gaastra 2003, 34 (table 6).

13. Hart 1993; Fritschy 2003; Feenstra 2018.

14. Spanninga 2012, 200–216.

15. Prak and Van Zanden 2009.

16. J. de Vries 2019, chs. 4–6, 14; 2009.

17. Fritschy 2009, 70–71.

18. Fritschy 2003, 69; 2009, 59–61.

19. Adams 2005; also Brandon 2015, ch. 1.

20. Klein 1965–66.

21. Data from Zandvliet 2018, 130–257.

22. For the early stages, around 1600, see Enthoven (1999).

23. Dijk and Roorda 1976.

24. Data from Zandvliet 2018, 130–72.

25. Rowen 1988, 67.

26. Colenbrander 2013, 24, 49, 54; Davids 2008, 150–53; see also Pfister 2008, 173–74.

27. Poelwijk 2003, 49–56.

28. Davids 2008, 150–74. On silk, see also Colenbrander (2013).

29. Davids 2008, 404.

30. Davids 2008, 127, 132, 142, 159, 169, 177, 184.

31. Kuijpers 1997, 511 (table 2).

32. De Moor and Van Zanden 2010, 207.

33. Davids 2001, 310–11.

34. Davids 2007.

35. Zanden 2009a, 155 (table 6).

36. Gelderblom 2011; see also Klein 1992; Klein and Veluwenkamp 1992.

37. Davids 1995a. There are more examples in Lesger and Noordegraaf (1999).

38. D. van der Linden 2015, 46–62.

39. Prak et al. 2006.

40. De Munck, Lourens, and Lucassen 2006, 39.

41. Most comprehensively in Ogilvie 2019.

42. Epstein 1998; see also Epstein and Prak 2008; Prak and Wallis 2019.

43. Bos 1998, ch. 3.

44. Lourens and Lucassen 2000.

45. Kuijpers 2005, 226–36.

46. Kuijpers 2005, 236–44.

47. Prak 2002.

48. See also Prak et al. 2020.

49. Prak 2008.

50. Rasterhoff 2017, 173 (table 6.1) and 217 (table 8.1); Prak 2008, 151–54.

51. Rasterhoff 2017, chs. 6–9; Montias 1987.

52. L. Lucassen and De Vries 1996.

53. B. de Vries et al., 2003.

54. Davids 1996, 101–2.

55. Unger 1978.

56. Wegener Sleeswyk 2003.

57. Davids 2012, 317.

58. Deurloo 1971.

59. Brandon 2015, 170, 182.

60. We are following here the argument of De Munck (2018).

61. What we call "republicanism" here is also labelled "corporatism" in the literature: De Munck 2018, ch. 4; Najemy 1982.

62. See the essays collected in Haitsma Mulier and Velema (1999), especially those by Martin van Gelderen, Hans W. Blom, and G. O. van de Klashorst.

63. Prak 2018, pt. 2.

64. Davids 2008, ch. 6; also Davids 1995b.

65. Quoted in J. de Vries and Van der Woude 1997, 609; see also Lourens and Lucassen 1992.

66. Lottum 2007; also Janssen 2017.

67. Krugman 1992; also Storper 2013, ch. 3.

68. Zanden 1993, ch. 3.

69. Sogner 1993.

70. Kuijpers 2005, 221, 248–52; Bruijn, Gaastra, and Schöffer 1987, 172.

71. Kuijpers 2005, 252–57; Heuvel 2007, ch. 3.

72. Van de Pol, 2011.

73. J. de Vries and Van der Woude 1997, 610–13.

74. J. de Vries and Van der Woude 1997, 627–30.

75. J. de Vries 2019, 346.

76. Nederveen Meerkerk 2010; Pleijt and Van Zanden 2018.

77. Schmidt 2001.

78. J. de Vries 2008, 87–92; see also Broadberry et al. 2015, 264.

79. Allen 2001, 428.

80. Zanden and Tielhof 2009; Tielhof and Van Zanden 2011, 78–79; also Wegener Sleeswyk 2003.

81. Surveys in Prak 1999a; Heerma van Voss and Van Leeuwen 2012.

82. Wijngaarden 2000, 256.

83. Wijngaarden 2000, 155.

84. Vlis 2001, 188.

85. Vlis 2001, 188.

86. Leeuwen 1996, 140 (quotes); Leeuwen 2012. See also the contributions by Looijesteijn, Nederveen Meerkerk, and Teeuwen to the special issue of *Continuity and Change* 27 (2012).

87. Teeuwen 2012, 2016.

88. Dekker 1982, 23.

89. Leeuwen 1996, 153.

90. Spierenburg 1991, 25–26, ch. 3.

91. Prak and Kuijpers 2001, 128–30.

92. Bavel and Rijpma 2016, 180, 182–83.

93. Epstein 2000, ch. 2.

94. Ogilvie 2019, esp. ch. 2.

95. Lindert 2004.

96. Tilly 1990; also Bogart et al. 2010, 72–73.

Chapter 8

1. Soens 2018.

2. Piketty 2014.

3. Scheidel 2017; but see Bavel and Scheffer 2021.

4. Acemoglu and Robinson 2012.

5. Bavel 2016.

6. Allen 2001. There is a much more detailed comparison of real wages in western Europe in Zegarra (2022).

7. Zanden 1995; Soltow and Van Zanden 1998.

8. The Gini for the entire province was higher than that of individual cities and villages, because of the gap in the average income between cities and countryside. These Ginis were calculated from tax data covering rents from real estate.

9. Soltow and Van Zanden 1998, 25–35.

10. Soltow and Van Zanden 1998, 38. The threshold for being included in the wealth tax was usually 1,000 guilders, which was a considerable sum (three times the annual wage income of an unskilled laborer), which explains why only a small part of the population paid this tax.

11. Soltow and Van Zanden 1998, 53.

12. Alfani and Ryckbosch 2016.

13. Milanovic, Lindert, and Williamson 2011.

14. Bavel 2016.

15. Zanden 1985.

16. Wallerstein 1980, 38.

17. Kennedy 1987.

18. Israel 1989, ch. 9.

19. Hart 1991; also Jardine 2008; Scott 2019, esp. 122.

20. Zanden and Van Leeuwen 2012, 126 (table 4).

21. This view can be found in J. de Vries and Van der Woude (1997, 681–83), and also J. de Vries (1976).

22. Brusse and Mijnhardt 2011.

23. J. de Vries and Van der Woude 1997, 223–34.

24. J. de Vries 2003, 51–52 (table 2.3) and 56–57 (table 2.4).

25. Gaastra 2016, 133–48 (tables 18 and 20).

26. Zanden 1996.

27. Zanden 1996.

28. Bruijn, Gaastra, and Schöffer 1979.

29. R. van Gelder 1997, ch. 2.

30. Rossum 2015, 23 (table 2).

31. See Fatah-Black 2015, 2019.

32. Fatah-Black 2019, 49 (table 2.1), 94 (table 3.2), 132 (table 4.2).

33. Brandon and Bosma 2019.

34. Fourie and Van Zanden 2013, 477.

35. Brandon and Bosma 2019.

36. Voort 1973; Stipriaan 1995; Fatah-Black 2019, ch. 4; J. de Vries and Van der Woude 1997, 475.

37. The most important work on this topic remains Riley (1980).

38. Prak 1985, 135–37.

39. J. de Vries and Van der Woude 1997, 121 (table 4.8).

40. Zanden and Van Riel 2000.

41. Following Zanden (1993).

42. *Waaragtig onderzoek wegens het verzuim*, 1748.

43. Streng 1997, 173 (table 4.8).

44. Noordam 1994, 41–45.

45. Dijk and Roorda 1976.

46. Prak 1994, 75, 82–83.

47. Noordam 1994, 91 (table 15); also Burke 1974, 113.

48. Prak 1985, 117; also Kooijmans 1985; Jong 1985.

49. Hovy 1966; also Klein 1992; Rommelse 2010.

50. Zanden and Van Riel 2000, 11–14.

51. Fritschy and Van der Voort 1997, 70; Aalbers 1977.

52. Prak 1985, 137.

53. Gelderblom and Jonker 2011.

54. Prak and Van Zanden 2009.

55. Hovy 1980.

56. About the informal centralization under the stadtholders, see Gabriëls (1989).

57. Diamond 2005, 519.

58. Soens 2009.

59. Soens 2018.

60. Tielhof 2021; we thank the author for sharing her manuscript with us.

61. Tielhof, 118, 126.

62. Tielhof, chs. 5 and 6.

63. De Munck, Lourens, and Lucassen 2006, 39–40 (tables 2.2 and 2.3); see also J. de Vries 1993; J. de Vries and Van der Woude 1997, 632–54.

64. On these early labor unions, see Lis and Soly (1994).

65. J. de Vries 1993.

66. Leeuwen 2016, ch. 2; Prak 2020.

67. Kuijpers 2005, 129–30; Panhuysen 2000, 164; P. Groot 2020, 22 (table 2).

68. Leeb 1973.

69. Kloek and Mijnhardt 2004, ch. 11.

70. Capellen tot den Poll (1781) 1987.

71. Gabriëls 1989, 109–112.

72. Capellen tot den Poll (1781) 1987, 21 (1781 pagination).

73. Capellen tot den Poll (1781) 1987, 25–26 (1781 pagination).

74. Te Brake 1989.

75. Prak 1999b, ch. 11. For a synthesis of the modern literature on the Dutch Patriot movement, see Rosendaal (2005, ch. 1). For the course of events, see also Schama (1977).

76. *Ontwerp om de Republiek*, 1785; see Prak 1991, 89–91.

77. *Ontwerp om de Republiek*, 1785, 48–49.

78. Rosendaal 2003, 145, 156.

79. Wiskerke 1938; M. de Boer 1932. See also Prak 1999b; Brandon and Fatah-Black 2016.

80. Alfani and Ryckbosch 2016

81. Following Zanden, Buringh, and Bosker 2012.

82. Rossum 2015, 23 (table 2).

83. See Kralingen 2014.

84. Hoonhout 2018, 326.

85. Hoonhout 2018, 326.

86. Hoonhout 2018, 323–28.

87. Drescher 2009.

Chapter 9

1. Duby, 1974; Campbell 2016.

2. Buringh et al. 2020.

3. Epstein 2001.

4. See also J. de Vries 2001a.

5. Blondé et al. 2020.

BIBLIOGRAPHY

Aalbers, J. 1977. "Holland's Financial Problems (1713–1733) and the Wars against Louis XIV.," In *Britain and the Netherlands: War and Society*, edited by A. Duke and C. Tamse, 79–93. The Hague, Nijhoff.

Acemoglu, Daron, and James C. Robinson. 2012. *Why Nations Fail: The Origins of Power, Prosperity and Poverty*. London: Profile Books.

Adams, Julia. 2005. *The Familial State: Ruling Families and Merchant Capitalism in Early Modern Europe*. Ithaca, NY: Cornell University Press.

Akkerman, J. 1962. "Het koopmansgilde van Tiel omstreeks het jaar 1000." *Tijdschrift voor rechtsgeschiedenis* 30: 409–71.

Alfani, Guido, and Wouter Ryckbosch. 2016. "Growing Apart in Early Modern Europe? A Comparison of Inequality Trends in Italy and the Low Countries, 1500–1800." *Explorations in Economic History* 62: 143–53.

Allen, Robert C. 2001. "The Great Divergence in European Wages and Prices from the Middle Ages to the First World War." *Explorations in Economic History* 38: 411–47.

Álvarez-Nogal, Carlos, and Leandro Prados de la Escosura. 2013. "The Rise and Fall of Spain (1270–1850)." *Economic History Review* 66: 1–37.

Arnade, Peter. 2008. *Beggars, Iconoclasts and Civic Patriots: The Political Culture of the Dutch Revolt*. Ithaca, NY: Cornell University Press.

Arrighi, Giovanni. 1994. *The Long Twentieth Century: Money, Power, and the Origins of Our Times*. London: Verso.

Aston, T. H., and C.H.E. Philpin, eds. 1987. *The Brenner Debate: Agrarian Class Structure and Economic Development in Pre-Industrial Europe*. Cambridge: Cambridge University Press.

Baart, J. 1984. "De ontstaansgeschiedenis van de stad Amsterdam." In *Van stadskern tot stadsgewest: Stedebouwkundige geschiedenis van Amsterdam*, edited by Michiel Jonker, Leo Noordegraaf, and Michiel Wagenaar, Amsterdamse Historische Reeks, Grote Serie, vol. 1, 16–34. Amsterdam: Verloren.

Baay, Reggie. 2015. *Daar werd wat gruwelijks verricht: Slavernij in Nederlands-Indië*. Amsterdam: Atheneum-Polak and Van Gennep.

Baten, Jörg, Winny Bierman, Jan Luiten van Zanden, and Peter Foldvari. 2014. "Personal Security since 1820." In *How Was Life? Global Well-Being since 1820*, edited by Jan Luiten van Zanden, Jörg Baten, Marco Mira d'Ercole, Auke Rijpma, Conal Smith, and Marcel Timmer, 139–58. Paris: OECD.

Bavel, Bas van. 2002. "People and Land: Rural Population Developments and Property Structures in the Low Countries, c. 1300–c. 1600." *Continuity and Change* 17: 9–37.

———. 2003. "Early Proto-industrialization in the Low Countries: The Importance and Nature of Market-Oriented Non-agricultural Activities in the Countryside in Flanders and Holland, c. 1250–1570." *Revue belge de philologie et d'histoire* 81: 181–237.

———. 2006. "Rural Wage Labour in the Sixteenth-Century Low Countries: An Assessment of the Importance and Nature of Wage Labour in the Countryside of Holland, Guelders and Flanders." *Continuity and Change* 21: 37–72.

———. 2007. "The Transition in the Low Countries: Rural Wage Labour as an Indicator of the Rise of Capitalism in the Countryside, 1300–1700." In "Rodney Hilton's Middle Ages," edited by Christopher Dyer, Peter Coss, and Chris Wickham. Supplement, *Past and Present* 195 (S2): 286–303.

———. 2010a. *Manors and Markets: Economy and Society in the Low Countries, 500–1600.* Oxford: Oxford University Press.

———. 2010b. "The Medieval Origins of Capitalism in the Netherlands." *BMGN: Low Countries Historical Review* 125: 45–79.

———. 2016. *The Invisible Hand? How Market Economies Have Emerged and Declined since AD 500.* Oxford: Oxford University Press.

Bavel, Bas van, Jessica Dijkman, Erika Kuijpers, and Jaco Zuijderduijn. 2012. "The Organisation of Markets as a Key Factor in the Rise of Holland from the Fourteenth to the Sixteenth Century: A Test Case for an Institutional Approach." *Continuity and Change* 27: 347–78.

Bavel, Bas van, and Auke Rijpma. 2016. "How Important Were Formalized Charity and Social Spending before the Rise of the Welfare State? A Long-Run Analysis of Selected Western European Cases, 1400–1850." *Economic History Review* 69: 159–87.

Bavel, Bas van, and Martin Scheffer. 2021. "Historical Effects of Shocks on Inequality: The Great Leveller Revisited." *Humanities and Social Science Communications* 8: 76.

Bavel, Bas van, and Jan Luiten van Zanden. 2004. "The Jump-Start of the Holland Economy during the Late-Medieval Crisis, c. 1350–1500." *Economic History Review* 57: 503–32.

Beckert, Sven. 2014. *Empire of Cotton: A History of Global Capitalism.* New York: Alfred A. Knopf.

Beckert, Sven, and Seth Rockman, eds. 2016. *Slavery's Capitalism: A New History of American Economic Development.* Philadelphia: University of Pennsylvania Press.

Benedict, Philip. 1993. "The Historiography of Continental Calvinism." In *Weber's Protestant Ethic: Origins, Evidence, Contexts,* edited by Hartmut Lehmann and Günther Roth, 305–25. Cambridge: Cambridge University Press.

Bennett, Judith M. 2010. "Compulsory Service in Late Medieval England." *Past and Present* 209: 7–51.

Berman, Harold. 1983. *Law and Revolution: The Formation of the Western Legal Tradition.* Cambridge, MA: Harvard University Press.

Bloch, Marc. 1961. *Feudal Society.* Translated by L. A. Manyon. 2 vols. London: Routledge and Kegan Paul.

Blockmans, Wim. 2020. *Medezeggenschap: Politieke participatie in Europa voor 1800.* Amsterdam: Prometheus.

Blok, D. 1985. "De vroege Middeleeuwen tot ca. 1150." In *Geschiedenis van Drenthe,* edited by J. Heringa, 141–70. Meppel, Netherlands: Boom.

Blondé, Bruno, Marc Boone, and Anne-Laure Van Bruaene, eds. 2018. *City and Society in the Low Countries, 1100–1600.* Cambridge: Cambridge University Press.

Blondé, Bruno, Sam Geens, Hilde Greefs, Wouter Ryckbosch, Tim Soens, and Peter Stabel. 2020. "The Low Countries' Paradox." In *Inequality and the City in the Low Countries (1200–2000),* edited by Bruno Blondé, Sam Geens, Hilde Greefs, Wouter Ryckbosch, Tim Soens, and Peter Stabel, 15–45. Turnhout, Belgium: Brepols.

Blussé, Leonard. 1986. *Strange Company: Chinese Settlers, Mestizo Women and the Dutch in VOC Batavia.* Dordrecht: Foris.

Bodian, Miriam. 1997. *Hebrews of the Portuguese Nation: Conversos and Community in Early Modern Amsterdam.* Bloomington: Indiana University Press.

Boer, Dick de. 1978. *Graaf en Grafiek: Sociale en economische ontwikkelingen in het Middeleeuwse "Noordholland" tussen plusminus 1345 en plusminus 1415*. Leiden: New Rhine.

Boer, M. G. de. 1932. "De ondergang der Amsterdamsche gilden." *Tijdschrift voor geschiedenis* 47: 129–49 and 225–45.

Bogart, Dan, Mauricio Drelichman, Oscar Gelderblom, and Jean-Laurent Rosenthal. 2010. "State and Private Institutions." In *The Cambridge Economic History of Europe*, vol. 1, *1700–1870*, edited by Stephen Broadberry and Kevin H. O'Rourke, 70–95. Cambridge: Cambridge University Press.

Bolt, Jutta, and Jan Luiten van Zanden. 2020. "The Maddison Project: Maddison Style Estimates of the Evolution of the World Economy; A New 2020 Update." Maddison Project Working Paper WP-15.

Boone, Marc. 2010. "A Medieval Metropolis." In *Ghent, a City of All Times*, edited by Marc Boone and Gita Deneckere, 81–105. Brussels: Mercatorfonds.

Boone, Marc, and Hanno Brand. 1992. "De ondermijning van het Groot Privilege van Holland, Zeeland en West Friesland volgens de instructie van 21 december 1477." *Holland* 24: 2–21.

Boone, Marc, and Maarten Prak. 1995. "Rulers, Patricians and Burghers: The Great and Little Traditions of Urban Revolt in the Low Countries." In *A Miracle Mirrored: The Dutch Republic in European Perspective*, edited by Karel Davids and Jan Lucassen, 99–134. Cambridge: Cambridge University Press.

Bos, Sandra. 1998. *"Uyt liefde tot malcander": Onderlinge hulpverlening binnen de Noord-Nederlandse gilden in internationaal perspectief (1570–1820)*. Amsterdam: IISG.

———. 2006. "A Tradition of Giving and Receiving: Mutual Aid within the Guild System." In *Craft Guilds in the Early Modern Low Countries: Work, Power and Representation*, edited by Maarten Prak, Catharina Lis, Jan Lucassen, and Hugo Soly, 174–93. Aldershot, UK: Ashgate.

Bowles, Samuel. 2016. *The Moral Economy: Why Good Incentives Are No Substitute for Good Citizens*. New Haven, CT: Yale University Press.

Brandon, Pepijn. 2015. *War, Capital, and the Dutch State (1588–1795)*. Chicago: Haymarket Books.

Brandon, Pepijn, and Ulbe Bosma. 2019. "De betekenis van de Atlantische slavernij voor de Nederlandse economie in de tweede helft van de achttiende eeuw." *TSEG—Low Countries Journal of Social and Economic History* 16: 5–46.

Brandon, Pepijn, and Karwan Fatah-Black. 2016. "'The Supreme Power of Local People': Local Autonomy and Radical Democracy in the Batavian Revolution (1795–1798)." *Atlantic Studies* 13: 370–88.

Braudel, Fernand. 1979. *Civilization and Capitalism, 15th–18th Century*. 3 vols. New York: Fontana.

Brenner, Robert. 1976. "Agrarian Class Structure and Economic Development in Pre-industrial Europe." *Past and Present* 70: 30–74.

Broadberry, Stephen, Bruce M. S. Campbell, Arthur Klein, Mark Overton, and Bas van Leeuwen. 2015. *British Economic Growth, 1270–1870*. Cambridge: Cambridge University Press.

Bruijn, Jaap R. 1993. *The Dutch Navy of the Seventeenth and Eighteenth Centuries*. Columbia: University of South Carolina Press.

Bruijn, Jaap R., Femme S. Gaastra, and Ivo Schöffer. 1979. *Dutch-Asiatic Shipping in the 17th and 18th Centuries*, vol. 3, *Homeward-Bound Voyages from Asia and the Cape to the Netherlands (1597–1795)*. The Hague: Martinus Nijhoff.

Bruijn, Jaap R., Femme S. Gaastra, and Ivo Schöffer, with assistance from A.C.J. Vermeulen. 1987. *Dutch-Asiatic Shipping in the 17th and 18th Centuries*, vol. 1, *Introductory Volume*. The Hague: Martinus Nijhoff.

Bruin, C. de, E. Persoons, and A. Weiler. 1984. *Geert Grote en de Moderne Devotie*. Zutphen, Netherlands: Walburg Pers.

Brusse, Paul, and Wijnand W. Mijnhardt. 2011. *Towards a New Template for Dutch History: De-urbanization and the Balance between City and Countryside*. Zwolle, Netherlands: Waanders.

Buringh, Eltjo. 2011. *Medieval Manuscript Production in the Latin West: Explorations with a Global Database*. Leiden: Brill.

Buringh, Eltjo, Bruce M. S. Campbell, Auke Rijpma, and Jan Luiten van Zanden. 2020. "Church Building and the Economy during Europe's 'Age of the Cathedrals', 700–1500 CE." *Explorations in Economic History* 76: 101316.

Buringh, Eltjo, and Jan Luiten van Zanden. 2009. "Charting the 'Rise of the West': Manuscripts and Printed Books in Europe, a Long-Term Perspective from the Sixth through Eighteenth Centuries." *Journal of Economic History* 69: 409–45.

Burke, Peter. 1974. *Venice and Amsterdam: A Study of Seventeenth-Century Elites*. London: Maurice Temple Smith.

Burnard, Trevor, and Giorgio Riello. 2020. "Slavery and the New History of Capitalism." *Journal of Global History* 15: 225–44.

Campbell, Bruce M. S. 2016. *The Great Transition: Climate, Disease and Society in the Late-Medieval World*. Cambridge: Cambridge University Press.

Camps, Hugo. 1995. *Het stadsrecht van Den Bosch van het begin (1184) tot het Privilegium Trinitatis (1330)*. Hilversum, Netherlands: Verloren.

Cantoni, Davide, Jeremiah Dittmar, and Noam Yuchtman. 2018. "Religious Competition and Reallocation: The Political Economy of Secularization in the Protestant Reformation." *Quarterly Journal of Economics* 133: 2037–96.

Capellen tot den Poll, Joan Derk van der. (1781) 1987. *Aan het volk van Nederland*. Introduced and annotated by H. Zwitzer. Amsterdam: Bataafsche Leeuw.

Chayanov, A.V. 1966. *A.V. Chayanov on the Theory of the Peasant Economy*. Edited by D. Torner, B. H. Kerblay, and R.E.F. Smith. Homewood, IL: American Economic Association.

Colenbrander, Sjoukje. 2013. *When Weaving Flourished: The Silk Industry in Amsterdam and Haarlem, 1585–1750*. Amsterdam: Aronson Concepts.

Cummins, Neil. 2017. "Lifespans of the European Elite, 800–1800." *Journal of Economic History* 77: 406–39.

Curtis, Daniel, and Jessica Dijkman. 2019. "The Escape from Famine in the Northern Netherlands: A Reconsideration Using the 1690s Harvest Failures and a Broader Northwest European Perspective." *Seventeenth Century* 23: 229–58.

Dari-Mattiacci, Giuseppe, Oscar Gelderblom, Joost Jonker, and Enrico C. Perotti. 2017. "The Emergence of the Corporate Form." *Journal of Law, Economics, and Organization* 33: 193–236.

Davids, C. A. 1995a. "Beginning Entrepreneurs and Municipal Governments in Holland at the Time of the Dutch Republic." In *Entrepreneurs and Entrepreneurship in Early Modern Times: Merchants and Industrialists within the Orbit of the Dutch Staple Market*, edited by Clé Lesger and Leo Noordegraaf, 167–83. The Hague: Stichting Hollandse Historische Reeks.

———. 1995b. "Shifts of Technological Leadership in Early Modern Europe." In *A Miracle Mirrored: The Dutch Republic in European Perspective*, edited by Karel Davids and Jan Lucassen, 338–66. Cambridge: Cambridge University Press.

———. 1996. "Neringen, hallen en gilden: Kapitalisten, kleine ondernemers en stedelijke overheid in de tijd van de Republiek." In *Kapitaal, ondernemerschap en beleid: Studies over economie en politiek in Nederland, Europa en Azië van 1500 tot heden*, edited by C. A. Davids, W. Fritschy, and L. A. van der Valk, 95–120. Hilversum, Netherlands: Verloren.

———. 2001. "Amsterdam as a Centre for Learning in the Dutch Golden Age, c. 1580–1700." In *Urban Achievement in Early Modern Europe: Golden Ages in Antwerp, Amsterdam and London*, edited by Patrick O'Brien, Derek Keen, Marjolein 't Hart, and Herman Van der Wee, 305–25. Cambridge: Cambridge University Press.

———. 2007. "Apprenticeship and Guild Control in the Netherlands, c. 1450–1800." In *Learning on the Shop Floor: Historical Perspectives on Apprenticeship*, edited by Bert De Munck, Steven L. Kaplan, and Hugo Soly, 65–84. New York: Berghahn.

———. 2008. *The Rise and Decline of Dutch Technological Leadership: Technology, Economy and Culture in the Netherlands, 1350–1800*. 2 vols. Leiden: Brill.

———. 2012. "Het geheim van het collectief: Technische vernieuwing in de Zaanstreek in de vroegmoderne tijd." In *Geschiedenis van de Zaanstreek*, edited by E. Beukers and C. van Stijl, 307–20. Zwolle, Netherlands: Waanders.

De Clippel, Karolien. 2006. "Two Sides of the Same Coin? Genre Painting in the North and South during the Sixteenth and Seventeenth Centuries." *Simiolus* 32: 17–34.

De Clippel, Karolien, Eric Jan Sluijter, and Filip Vermeylen, eds. 2015. "Art on the Move." Special issue, *De zeventiende eeuw* 31.

Dehing, Pit. 2012 *Amsterdam in Geld: Wisselbank en wisselkoersen, 1650–1725*. Hilversum, Netherlands: Verloren.

Dekker, Rudolf. 1982. *Holland in beroering: Oproeren in de 17de en 18de eeuw*. Baarn, Netherlands: Ambo.

De la Croix, David, and Omar Licandro. 2015. "The Longevity of Famous People from Hammurabi to Einstein." *Journal of Economic Growth* 20: 263–303.

De Moor, Tine. 2015. *The Dilemma of the Commoners: Understanding the Use of Common-Pool Resources in Long-Term Perspective*. Cambridge: Cambridge University Press.

De Moor, Tine, and Jan Luiten van Zanden. 2010. "'Every Woman Counts': A Gender-Analysis of Numeracy in the Low Countries during the Early Modern Period." *Journal of Interdisciplinary History* 41: 179–208.

———. 2012. "Girl Power: The European Marriage Pattern and Labour Markets in the North Sea Region in the Late Medieval and Early Modern Period." *Economic History Review* 65: 835–61.

De Munck, Bert. 2018. *Guilds, Labour and the Urban Body Politic: Fabricating Community in the Southern Netherlands, 1300–1800*. New York: Routledge.

De Munck, Bert, Piet Lourens, and Jan Lucassen. 2006. "The Establishment and Distribution of Craft Guilds in the Low Countries, 1000–1800." In *Craft Guilds in the Early Modern Low Countries: Work, Power, and Representation*, edited by Maarten Prak, Catharina Lis, Jan Lucassen, and Hugo Soly, 32–73. Aldershot, UK: Ashgate.

Deurloo, A. J. 1971. "Bijltjes en klouwers: Een bijdrage tot de geschiedenis der Amsterdamse scheepsbouw, in het bijzonder in de tweede helft der achttiende eeuw." *Economisch- en sociaal-historisch jaarboek* 34: 4–71.

Diamond, Jared. 2005. *Collapse: How Societies Choose to Fail or to Succeed*. Harmondsworth, UK: Allen Lane.

Diederiks, H. A., and P. C. Spierenburg. 1995. "Economische en sociale ontwikkelingen." In *Deugd boven geweld: Een geschiedenis van Haarlem, 1245–1995*, edited by G. van der Ree-Scholtens, 169–97. Hilversum, Netherlands: Verloren.

Diefenbach, Thomas. 2019. "Why Michels' 'Iron Law of Oligarchy' Is Not an Iron Law—and How Democratic Organizations Can Stay 'Oligarchy-Free.'" *Organization Studies* 40: 545–62.

Dijk, H. van, and D. J. Roorda. 1976. "Social Mobility under the Regents of the Republic." *Acta historiae Neerlandicae* 9: 76–102.

Dijkhof, Eef. 2004. "Op weg naar autonomie." In *Geschiedenis van Amsterdam*, vol. 1, *Een stad uit het niets—tot 1578*, edited by Marijke Carasso-Kok, 63–73. Amsterdam: Boom.

Dijkman, Jessica. 2011. *Shaping Medieval Markets: The Organisation of Commodities Markets in Holland, c. 1200–c. 1450*. Leiden: Brill.

———. 2021. "Managing Food Crises: Urban Relief Stock in Pre-industrial Holland." *Past and Present* 251: 41–74.

Dittmar, Jeremiah E. 2011. "Information Technology and Economic Change: The Impact of the Printing Press." *Quarterly Journal of Economics* 126: 1133–72.

Dittmar, Jeremiah E., and Ralf. R. Meisenzahl. 2020. "Public Goods Institutions, Human Capital, and Growth: Evidence from German History." *Review of Economic Studies* 87: 959–96.

Drescher, Seymour. 2009. *Abolition: A History of Slavery and Antislavery*. New York: Cambridge University Press.

Duby, Georges. 1974. *The Early Growth of European Economy: Warriors and Peasants from the Seventh to the Twelfth Centuries*. Ithaca, NY: Cornell University Press.

Dudok van Heel, S. 1981. "De familie van Pieter Cornelisz Hooft." *Jaarboek Centraal Bureau voor Genealogie* 35: 68–108.

Duindam, Jeroen. 2003. *Vienna and Versailles: The Courts of Europe's Dynastic Rivals, 1550–1780*. Cambridge: Cambridge University Press.

———. 2016. *Dynasties: A Global History of Power, 1300–1800*. Cambridge: Cambridge University Press.

Duplessis, Robert S. 2019. *Transitions to Capitalism in Early Modern Europe: Economies in the Era of Early Globalization, c. 1450–c. 1820*. 2nd ed. Cambridge: Cambridge University Press.

Elias, Johan. 1903–5. *De vroedschap van Amsterdam*. Haarlem: Loosjes.

Eltis, David. 1995. "The Total Product of Barbados, 1664–1701." *Journal of Economic History* 55: 321–38.

Emmer, Piet C. 2019. *Geschiedenis van de Nederlands slavenhandel*. Amsterdam: Nieuw Amsterdam.

Emmer, Pieter C., and Jos J. C. Gommans. 2021. *The Dutch Overseas Empire, 1600–1800*. Cambridge: Cambridge University Press.

Engelbrecht, E. A. 1973. *De vroedschap van Rotterdam, 1572–1795*. Rotterdam: Gemeentelijke Archiefdienst.

Enthoven, Victor. 1999. "Een symbiose tussen koopman en regent: De tweetrapsraket van de opkomst van de Republiek en Zeeland." In *Ondernemers & bestuurders: Economie en politiek in de Noordelijke Nederlanden in de late Middeleeuwen en vroegmoderne tijd*, edited by Clé Lesger and Leo Noordegraaf, 203–36. Amsterdam: NEHA.

Epstein, S. R. 1991. "Cities, Regions and the Late Medieval Crisis: Sicily and Tuscany Compared." *Past and Present* 130: 3–50.

———. 1998. "Craft Guilds, Apprenticeship, and Technological Change in Pre-industrial Europe." *Journal of Economic History* 53: 684–713.

———. 2000. *Freedom and Growth: The Rise of States and Markets in Europe, 1300–1750*. London: Routledge.

———. 2001. "The Late Medieval Crisis as an 'Integration Crisis.'" In *Early Modern Capitalism: Economic and Social Change in Europe, 1400–1800*, edited by Maarten Prak, 25–50. London: Routledge.

———. 2006. "The Rise of the West." In *An Anatomy of Power: The Social Theory of Michael Mann*, edited by John A. Hall and Ralph Schroeder, 233–62. Cambridge: Cambridge University Press.

———. 2007. "Rodney Hilton, Marxism and the Transition from Feudalism to Capitalism." In "Rodney Hilton's Middle Ages," edited by Christopher Dyer, Peter Coss, and Chris Wickham. Supplement, *Past and Present* 195 (S2): 248–69.

Epstein, S. R., and Maarten Prak, eds. 2008. *Guilds, Innovation and the European Economy, 1400–1800*. Cambridge: Cambridge University Press.

Fatah-Black, Karwan. 2015. *White Lies and Black Markets: Evading Metropolitan Authority in Colonial Suriname, 1650–1800*. Leiden: Brill.

———. 2019. *Sociëteit van Suriname, 1683–1795: Het bestuur van de kolonie in de achttiende eeuw*. Zutphen, Netherlands: Walburg Pers.

Feenstra, Alberto. 2018. "Between Shared and Conflicting Interests: The Political Economy of Markets for Public Debt in the Dutch Republic, 1600–1795." PhD dissertation, Universiteit van Amsterdam.

Feld, Maury D. 1977. *The Structure of Violence: Armed Forces as Social Systems*. Beverly Hills: Sage.

Fisman, Raymond, and Edward Miguel. 2007. "Corruption, Norms and Legal Enforcement: Evidence from Diplomatic Parking Tickets." *Journal of Political Economy* 115 (6): 1020–48.

Foldvari, Peter, Bas van Leeuwen, and Jan Luiten van Zanden. 2013. "The Contribution of Migration to Economic Development in Holland, 1570–1800." *De Economist* 161: 1–18.

Fourie, Johan, and Jan Luiten van Zanden. 2013. "GDP in the Dutch Cape Colony: The National Accounts of a Slave-Based Society." *South African Journal of Economics* 81: 467–90.

Frentrop, Paul. 2002. *Ondernemingen en hun aandeelhouders sinds de VOC*. Amsterdam: Prometheus.

Frijhoff, W.Th.M. 2008. "Was the Dutch Republic a Calvinist Community? The State, the Confessions and Culture in the Early Modern Netherlands." In *The Republican Alternative: The Netherlands and Switzerland Compared*, edited by André Holenstein, Thomas Maissen, and Maarten Prak, 99–122. Amsterdam: Amsterdam University Press.

Frijhoff, W.Th.M., Michel Groothedde, and Christiaan te Strake. 2011. *Historische atlas van Zutphen: Torenstad aan de Berkel*. Nijmegen, Netherlands: Vantilt.

Fritschy, Wantje. 2003. "A 'Financial Revolution' Reconsidered: Public Finance in Holland during the Dutch Revolt, 1568–1648." *Economic History Review* 56: 57–89.

———. 2009. "The Efficiency of Taxation in Holland." In *The Political Economy of the Dutch Republic*, edited by Oscar Gelderblom, 55–84. Farnham, UK: Ashgate.

———. 2017. *Public Finance of the Dutch Republic in Comparative Perspective: The Viability of an Early Modern Federal State (1570s–1795)*. Leiden: Brill.

Fritschy, Wantje, and René van der Voort. 1997. "From Fragmentation to Unification: Public Finance 1700–1914." In *A Financial History of The Netherlands*, edited by Marjolein 't Hart, Joost Jonker, and Jan Luiten van Zanden, 64–93. Cambridge: Cambridge University Press.

Fuks-Mansfeld, R. 1989. *De Sefardim in Amsterdam tot 1795: Aspecten van een joodse minderheid in een Hollandse stad*. Hilversum, Netherlands: Verloren.

Fynn-Paul, Jeffrey. 2009. "Empire, Monotheism and Slavery in the Greater Mediterranean Region from Antiquity through the Early Modern Era." *Past and Present* 205: 3–40.

Gaastra, Femme S. 1989. *Bewind en beleid bij de VOC: De financiële en commerciële politiek van de bewindhebbers, 1672–1702*. Zutphen, Netherlands: Walburg Pers.

———. 2003. *The Dutch East India Company: Expansion and Decline*. Zutphen, Netherlands: Walburg Pers.

———. 2016. *Geschiedenis van de VOC: Opkomst, bloei en ondergang*. Zutphen, Netherlands: Walburg Pers.

Gabriëls, A.C.M. 1989. *De heren als dienaren en de dienaar als heer: Het stadhouderlijk stelsel in de tweede helft van de achttiende eeuw*. Amsterdam: Stichting Hollandse Historische Reeks.

Gelder, H. Enno van. (1918) 1982. *De levensbeschouwing van Cornelis Pieterszoon Hooft, burgermeester van Amsterdam 1547–1626*. Utrecht: Hes.

———, ed. 1925. *Memoriën en adviezen van Cornelis Pietersz. Hooft*. Utrecht: Kemink.

Gelder, Roelof van. 1997. *Het Oost-Indisch avontuur: Duitsers in dienst van de VOC (1600–1800)*. Nijmegen, Netherlands: SUN.

Gelderblom, Oscar. 1999. "De deelname van Zuid-Nederlandse kooplieden aan het openbare leven van Amsterdam (1578–1650)." In *Ondernemers & bestuurders: Economie en politiek in de Noordelijke Nederlanden in de late Middeleeuwen en vroegmoderne tijd*, edited by Clé Lesger and Leo Noordegraaf, 237–58. Amsterdam: NEHA.

———. 2000. *Zuid-Nederlandse kooplieden en de opkomst van de Amsterdamse stapelmarkt (1578–1630)*. Hilversum, Netherlands: Verloren.

———. 2003. "From Antwerp to Amsterdam: The Contribution of Merchants from the Southern Netherlands to the Commercial Expansion of Amsterdam (c. 1540–1609)." *Review (Fernand Braudel Center)* 26: 247–83.

———. 2011. "Entrepreneurs in the Dutch Golden Age." In *The Invention of Enterprise: Entrepreneurship from Ancient Mesopotamia to Modern Times*, edited by William J. Baumol, David Landes, and Joel Mokyr, 156–82. Princeton, NJ: Princeton University Press.

———. 2013. *Cities of Commerce: The Institutional Foundations of International Trade in the Low Countries, 1250–1650*. Princeton, NJ: Princeton University Press.

Gelderblom, Oscar, Mark Hup, and Joost Jonker. 2018. "Public Functions, Private Markets: Credit Registration by Aldermen and Notaries in the Low Countries, 1500–1800." In *Financing in Europe: Evolution, Coexistence and Complementarity of Lending Practices from the Middle Ages to Modern Times*, edited by Marcella Lorenzini, Cinzia Lorandini, and D'Maris Coffmann, 163–94. Cham, Switzerland: Palgrave.

Gelderblom, Oscar, Abe de Jong, and Joost Jonker. 2011. "An Admiralty for Asia: Isaac Le Maire and Conflicting Conceptions about the Corporate Governance of the VOC." In *Origins of Shareholder Advocacy*, edited by Jonathan G. S. Koppell, 29–60. New York: Palgrave.

———. 2013. "The Formative Years of the Modern Corporation: The Dutch East India Company VOC, 1602–1623." *Journal of Economic History* 73: 1050–76.

Gelderblom, Oscar, and Joost Jonker. 2011. "Public Finance and Economic Growth: The Case of Holland in the Seventeenth Century." *Economic History Review* 71: 1–39.

———. 2014. "The Low Countries." In *The Cambridge History of Capitalism*, vol. 1, *The Rise of Capitalism: From Ancient Origins to 1848*, edited by Larry Neal and Jeffrey G. Williamson, 314–56. Cambridge: Cambridge University Press.

———. 2018. "Enter the Ghost: Cashless Payments in the Early Modern Low Countries, 1500–1800." In *Money, Currency and Crisis: In Search of Trust, 2000 BC to AD 2000*, edited by R. J. van der Spek and Bas van Leeuwen, 224–47. Abingdon, UK: Routledge

Gelderen, Martin van. 1999. "De Nederlandse Opstand (1555–1610): Van 'vrijheden,' naar 'oude vrijheid' en 'vrijheid der conscientien.'" In *Vrijheid: Een geschiedenis van de vijftiende tot de twintigste eeuw*, edited by E.O.G. Haitsma Mulier and W.R.E. Velema, 27–52. Amsterdam: Amsterdam University Press.

——— 2002. "Aristotelians, Monarchomachs and Republicans: Sovereignty and Respublica Mixta in Dutch and German Political Thought, 1580–1650." In *Republicanism: A Shared European Heritage*, edited by Van Gelderen and Quentin Skinner, vol. 1, 195–217. Cambridge: Cambridge University Press.

Gillard, Lucien. 2004. *La Banque d'Amsterdam et le florin européen au temps de la République néerlandaise (1610–1820)*. Paris: EHESS.

Goldstone, Jack A. 2021."Dating the Great Divergence." *Journal of Global History* 16: 266–85.

Goody, Jack. 1985. *The Development of the Family and Marriage in Europe*. Cambridge: Cambridge University Press.

Goor, Jur van. 1998. Review of *Calvinisme en koloniale stadscultuur: Batavia 1619–1725*, by H. E. Niemeijer. *Bijdragen en mededelingen betreffende de geschiedenis der Nederlanden* 113: 233–35.

———. 2015. *Jan Pieterszoon Coen, 1587–1629*. Amsterdam: Boom.

Gorski, Philip S. 2003. *The Disciplinary Revolution: Calvinism and the Rise of the State in Early Modern Europe*. Chicago: University of Chicago Press.

Grayson, J. C. 1980. "The Civic Militia in the County of Holland, 1560–81: Politics and Public Order in the Dutch Republic." *Bijdragen en mededelingen betreffende de geschiedenis der Nederlanden* 95: 35–63.

Greif, Avner. 2006a. "Family Structure, Corporations and Growth: The Origins and Implications of Corporations." *American Economic Review* 96: 308–12.

———. 2006b. *Institutions and the Path to the Modern Economy: Lessons from Medieval Trade*. Cambridge: Cambridge University Press.

Groenveld, S., and H.L.Ph. Leeuwenberg. 1979. "'Die originale unie metten acten daernaer gevolcht.'" In *De Unie van Utrecht: Wording en werking van een verbondsacte*, edited by Groenveld and Leeuwenberg, 5–55. The Hague: Martinus Nijhoff.

Groot, H. L. de. 2000. "Van strijdhamer tot bisschopsstaf: De vroegste geschiedenis tot circa 925." In *"Een paradijs vol weelde": Geschiedenis van de stad Utrecht*, edited by R. E. de Bruin, P. D. 't Hart, A. J. van den Hoven van Genderen, A. Pietersma, and J.E.A.L. Struick, 13–43. Utrecht: Matrijs.

Groot, Piet. 2020. "Newcomers, Migrants, Surgeons: Making Career in the Amsterdam Surgeons' Guild of the Eighteenth Century." *TSEG—Low Countries Journal of Social and Economic History* 17: 7–36.

Gunn, Steven, David Grummitt, and Hans Cools. 2007. *War, State and Society in England and the Netherlands, 1477–1559*. Oxford: Oxford University Press.

Haan, Frederik de. 1922. *Oud Batavia: Gedenkboek uitgegeven door het Bataviaasch Genootschap van Kunsten en Wetenschappen naar aanleiding van het driehonderdjarig bestaan der slad in 1919*. Batavia [Jakarta]: Kolff.

Haitsma Mulier, E.O.G. 1980. *The Myth of Venice and Dutch Republican Thought in the Seventeenth Century*. Assen, Netherlands: Van Gorcum.

Haitsma Mulier, E.O.G., and W.R.E. Velema, eds. 1999. *Vrijheid: Een geschiedenis van de vijftiende tot de twintigste eeuw*. Amsterdam: Amsterdam University Press.

Hall, Peter A., and David S. Soskice, eds. 2001. *Varieties of Capitalism: The Institutional Foundations of Comparative Advantage*. Oxford: Oxford University Press.

Hanus, Jord. 2010. "Affluence and Inequality in the Low Countries: The City of 's Hertogenbosch in the Long Sixteenth Century, 1500–1650." PhD dissertation, Universiteit Antwerpen.

Harris, Ron. 2020. *Going the Distance: Eurasian Trade and the Rise of the Business Corporation, 1400–1700*. Princeton, NJ: Princeton University Press.

Hart, Marjolein 't. 1991. "'The Devil or the Dutch': Holland's Impact on the Financial Revolution in England, 1643–1694." *Parliaments, Estates and Representation* 11: 39–52.

———. 1993. *The Making of a Bourgeois State: War, Politics and Finance during the Dutch Revolt*. Manchester: Manchester University Press.

———. 1994. "Intercity Rivalries and the Making of the Dutch State." In *Cities and the Rise of States in Europe, A.D. 1000 to 1800*, edited by Charles Tilly and Wim P. Blockmans, 196–217. Boulder, CO: Westview.

———. 2014. *The Dutch Wars of Independence: Warfare and Commerce in the Netherlands, 1570–1680*. London: Routledge.

Head, Thomas, and Richard Landes, eds. 1992. *The Peace of God: Social Violence and Religious Response in France around the Year 1000*. Ithaca, NY: Cornell University Press.

Heerma van Voss, Lex, and Marco H. D. van Leeuwen. 2012. "Charity in the Dutch Republic: An Introduction." *Continuity and Change* 27: 175–97.

Heijer, Henk den. 2021. *Nederlands slavernijverleden: Historische inzichten en het debat nu*. Zutphen, Netherlands: Walburg Pers.

Henstra, D. 2000. "The Evolution of the Money Standard in Medieval Frisia: A Treatise on the History of the Systems of Money of Account in the Former Frisia (c.600–c.1500)." PhD dissertation, Rijksuniversiteit Groningen.

Heringa, J. 1982. *De buurschap en haar marke*. Assen, Netherlands: Provinciaal Bestuur Drenthe.

Herlihy, David. 1997. *The Black Death and the Transformation of the West*. Cambridge, MA: Harvard University Press.

Heuvel, Danielle van den. 2007. *Women and Entrepreneurship: Female Traders in the Northern Netherlands, c. 1580–1815*. Amsterdam: Aksant.

Hondius, D. 2005. "Afrikanen in Zeeland, Moren in Middelburg in Zeeland." *Zeeland* 14: 13–25.

Hoonhout, Bram. 2018. "1776: 'Vrije grond' onbereikbaar voor slaven." In *Wereldgeschiedenis van Nederland*, edited by Lex Heerma van Voss, 323–28. Amsterdam: Ambo Anthos.

Hovy, J. 1966. *Het voorstel van 1751 voor de instelling van een beperkt vrijhavestelsel (propositae tot een gelimiteerd porto-franco)*. Groningen, Netherlands: Wolters Noordhoff.

———. 1980. "Institutioneel onvermogen in de 18de eeuw." In *Algemene geschiedenis der Nederlanden*, edited by D. Blok, W. Prevenier, D. J. Roorda, A. M. van der Woude, J. A. Van Houtte, H.F.J.M. van den Eerenbeemt, Th. Van Tijn, and H. Balthazar, vol. 9, 126–38. Haarlem, Netherlands: Unieboek.

Howell, Martha C. 2010. *Commerce before Capitalism in Europe, 1300–1600*. Cambridge: Cambridge University Press.

Hsia, Ronnie Po-Chia, and Henk F. K. van Nierop, eds. 2002. *Calvinism and Religious Toleration in the Dutch Golden Age*. Cambridge: Cambridge University Press.

Informacie up den staet faculteyt ende gelegenheyt van de steden ende dorpen van Hollant ende Vrieslant om daernae te reguleren de nyeuwe schiltaele. Gedaen in den jaere MDXIV. 1866. Leiden: Maatschappij der Nederlandsche Letterkunde, under the direction of R. Fruin. http://www.iisg.nl/nationalaccounts/enqueste/.

Israel, Jonathan I. 1982. *The Dutch Republic and the Hispanic World, 1606–1661*. Oxford: Oxford University Press.

———. 1983. "The Economic Contribution of Dutch Sephardi Jewry to Holland's Golden Age, 1595–1713." *Tijdschrift voor geschiedenis* 96: 505–35.

———. 1989. *Dutch Primacy in World Trade, 1585–1740*. Oxford: Oxford University Press.

———. 1995. *The Dutch Republic, Its Rise, Greatness, and Fall, 1477–1806*. Oxford: Oxford University Press.

Janssen, Geert H. 2017. "The Republic of Refugees: Early Modern Migrations and the Dutch Experience." *Historical Journal* 60: 233–52.

Jardine, Lisa. 2008. *Going Dutch: How England Plundered Holland's Glory*. London: Harper Collins.

Jobse-Van Putten, Jozien. 1995. *Eenvoudig maar voedzaam: Cultuurgeschiedenis van de dagelijkse maaltijd in Nederland*. Nijmegen, Netherlands: SUN.

Jong, J. J. de. 1985. *Met goed fatsoen: De elite in een Hollandse stad, Gouda 1700–1780*. The Hague: De Bataafsche Leeuw.

Jongh, Johan Matthijs de. 2011. "Shareholder Activists Avant la Lettre: The 'Complaining Participants' in the Dutch East India Company, 1622–1625." In *Origins of Shareholder Advocacy*, edited by Jonathan G. S. Koppell, 61–88. New York: Palgrave.

Joose, L. J. 2011. "Predikanten, slavernij en slavenhandel, 1640–1740." Leendert J. Joosse's website, July 2011. https://www.ljjoosse.nl/wp-content/uploads/2011/07/Kerk-en-slavernij.pdf.

Kan, F. van. 1988. *Sleutels tot de macht: De ontwikkeling van het Leidse patriciaat tot 1420*. Hilversum, Netherlands: Verloren.

Kaplan, Benjamin. 1995. *Calvinists and Libertines: Confession and Community in Utrecht, 1578–1620*. Oxford: Oxford University Press.

———. 2007. *Divided by Faith: Religious Conflict and the Practice of Toleration in Early Modern Europe*. Cambridge, MA: Harvard University Press.

Kaptein, Herman. 1998. *De Hollandse textielnijverheid 1350–1600: Conjunctuur en continuïteit*. Hilversum, Netherlands: Verloren.

———. 2004. "Poort van Holland: De economische ontwikkeling, 1200–1578." In *Geschiedenis van Amsterdam*, vol. 1, *Een stad uit het niets—tot 1578*, edited by Marijke Carasso-Kok, 109–73. Amsterdam: Boom.

Kelly, Morgan. 1997. "The Dynamics of Smithian Growth." *Quarterly Journal of Economics* 112: 939–64.

Kennedy, Paul. 1987. *The Rise and Fall of the Great Powers: Economic Change and Military Conflict from 1500 to 2000*. New York: Vintage Books.

Klein, P. W. 1965–66. "De heffing van de 100e en 200e penning van het vermogen te Gouda, 1599–1722." *Economisch-historisch jaarboek* 31: 41–62.

———. 1992. "A New Look at an Old Subject: Dutch Trade Policies in the Age of Mercantilism." In *State and Trade: Government and the Economy in Britain and the Netherlands since the Middle Ages*, Britain and the Netherlands 10, edited by Simon Groenveld and Michael Wintle, 39–49. Zutphen, Netherlands: Walburg Pers.

Klein, P. W., and Jan Willem Veluwenkamp. 1992. "The Role of the Entrepreneur in the Economic Expansion of the Dutch Republic." In *The Dutch Economy in the Golden Age: Nine Essays*, edited by Karel Davids and Leo Noordegraaf, 27–54. Amsterdam: NEHA.

Kloek, Joost, and W. W. Mijnhardt. 2004. *1800: Blueprints for a National Community*. Assen, Netherlands: Van Gorcum.

Koekkoek, René, Anne-Isabelle Richard, and Arthur Weststeijn, eds. 2019. *The Dutch Empire between Ideas and Practice, 1600–1200*. Cham, Switzerland: Palgrave.

Koene, Bert. 2009. *Goede luiden en gemene onderzaten: Assendelft vanaf zijn ontstaan tot de nadagen van de Gouden Eeuw*. Hilversum, Netherlands: Verloren.

Kokken, H. 1991. *Steden en Staten: Dagvaarten van steden en Staten van Holland onder Maria van Bourgondië en het eerste regentschap van Maximiliaan van Oostenrijk (1477–1494)*. The Hague: Stichting Hollandse Historische Reeks.

Kooijmans, Luuc. 1985. *Onder regenten: De elite in een Hollandse stad Hoorn, 1700–1780*. Amsterdam: De Bataafsche Leeuw.

Koopmans, J. 1990. *De Staten van Holland en de Opstand: De ontwikkeling van hun functies en organisatie in de periode 1544–1588*. The Hague: Stichting Hollandse Historische Reeks.

Kralingen, Hans-Jan van. 2014. Some Remarks on Slavery and Legal History." *Leidenlawblog*, March 5, 2014. https://leidenlawblog.nl/articles/some-remarks-on-slavery-and-legal-history.

Krugman, Paul. 1992. *Geography and Trade*. Leuven, Belgium: Leuven University Press.

Kuijpers, Erika. 1997. "Lezen en schrijven: Onderzoek naar het alfabetiseringsniveau in zeventiende-eeuws Amsterdam." *Tijdschrift voor sociale geschiedenis* 23: 490–522.

———. 2005. *Migrantenstad: Immigratie en sociale verhoudingen in 17e-eeuws Amsterdam*. Hilversum, Netherlands: Verloren.

Kuijpers, Erika, and Maarten Prak. 2004. "Gevestigden en buitenstaanders." In *Geschiedenis van Amsterdam*, vol. 2a, *Centrum van de wereld, 1578–1650*, edited by W. Frijhoff and Prak, 189–239. Amsterdam: SUN.

Kuiper, Yme, and Ben Olde Meierink, eds. 2015. *Buitenplaatsen in de Gouden Eeuw: De rijkdom van het buitenleven Republiek*. Hilversum, Netherlands: Verloren.

Langen, G. de, and P. Noomen. 1996. "Stinzen, states en versterkingen." In *Verborgen verleden belicht*, edited by G. van Langen et al., 43–57. Leeuwarden, Netherlands: Provincie Friesland.

Lantschner, Patrick. 2015. *The Logic of Political Conflict in Medieval Cities: Italy and the Southern Low Countries, 1370–1440*. Oxford: Oxford University Press.

Leeb, I. Leonard. 1973. *The Ideological Origins of the Batavian Revolution: History and Politics in the Dutch Republic, 1747–1800*. The Hague: Martinus Nijhoff.

Leeuwen, Marco H. D. van. 1996. "Amsterdam en de armenzorg tijdens de Republiek." *NEHA jaarboek* 59: 132–61.

———. 2012. "Giving in Early Modern History: Philanthropy in Amsterdam in the Golden Age." *Continuity and Change* 27: 301–43.

———. 2016. *Mutual Insurance, 1550–2015: From Guild Welfare and Friendly Societies to Contemporary Micro-insurance*. London: Palgrave Macmillan.

Lesger, Clé L. 2006. *The Rise of the Amsterdam Market and Information Exchange: Merchants, Commercial Expansion and Change in the Spatial Economy of the Low Countries, c.1550–1630.* Aldershot, UK: Ashgate.

Lesger, Clé L., and Leo Noordegraaf, eds. 1999. *Ondernemers en bestuurders: Economie en politiek in de Noordelijke Nederlanden in de late Middeleeuwen en vroegmoderne tijd.* Amsterdam: NEHA.

Lewis, Bernard. 1982. *The Muslim Discovery of Europe.* New York: Weidenfeld and Nicolson.

Linden, David van der. 2015. *Experiencing Exile: Huguenot Refugees in the Dutch Republic, 1680–1700.* Farnham, UK: Ashgate.

Linden, H. van der. 1956. *De cope: Bijdrage tot de rechtsgeschiedenis van de openlegging der Hollands-Utrechtse laagvlakte.* Assen, Netherlands: Van Gorcum.

Linden, Marcel van der. 1997. "Marx and Engels, Dutch Marxism and the 'Model Capitalist Nation of the seventeenth Century.'" *Science and Society* 61: 161–92.

Lindert, Peter H. 2004. *Growing Public: Social Spending and Economic Growth since the Eighteenth Century,* vol. 1, *The Story.* Cambridge: Cambridge University Press.

Lis, Catharina, and Hugo Soly. 1979. *Poverty and Capitalism in Pre-industrial Europe.* Brighton, UK: Harvester.

———. 1994. "'An Irresistable Phalanx': Journeymen Associations in Western Europe, 1300–1800." In "Before the Unions: Wage Earners and Collective Action in Europe, 1300–1850," edited by Catharina Lis, Jan Lucassen and Hugo Soly. Supplement, *International Review of Social History* 39 (S2): 11–52.

Looijesteijn, Henk. 2012. "Funding and Founding Private Charities: Leiden Almshouses and Their Founders, 1450–1800." *Continuity and Change* 27: 199–239.

Lottum, Jelle van. 2007. *Across the North Sea: The Impact of the Dutch Republic on International Labour Migration, c.1550–1850.* Amsterdam: Aksant.

Lourens, Piet, and Jan Lucassen. 1992. "Marx als Historiker der niederländischen Republik." In *Die Rezeption der Marxschen Theorie in den Niederlanden,* Schriften aus dem Karl-Marx-Haus 45, edited by Marcel van der Linden, 430–54. Trier, Germany: Karl-Marx-Haus.

———. 1997. *Inwoneraantallen van Nederlandse steden ca. 1300–1800.* Amsterdam: NEHA.

———. 2000. "'Zunftlandschaften' in den Niederlanden und im benachbarten Deutschland." In *Zunftlandschaften in Deutschland und den Niederlanden im Vergleich,* Schriften der historischen Kommission für Westfalen 17, edited by Wilfried Reininghaus, 11–43. Münster, Germany: Aschendorf.

Lucassen, Jan. 2002. "Holland, een open gewest: Immigratie en bevolkingsontwikkeling." In *Geschiedenis van Holland,* vol. 2, *1572 tot 1795,* edited by Timo de Nijs and Eelco Beukers, 181–215. Hilversum, Netherlands: Verloren.

———. 2014. "Deep Monetisation: The Case of the Netherlands, 1200–1940." *Tijdschrift voor economische en sociale geschiedenis* 11: 73–121.

Lucassen, Leo, and Boudien de Vries. 1996. "Leiden als middelpunt van een Westeuropees textiel-migratiesysteem, 1585–1650." *Tijdschrift voor sociale geschiedenis* 22: 138–67.

Maat, G.J.R. 2005. "Two Millennia of Male Stature Development and Population Health and Wealth in the Low Countries." *International Journal of Osteoarcheology* 15 (4): 276–90.

MacCulloch, Diarmaid. 2003. *Reformation: Europe's House Divided, 1490–1700.* London: Allen Lane.

Maddison, Angus. 2004. *The World Economy: Historical Statistics.* Paris: OECD.

Malanima, Paolo. 2011. "The Long Decline of a Leading Economy: GDP in Central and Northern Italy, 1300–1913." *European Review of Economic History* 15: 169–219.

Meij, J. de. 1980. *De watergeuzen: Piraten en bevrijders.* Haarlem, Netherlands: Fibula-Van Dishoeck.

Meinzer, Nicholas J., Richard H. Steckel, and Jörg Baten. 2018. "Agricultural Specialization, Urbanization, Workload, and Stature." In *The Backbone of Europe: Health, Diet, Work and Violence over Two Millennia*, edited by Steckel, Clark Spencer Larsen, Charlotte A. Roberts, and Baten, 231–52. Cambridge: Cambridge University Press.

Melker, Bas de. 2004. "Burgers en devotie, 1340-1520." In *Geschiedenis van Amsterdam*, vol. 1, *Een stad uit het niets—tot 1578*, edited by Marijke Carasso-Kok, 251–311. Amsterdam: Boom.

Milanovic, Branko. 2019. *Capitalism Alone: The Future of the System That Rules the World*. Cambridge, MA: Harvard University Press.

Milanovic, Branko, Peter Lindert, and Jeffrey Williamson. 2011. "Pre-industrial Inequality." *Economic Journal* 121: 255–72.

Mokyr, Joel. 2018. "The Past and the Future of Innovation: Some Lessons from Economic History." *Explorations in Economic History* 69: 13–26.

Mol, Hans. 2001. "Friese krijgers en de kruistochten." *Jaarboek voor middeleeuwse geschiedenis* 4: 86–117.

———. 2004. "Friezen en de zeggenschap over hun kerken in de Middeleeuwen." Inaugural lecture, Universiteit Leiden.

Montias, John Michael. 1987. "Cost and Value in Seventeenth-Century Dutch Art." *Art History* 10: 455–66.

Mooij, J. 2009. "Banck van Wissel: Het begin van een fenomeen." In *De Wisselbank: Van stadsbank tot bank van de wereld*, edited by M. van Nieuwkerk and C. Kroeze, 28–37. Amsterdam: De Nederlandsche Bank.

Mostert, Marco. 2009. *In de marge van de beschaving: De geschiedenis van Nederland, 0–1000*. Amsterdam: Prometheus.

Munro, John H. 2003. "The Medieval Origins of the Financial Revolution: Usury, Rentes, and Negotiability." *International History Review* 25: 505–62.

Najemy, John M. 1982. *Corporatism and Consensus in Florentine Electoral Politics, 1280–1400*. Chapel Hill: University of North Carolina Press.

Neal, Larry M., and Jeffrey G. Williamson, eds. 2014. *The Cambridge History of Capitalism*. 2 vols. Cambridge: Cambridge University Press.

Nederveen Meerkerk, Elise van. 2010. "Market Wage or Discrimination? The Remuneration of Male and Female Wool Spinners in the Seventeenth-Century Dutch Republic." *Economic History Review* 63: 165–86.

———. 2012. "The Will to Give: Charitable Bequests, Inter Vivos Gifts and Community Building in the Dutch Republic, c. 1600–1800." *Continuity and Change* 27: 241–70.

Niemeijer, H. E. 1996. "Calvinisme en koloniale stadscultuur: Batavia, 1619–1725." PhD dissertation, Universiteit van Amsterdam.

———. 2005. *Batavia: Een koloniale samenleving in de 17de eeuw*. Amsterdam: Balans.

Nierop, H.F.K. van. 2000. *Het foute Amsterdam*. Amsterdam: Vossius Pers.

Nieuwkerk, M. van. 2009. "Van Stadsbank tot Bank van de Wereld." In *De Wisselbank: Van Stadsbank tot Bank van de Wereld*, edited by Nieuwkerk and C. Kroeze, 12–27. Amsterdam: De Nederlandsche Bank.

Nimwegen, Olaf van. 2010. *The Dutch Army and the Military Revolutions, 1588–1688*. Martlesham, UK: Boydell.

Nipperdey, Thomas. 1993. "Max Weber, Protestantism, and the Context of the Debate around 1900." In *Weber's Protestant Ethic: Origins, Evidence, Contexts*, edited by Hartmut Lehmann and Günther Roth, 73–81. Cambridge: Cambridge University Press.

Noordam, Dirk Jaap. 1994. *Geringde buffels en heren van stand: Het patriciaat van Leiden, 1574–1700*. Hilversum, Netherlands: Verloren.

Noordegraaf, Leo, and Jan Luiten van Zanden. 1995. "Early Modern Economic Growth and the Standard of Living: Did Labor Benefit from Holland's Golden Age?" In *A Miracle Mirrored: The Dutch Republic in European Perspective*, edited by Karel Davids and Jan Lucassen, 410–37. Cambridge: Cambridge University Press.

North, Douglass. 1981. *Structure and Change in Economic History*. New York: Norton.

———. 1990. *Institutions, Institutional Change and Economic Performance*. Cambridge: Cambridge University Press.

North, Douglass, and Barry Weingast. 1989. "Constitutions and Commitment: The Evolution of Institutions Governing Public Choice in Seventeenth-Century England." *Journal of Economic History* 49: 803–32.

Nunn, Nathan. 2008a. "The Long-term Effects of Africa's Slave Trades." *Quarterly Journal of Economics* 123: 139–76.

———. 2008b. "Slavery, Inequality, and Economic Development in the Americas: An Examination of the Engerman-Sokoloff Hypothesis." In *Institutions and Economic Performance*, edited by Elhanan Helpman, 148–80. Cambridge: Cambridge University Press.

Ogilvie, Sheilagh. 2019. *The European Guilds: An Economic Analysis*. Princeton, NJ: Princeton University Press.

Ontwerp om de Republiek door eene heilzaame vereeniging der belangen van regent en burger van binnen gelukkig en van buiten gedugt te maaken. 1785. Leiden.

Ostrom, Elinor. 1990. *Governing the Commons: The Evolution of Institutions for Collective Action*. Cambridge: Cambridge University Press.

Panhuysen, Bibi. 2000. *Maatwerk: Kleermakers, naaisters, oudkleerkopers en de gilden (1500–1800)*. Amsterdam: IISG.

Paping, Richard. 2014. "General Dutch Population Development, 1400–1850: Cities and Countryside." Paper presented at the First Conference of the European Society of Historical Demography (ESHD), Sassari/Alghero, Sardinia, September 25, 2014.

Parker, Charles H. 1998. *The Reformation of Community: Social Welfare and Calvinist Charity in Holland, 1572–1620*. Cambridge: Cambridge University Press.

Parker, Geoffrey. 1977. *The Dutch Revolt*. London: Allen Lane.

———. 1988. *The Military Revolution: Military Innovation and the Rise of the West, 1500–1800*. Cambridge: Cambridge University Press.

Pettegree, Andrew, and Arthur der Weduwen. 2019. *The Bookshop of the World: Making and Trading Books in the Dutch Golden Age*. New Haven, CT: Yale University Press.

Pfister, Ulrich. 2008. "Craft Guilds and Technological Change: The Engine Loom in the European Silk Ribbon Industry in the Seventeenth and Eighteenth Centuries." In *Guilds, Innovation and the European Economy, 1400–1800*, edited by S. R. Epstein and Maarten Prak, 172–98. Cambridge: Cambridge University Press.

Piketty, Thomas. 2014. *Capital in the Twenty-First Century*. Cambridge, MA: Belknap.

Pinker, Steven. 2012. *The Better Angels of Our Nature: Why Violence Has Declined*. New York: Viking.

Pirenne, Henri. 1927. *Les villes au moyen âge: Essai d'histoire économique et sociale*. Brussels: Maurice Lamartin.

Pleijt, Alexandra de, and Jan Luiten van Zanden. 2018. "Two Worlds of Female Labour: Gender Wage Inequality in Western Europe, 1300–1800." *Economic History Review* 74: 611–38.

———. 2019. "Preindustrial Economic Growth, ca. 1270–1820." In *Handbook of Cliometrics*, edited by Claude Diebolt and Michael John Haupert, 423–38. Cham, Switzerland: Springer.

Poelwijk, Arjan. 2003. *"In dienste van het Suyckerbacken": De Amsterdamse suikernijverheid en haar ondernemers, 1580–1630*. Hilversum, Netherlands: Verloren.

Pollmann, Judith. 2019. "Oranje en de eerste statenvergadering: Een goed verborgen revolutie." In *Willem van Oranje en de eerste statenvergadering 1572 Dordrecht*, edited by C. A. Tamse, 7–33. The Hague: Prins Willem de Eerste Herinneringsstichting.

Prados de la Escosura, Leandro, and Carlos Vladimir Rodriguez-Caballero. 2020. "Growth, War, and Pandemics: Europe in the Very Long-Run." Centre for Economic Policy Research Discussion Paper no. DP14816.

Prak, Maarten. 1985. *Gezeten burgers: De elite in een Hollandse stad; Leiden, 1700–1780*. Dieren: Bataafsche Leeuw.

———. 1991. "Citizen Radicalism and Democracy in the Dutch Republic: The Patriot Movement of the 1780's." *Theory and Society* 20: 73–102.

———. 1994. "Verfassungsnorm und Verfassungsrealität in den niederländischen Städten des späten 17. und 18. Jahrhunderts: Die Oligarchie in Amsterdam, Rotterdam, Deventer und Zutphen 1672/75–1795." In *Verwaltung und Politik in Städten Mitteleuropas: Beiträge zu Verfassungsnorm und Verfassungswirklichkeit in altständischer Zeit*, edited by Wilfried Ehbrecht, 55–83. Cologne: Böhlau.

———. 1999a. "The Carrot and the Stick: Social Control and Poor Relief in the Dutch Republic, Sixteenth to Eighteenth Centuries." In *Institutionen, Instrumente und Akteure sozialer Kontrolle und Disziplinierung im frühneuzeitlichen Europa / Institutions, Instruments and Agents of Social Control and Discipline in Early Modern Europe*, Ius Commune: Studien zur Europäischen Rechtsgeschichte 127, edited by Heinz Schilling, 149–66. Frankfurt am Main.

———. 1999b. *Republikeinse veelheid, democratisch enkelvoud: Sociale verandering in het revolutietijdperk; 's-Hertogenbosch, 1770–1820*. Nijmegen, Netherlands: SUN.

———. 2002. "The Politics of Intolerance: Citizenship and Religion in the Dutch Republic (17th–18th C.)." In *Calvinism and Religious Toleration in the Dutch Golden Age*, edited by Ronnie Po-chia Hsia and Henk F. K. van Nierop, 159–75. Cambridge: Cambridge University Press.

———. 2008. "Painters, Guilds and the Art Market during the Dutch Golden Age." In *Guilds, Innovation and the European Economy*, edited by S. R. Epstein and Prak, 143–71. Cambridge: Cambridge University Press

———. 2015. Review of *The Cambridge History of Capitalism*, vol. 1, *The Rise of Capitalism: From Ancient Origins to 1848*; vol. 2, *The Spread of Capitalism: From 1848 to the Present*, by Larry Neal and Jeffrey G. Williamson. *Journal of Global History* 10: 506–8.

———. 2018. *Citizens without Nations: Urban Citizenship in Europe and the World before the French Revolution*. Cambridge: Cambridge University Press.

———. 2020. "Guilds and Mutual Aid in the Northern Netherlands." In *Professional Guilds and the History of Insurance: A Comparative Analysis*, Studien zur vergleichenden Geschichte des Versicherungsrechts 7, edited by Phillip Hellwege, 47–62. Berlin: Duncker und Humblot.

———. 2023. *The Dutch Republic in the Seventeenth Century*. 2nd ed. Cambridge: Cambridge University Press.

Prak, Maarten, Clare Haru Crowston, Bert De Munck, Christopher Kissane, Chris Minns, Ruben Schalk, and Patrick Wallis. 2020. "Access to the Trade: Monopoly and Mobility in European Craft Guilds in the Seventeenth and Eighteenth Centuries." *Journal of Social History* 54: 421–52.

Prak, Maarten, and Erika Kuijpers. 2001. "Burger, ingezetene, vreemdeling: Burgerschap in Amsterdam in de 17e en 18e eeuw." In *Burger: Een geschiedenis van het begrip "burger" in de Nederlanden van de Middeleeuwen tot de 21ste eeuw*, edited by Joost Kloek and Karin Tilmans, 113–32. Amsterdam: Amsterdam University Press.

Prak, Maarten, Catharina Lis, Jan Lucassen, and Hugo Soly, eds. 2006. *Craft Guilds in the Early Modern Low Countries: Work, Power and Representation*. Aldershot, UK: Ashgate.

Prak, Maarten, and Patrick Wallis, eds. 2019. *Apprenticeship in Early Modern Europe*. Cambridge: Cambridge University Press.

Prak, Maarten, and Jan Luiten van Zanden. 2009. "Tax Morale and Citizenship in the Dutch Republic." In *The Political Economy of the Dutch Republic*, edited by Oscar Gelderblom, 143–65. Farnham, UK: Ashgate.

Prevenier, Walter, and Wim Blockmans. 2000. *De Bourgondiërs: De Nederlanden op weg naar een eenheid, 1384–1530*. Amsterdam: Meulenhoff.

Price, J. L. 1994. *Holland and the Dutch Republic in the Seventeenth Century: The Politics of Particularism*. Oxford: Clarendon.

Putnam, Robert D. 1994. *Making Democracy Work: Civic Traditions in Modern Italy*. Princeton, NJ: Princeton University Press.

Quinn, Stephen, and William Roberds. 2014. "The Bank of Amsterdam through the Lens of Monetary Competition." In *Explaining Monetary and Financial Innovations*, edited by Peter Bernholz and Roland Vaubel, 283–300. Cham, Switzerland: Springer.

Rasterhoff, Clara. 2017. *Painting and Publishing as Cultural Industries: The Fabric of Creativity in the Dutch Republic, 1580–1800*. Amsterdam: Amsterdam University Press.

Reynolds, Susan. 1994. *Fiefs and Vassals: The Medieval Evidence Reinterpreted*. Oxford: Oxford University Press.

Richardson, Gary, and Michael McBride. 2009. "Religion, Longevity and Cooperation: The Case of the Craft Guild." *Journal of Economic Behavior and Organization* 71: 172–86.

Rij, H. van, ed. 1999. *Gebeurtenissen van deze tijd: Een fragment over bisschop Diederik I van Metz en de mirakelen van de heilige Walburg in Tiel*. Hilversum, Netherlands: Verloren.

Riley, James C. 1980. *International Government Finance and the Amsterdam Capital Market, 1740–1815*. Cambridge: Cambridge University Press.

Rommelse, Gijs. 2010. "The Role of Mercantilism in Anglo-Dutch Relations, 1650–1674." *Economic History Review* 63: 591–611.

Rommes, Ronald. 2015. "Plague in Northwestern Europe: The Dutch Experience, 1350–1670." *Popolazione e storia* 16 (2): 47–71.

Roosen, Joris, and Daniel Curtis. 2019. "The 'Light Touch' of the Black Death in the Southern Netherlands: An Urban Trick?" *Economic History Review* 72: 32–56.

Rooze-Stouthamer, C. 2009. *Opmaat tot de Opstand: Zeeland en het centraal gezag (1566–1572)*. Hilversum, Netherlands: Verloren.

Rosendaal, Joost. 2003. *Bataven: Nederlandse vluchtelingen in Frankrijk, 1787–1795*. Nijmegen, Netherlands: Vantilt.

———. 2005. *De Nederlandse revolutie: Vrijheid, volk en vaderland, 1783–1799*. Nijmegen, Netherlands: Vantilt.

Rossum, Mattthias van. 2015. *Kleurrijke tragiek: De geschiedenis van de slavernij in Azië onder de VOC*. Hilversum, Netherlands: Verloren.

Rowen, Herbert H., ed. 1972. *The Low Countries in Early Modern Times*. London: Macmillan.

———. 1988. *The Princes of Orange: The Stadholders in the Dutch Republic*. Cambridge: Cambridge University Press.

Schaïk, Remi van. 1989. "Zutphens geschiedenis: Van de elfde tot het einde van de zestiende eeuw." In *Geschiedenis van Zutphen*, edited by W.Th.M. Frijhoff, 48–83. Zutphen, Netherlands: Walburg Pers.

———. 1993. "Taxation, Public Finances and the State-Making Process in the Late Middle Ages: The Case of the Duchy of Guelders." *Journal of Medieval History* 19: 251–71.

———. 2008. "Consolidatie en bloei: De periode van de dertiende en begin veertiende eeuw." In *Geschiedenis van Groningen*, edited by Maarten Duijvendak, 169–227. Zwolle, Netherlands: Waanders.

Schama, Simon. 1977. *Patriots and Liberators: Revolution in the Netherlands, 1780–1813*. New York: Alfred Knopf.

———. 1987. *The Embarrassment of Riches: An Interpretation of Dutch Culture in the Golden Age*. New York: Alfred Knopf.

Scheidel, Walter. 2017. *The Great Leveler: Violence and the History of Inequality from the Stone Age to the Twenty-First Century*. Princeton, NJ: Princeton University Press.

Schilling, Heinz. 1980. "Calvinistische Presbyterien in Städten der Frühneuzeit—eine kirchliche Alternativform zur bürgerlichen Repräsentation? (Mit einer quantifizierenden Untersuchung zur holländischen Stadt Leiden.)" In *Städtische Führungsgruppen und Gemeinde in der werdenden Neuzeit*, Städteforschung A/9, edited by Wilfried Ehbrecht, 385–444. Cologne: Böhlau.

———. 1992 *Religion, Political Culture and the Emergence of Early Modern Society: Essays in German and Dutch History*. Leiden: Brill.

Schilstra, J. 1974. *In de ban van de dijk: De Westfriese omringdijk*. Hoorn, Netherlands: n.p.

Schmidt, Ariadne. 2001. *Overleven na de dood: Weduwen in Leiden in de Gouden Eeuw*. Amsterdam: Prometheus.

Schulz, Jonathan F., Duman Bahrami-Rad, Jonathan P. Beauchamp, and Joseph Henrich. 2019. "The Church, Intensive Kinship, and Global Psychological Variation." *Science* 366 (6466). https://doi.org/10.1126/science.aau5141.

Scott, Jonathan. 2019. *How the Old World Ended: The Anglo-Dutch-American Revolution, 1500–1800*. New Haven, CT: Yale University Press.

Semih Akçomak, İ., Dinand Webbink, and Bas ter Weel. 2016. "Why Did the Netherlands Develop So Early? The Legacy of the Brethern of the Common Life." *Economic Journal* 126 (593): 821–60.

Sen, Amartya. 2001. *Development as Freedom*. Oxford: Oxford University Press.

Sicking, Louis. 2004. *Neptune and the Netherlands: State, Economy, and War at Sea in the Renaissance*. Leiden: Brill.

Slicher van Bath, B. H. 1945. *Mensch en land in de Middeleeuwen: Bijdrage tot een geschiedenis der nederzettingen in oostelijk Nederland*. Assen, Netherlands: Van Gorcum.

———. 1948. *Boerenvrijheid*. Groningen, Netherlands: Wolters.

Sluyterman, Keetie, ed. 2015. *Varieties of Capitalism and Business History: The Dutch Case*. London: Routledge.

Smith, Adam. (1776) 1986. *An Inquiry into the Nature and Causes of the Wealth of Nations*. Harmondsworth, UK: Penguin.

Smithuis, Justine. 2019. "Urban Politics and the Role of Guilds in the City of Utrecht (1250–1450)." PhD dissertation, Universiteit Leiden.

Soens, Tim. 2009. *Spade in de dijk? Waterbeheer en rurale samenleving in de Vlaamse kustvlakte (1280–1580)*. Ghent: Academia Press.

———. 2018. "Waddenzee wordt Moordzee." *Tijdschrift voor geschiedenis* 131: 605–30.

Sogner, Solvi. 1993. "Young in Europe around 1700: Norwegian Sailors and Servant Girls Seeking Employment in Amsterdam." In *Mesurer et comprendre: Mélanges en l'honneur de Jacques Dupâquier*, edited by Jean-Pierre Bardet, François Lebrun, and René le Mée, 515–32. Paris: Presses universitaires de France.

Soltow, Lee, and Jan Luiten van Zanden. 1998. *Income and Wealth: Inequality in the Netherlands, 16th–20th Century*. Amsterdam: Het Spinhuis.

Spaans, Joke. 1989. *Haarlem na de Reformatie: Stedelijke cultuur en kerkelijk leven, 1577–1620*. The Hague: Stichting Hollandse Historische Reeks.

Spanninga, Hotso. 2012. *Gulden vrijheid? Politieke cultuur en staatsvorming in Friesland, 1600–1640*. Hilversum, Netherlands: Verloren.

Spek, Theo. 2004. *Het Drentse esdorpenlandschap: Een historisch-geografische studie*. 2 vols. Utrecht: Matrijs.

Spierenburg, Pieter. 1991. *The Prison Experience: Disciplinary Institutions and Their Inmates in Early Modern Europe*. New Brunswick, NJ: Rutgers University Press.

Stanton, Elizabeth A. 2007. "The Human Development Index: A History." Political Economy Research Institute Working Papers 127.

Stasavage, David. 2011. *States of Credit: Size, Power, and the Development of European Polities*. Princeton, NJ: Princeton University Press.

Stayer, J. M. 1995. "The Radical Reformation." In *Handbook of European History, 1400–1600: Late Middle Ages, Renaissance and Reformation*, edited by Thomas A. Brady, Heiko A. Oberman, and James D. Tracy, vol. 2, 249–82. Leiden: Brill.

Steensel, Arie van. 2014. "Origins and Transformations: Recent Historiography on the Nobility in the Medieval Low Countries." *History Compass* 12: 263–99.

Steur, J. 1984. *Herstel of ondergang: De voorstellen tot redres van de Verenigde Oost-Indische Compagnie, 1740–1795*. Utrecht: Hes.

Stipriaan, Alex van. 1995. "Debunking Debts, Image and Reality of a Colonial Crisis: Suriname at the End of the 18th Century." *Itinerario* 19: 69–84.

Storper, Michael. 2013. *The Keys to the City: How Economics, Institutions, Social Interaction, and Politics Shape Development*. Princeton, NJ: Princeton University Press.

Streng, J. 1997. *"Stemme in staat": De bestuurlijke elite in de stadsrepubliek Zwolle, 1579–1795*. Hilversum, Netherlands: Verloren.

Sweezy, Paul, Maurice Dobb, Kohachiro Takahashi, Rodney Hilton, Christopher Hill, Georges Lefebvre, Giuliano Procaci, Eric Hobsbawm, and John Merrington. 1978. *The Transition from Feudalism to Capitalism*. London: Verso.

Te Brake, Wayne P. 1989. *Regents and Rebels: The Revolutionary World of an Eighteenth-Century Dutch City*. Oxford: Blackwell.

———. 1998. *Shaping History: Ordinary People in European Politics, 1500–1700*. Berkeley: University of California Press.

———. 2017. *Religious War and Religious Peace in Early Modern Europe*. Cambridge: Cambridge University Press.

Teeuwen, Daniëlle. 2012. "Collections for the Poor: Monetary Charitable Donations in Dutch Towns, c. 1600–1800." *Continuity and Change* 27: 271–99.

———. 2016. *Financing Poor Relief through Charitable Collections in Dutch Towns, c. 1600–1800*. Amsterdam: Amsterdam University Press.

Temin, Peter. 2015. "The Cambridge History of 'Capitalism.'" *Journal of Economic Literature* 53: 996–1016.

Temple, William. 1972. *Observations upon the United Provinces of the Netherlands*. Edited by G. Clark. Oxford: Clarendon.

Tielhof, Milja van. 1995. *De Hollandse graanhandel, 1470–1570: Koren op de Amsterdamse molen*. The Hague: Stichting Hollandse Historische Reeks.

———. 2002. *The "Mother of All Trades": The Baltic Grain Trade in Amsterdam from the Late 16th to the Early 19th Century*. Leiden: Brill.

———. 2021. *Consensus en conflict: Geschiedenis van het Nederlandse waterbeheer, 1200–1800*. Hilversum, Netherlands: Verloren.

Tielhof, Milja van, and Petra van Dam. 2006. *Waterstaat in stedenland: Het hoogheemraadschap Rijnland voor 1857*. Utrecht: Matrijs.

Tielhof, Milja van, and Jan Luiten van Zanden. 2011. "Productivity Changes in Shipping in the Dutch Republic: The Evidence from Freight Rates, 1550–1800." In *Shipping and Economic Growth, 1350–1800*, edited by Richard W. Unger, 47–80. Leiden: Brill.

Tilly, Charles. 1990. *Coercion, Capital, and European States, AD 990–1990*. Oxford: Basil Blackwell.

Tracy, James D. 1985. *A Financial Revolution in the Habsburg Netherlands:* Renten *and* Renteniers *in the County of Holland, 1515–1565*. Berkeley: University of California Press.

———. 1990. *Holland under Habsburg Rule: The Formation of a Body Politic*. Berkeley: University of California Press.

———. 2008. *The Founding of the Dutch Republic: War, Finance, and Politics in Holland, 1572–1588*. Oxford: Oxford University Press.

Tromp, H.M.J. 1991. "Drenthe, Coevorden en de bisschop, 1150–1395." In *Geschiedenis van Drenthe*, edited by J. Heringa, 171–96. Amsterdam: Boom.

Unger, Richard W. 1978. *Dutch Shipbuilding before 1800: Ships and Guilds*. Assen, Netherlands: Van Gorcum.

Van de Pol, Lotte. 2011. *The Burgher and the Whore: Prostitution in Early Modern Amsterdam*. Oxford: Oxford University Press.

Van der Wee, Herman. 1963. *The Growth of the Antwerp Market and the European Economy (Fourteenth–Sixteenth Centuries)*. The Hague: Nijhoff.

Van Dijck, Maarten F. 2020. "Violent Classes? Interpersonal Violence and Social Inequality in Mechelen, 1350–1700." In *Inequality and the City in the Low Countries (1200–2020)*, edited by Bruno Blondé, Sam Geens, Hilde Greefs, Wouter Ryckbosch, Tim Soens, and Peter Stabel, 329–43. Turnhout, Belgium: Brepols.

Ven, Gerard P. van de, ed. 2004. *Man-Made Low Lands: History of Water Management and Land Reclamation in the Netherlands*. Utrecht: Matrijs.

Verkerk, C. 1998. "De vroegste vermelding van de tol van Geervliet." In *Datum et Actum: Essays Presented to Jaap Kruisheer on the Occasion of his Sixty-Fifth Birthday*, edited by D. Blok, J.W.J. Burgers, E. C. Dijkhof, P. A. Henderikx, and G. van Herwijnen, 431–45. Amsterdam: Meertens Instituut.

Vliet, Kaj van. 2000. "De stad van de bisschop, circa 925–1122." In *"Een paradijs vol weelde": Geschiedenis van de stad Utrecht*, edited by R. E. de Bruin, P. D. 't Hart, A. J. van den Hoven van Genderen, A. Pietersma, and J.E.A.L. Struick, 45–71. Utrecht: Matrijs.

Vlis, Ingrid van der. 2001. *Leven in armoede: Delfste bedeelden in de zeventiende eeuw*. Amsterdam: Prometheus.

Voigtländer, Nico, and Hans-Joachim Voth. 2013. "The three Horsemen of Riches: Plague, War, and Urbanization in Early Modern Europe." *Review of Economic Studies* 80: 774–811.

Voort, J. P. van der. 1973. "De Westindische plantages van 1720–1795: Financiën en handel." PhD dissertation, Radboud Universiteit Nijmegen.

Vries, Boudien de, Jan Lucassen, Piet Lourens, and Harm Nijboer. 2003. "Het economische leven: Spectaculair succes en diep verval." In *Leiden: De geschiedenis van een Hollandse stad*, vol. 2, *1574–1795*, edited by Simon Groenveld, 85–98. Leiden: Stichting Geschiedschrijving Leiden.

Vries, Jan de. 1974. *The Dutch Rural Economy in the Golden Age, 1500–1700*. New Haven, CT: Yale University Press.

———. 1976. *The Economy of Europe in an Age of Crisis, 1600–1750*. Cambridge: Cambridge University Press.

———. 1978. *Barges and Capitalism: Passenger Transportation in the Dutch Economy, 1632–1839*. Utrecht: Hes.

———. 1993. "The Labour Market." In *The Dutch Economy in the Golden Age: Nine Essays*, edited by Karel Davids and Leo Noordegraaf, 55–78. Amsterdam: NEHA.

———. 2001a. "Economic Growth before and after the Industrial Revolution: A Modest Proposal." In *Early Modern Capitalism: Economic and Social Change in Europe, 1400–1800*, edited by Maarten Prak, 177–94. London: Routledge.

———. 2001b. "The Transition to Capitalism in a Land without Feudalism." In *Peasants into Farmers? The Transformation of Rural Economy and Society in the Low Countries (Middle Ages–19th Century) in Light of the Brenner Debate*, CORN series 4, edited by Peter Hoppenbrouwers and Jan Luiten van Zanden, 67–84. Turnhout, Belgium: Brepols.

———. 2003. "Connecting Europe and Asia: A Quantitative Analysis of the Cape-Route Trade." In *Global Connections and Monetary History, 1470–1800*, edited by Dennis O. Flynn, Arturo Giráldez, and Richard von Glahn, 35–106. Aldershot, UK: Ashgate.

———. 2008. *The Industrious Revolution: Consumer Behavior and the Household Economy, 1650 to the Present*. Cambridge: Cambridge University Press.

———. 2009. "The Political Economy of Bread in the Dutch Republic." In *The Political Economy of the Dutch Republic*, edited by Oscar Gelderblom, 85–114. Farnham, UK: Ashgate.

———. 2014. "The Netherlands and the Polder Model: Questioning the Polder Model Concept." *BMGN: Low Countries Historical Review* 129: 99–111.

———. 2019. *The Price of Bread: Regulating the Market in the Dutch Republic*. Cambridge: Cambridge University Press.

Vries, Jan de, and Ad van der Woude. 1997. *The First Modern Economy: Success, Failure, and Perseverance of the Dutch Economy, 1500–1815*. Cambridge: Cambridge University Press.

Waaragtig onderzoek wegens het verzuim in het waarnemen der oude handvesten van Leiden. 1748. Knuttel 18117. Leiden.

Wallerstein, Immanuel. 1980. *The Modern World-System*, vol. 2, *Mercantilism and the Consolidation of the European World-Economy, 1600–1750*. New York: Academic Press.

Weber, Max. (1905) 2002. *The Protestant Ethic and the "Spirit of Capitalism" and Other Writings*. Translated and edited by Peter Baehr and Gordon C. Wells. Harmondsworth, UK: Allen Lane.

Wegener Sleeswyk, André. 2003. *De gouden eeuw van het fluitschip*. Franeker, Netherlands: Van Wijnen.

Weststrate, Job. 2008. *In het kielzog van moderne markten: Handel en scheepvaart op de Rijn, Waal en IJssel, ca. 1360–1560*. Hilversum, Netherlands: Verloren.

———. 2010. "De marktpositie van Deventer van de veertiende eeuw tot het begin van de Opstand." In *Bourgondië voorbij: De Nederlanden, 1250–1650*, edited by Mario Damen and Louis Sicking, 263–77. Hilversum, Netherlands: Verloren.

Wickham, Chris. 2015. *Sleepwalking into a New World: The Emergence of Italian City Communes in the Twelfth Century*. Princeton, NJ: Princeton University Press.

———. 2021. "How Did the Feudal Economy Work? The Economic Logic of Medieval Societies." *Past and Present* 251: 1–40.

Wijngaarden, Hilde van. 2000. *Zorg voor de kost: Armenzorg, arbeid en onderlinge hulp in Zwolle, 1650–1700*. Amsterdam: Bert Bakker.

Wiskerke, C. 1938. *De afschaffing der gilden in Nederland*. Amsterdam: Paris.

Woude, A. M. van der. 1972. *Het Noorderkwartier: Een regionaal-historisch onderzoek in de demografische en economische geschiedenis van westelijk Nederland*. AAG Bijdragen 16. Wageningen, Netherlands: Afdeling Agrarische Geschiedenis.

———. 1982. "Population Developments in the Northern Netherlands (1500–1800) and the Validity of the 'Urban Graveyard' Effect." *Annales de démographie historique* 1982: 55–75.

———. 1991. "The Volume and Value of Paintings in Holland at the Time of the Dutch Republic." In *Art in History, History in Art: Studies in Seventeenth-Century Dutch Culture*, edited by David Freedberg and Jan de Vries, 285–329. Santa Monica, CA: Getty Center for the History of Art and the Humanities.

Wubs-Mrozewicz, J. 2008. *Traders, Ties and Tensions: The Interaction of Lübeckers, Overijsselers and Hollanders in Late Medieval Bergen*. Hilversum, Netherlands: Verloren.

Zanden, Jan Luiten van. 1985. *De economische ontwikkeling van de Nederlandse landbouw in de negentiende eeuw, 1800–1914*. AAG Bijdragen 25. Wageningen, Netherlands: Afdeling Agrarische Geschiedenis.

———. 1988. "Op zoek naar de 'missing link': Hypothesen over de opkomst van Holland in de late Middeleeuwen en de vroeg-moderne tijd." *Tijdschrift voor sociale geschiedenis* 14: 359–87.

———. 1993. *The Rise and Decline of Holland's Economy: Merchant Capitalism and the Labour Market*. Manchester: Manchester University Press.

———. 1995. "Tracing the Beginning of the Kuznets Curve: Western Europe during the Early Modern Period." *Economic History Review* 47: 643–64.

———. 1996. "Over de rationaliteit van het ondernemersgedrag van de VOC: Enkele empirische bevindingen." In *Kapitaal, ondernemerschap en beleid: Studies over economie en politiek in Nederland, Europa en Azië van 1500 tot heden*, edited by C. A. Davids, W. Fritschy, and L. A. van der Valk, 409–22. Hilversum, Netherlands: Verloren.

———. 1999. "The Paradox of the Marks: The Exploitation of Commons in the Eastern Netherlands, 1250–1850." *Agricultural History Review* 47: 125–44.

———. 2001. "Early Modern Economic Growth: A Survey of the European Economy." In *Early Modern Capitalism: Economic and Social Change in Europe*, edited by Maarten Prak, 69–88. London: Routledge.

———. 2002a. "The 'Revolt of the Early Modernists' and the 'First Modern Economy': An Assessment." *Economic History Review* 55: 619–41.

———. 2002b. "Taking the Measure of the Early Modern Economy: Historical National Accounts for Holland in 1510/1514." *European Review of Economic History* 6: 131–63.

———. 2004. "On the Efficiency of Markets for Agricultural Products: Rice Prices and Capital Markets in Java, 1823–1853." *Journal of Economic History* 64: 1028–55.

———. 2005. *The Economic History of the Netherlands, 1914–1995: A Small Open Economy in the 'Long' Twentieth Century*. London: Routledge.

———. 2009a. *The Long Road to the Industrial Revolution: The European Economy in Global Perspective*. Leiden: Brill.

———. 2009b. "The Skill Premium and the 'Great Divergence.'" *European Review of Economic History* 13: 121–53.

Zanden, Jan Luiten van, Jörg Baten, Marco Mira d'Ercole, Auke Rijpma, Conal Smith, and Marcel Timmer, eds. 2014. *How Was Life? Global Well-Being since 1820*. Paris: OECD.

Zanden, Jan Luiten van, Eltjo Buringh, and Maarten Bosker. 2012. "The Rise and Decline of European Parliaments, 1188–1789." *Economic History Review* 65: 835–61.

Zanden, Jan Luiten van, Tine De Moor, and Sarah Carmichael. 2019. *Capital Women: The European Marriage Pattern, Female Empowerment and Economic Development in Western Europe, 1300–1800*. Oxford: Oxford University Press.

Zanden, Jan Luiten van, and Emanuele Felice. 2019. "Benchmarking the Middle Ages: 15th Century Tuscany in European Perspective." Centre for Global Economic History working paper no. 81.

Zanden, Jan Luiten van, and Bas van Leeuwen. 2012. "Persistent but Not Consistent: The Growth of National Income in Holland, 1347–1807." *Explorations in Economic History* 49: 119–130.

Zanden, Jan Luiten van, and Maarten Prak. 2006. "Towards an Economic Interpretation of Citizenship: The Dutch Republic between Medieval Communes and Modern Nation-States." *European Review of Economic History* 10: 111–45.

Zanden, Jan Luiten van, and Arthur van Riel. 2000. *The Strictures of Inheritance: The Dutch Economy in the Nineteenth Century*. Princeton, NJ: Princeton University Press.

Zanden, Jan Luiten van, Auke Rijpma, and Jan Kok, eds. 2017. *Agency, Gender and Economic Development in the World Economy, 1850–2000: Testing the Sen Hypothesis*. London: Routledge.

Zanden, Jan Luiten van, and Milja van Tielhof. 2009. "Roots of Growth and Productivity Change in Dutch Shipping Industry, 1500–1800." *Explorations in Economic History* 46: 389–403.

Zanden, Jan Luiten van, Jaco Zuijderduijn, and Tine De Moor. 2012. "Small Is Beautiful: The Efficiency of Credit Markets in Late Medieval Holland." *European Review of Economic History* 16: 3–22.

Zandvliet, Kees. 2018. *De 500 rijksten van de Republiek: Rijkdom, geloof, macht en cultuur*. Zutphen, Netherlands: Walburg Pers.

Zegarra, Luis Felipe. 2022. "Living Costs and Welfare Ratios in Western Europe: New Estimates Using a Linear Programming Model." *European Review of Economic History* 25: 38–61.

Zijl, Theodore P. van. 1963. *Gerard Groote: Ascetic and Reformer (1340–1484)*. Washington, DC: Catholic University of America Press.

Zijlstra, Samme. 2000. *Om de ware gemeente en de oude gronden: Geschiedenis van de dopersen in de Nederlanden, 1531–1675*. Hilversum, Netherlands: Verloren.

Zuijderduijn, C. J. 2008. *Medieval Capital Markets: Markets for Renten, State Formation and Private Investment in Holland (1300–1550)*. Leiden: Brill.

Zwitzer, H. 1991. *"De militie van den staat": Het leger van de Republiek der Verenigde Nederlanden*. Amsterdam: Bataafsche Leeuw.

INDEX

Page numbers in *italics* indicate figures and tables.

The Princeton Economic History of The Western World

Joel Mokyr, Series Editor

Recent titles

A NOTE ON THE TYPE

This book has been composed in Adobe Text and Gotham.
Adobe Text, designed by Robert Slimbach for Adobe,
bridges the gap between fifteenth- and sixteenth-century
calligraphic and eighteenth-century Modern styles.
Gotham, inspired by New York street signs, was designed
by Tobias Frere-Jones for Hoefler & Co.

GPSR Authorized Representative: Easy Access System Europe - Mustamäe tee
50, 10621 Tallinn, Estonia, gpsr.requests@easproject.com

www.ingramcontent.com/pod-product-compliance
Ingram Content Group UK Ltd.
Pitfield, Milton Keynes, MK11 3LW, UK
UKHW042250300325
456820UK00007B/37/J